UNIVERSITY *of* NEBRASKA

1995 NATIONAL CHAMPIONS

UNIVERSITY *of* NEBRASKA

1995 NATIONAL CHAMPIONS

Acknowledgments

Dear Husker fan,

It is with great pleasure and pride that we present the University of Nebraska National Champion 1995 book. We wanted to produce for you, the most dedicated and enthusiastic of fans, the most comprehensive book possible on Nebraska's incredible second-consecutive championship season. On these pages, you will be able to relive every second of the Huskers' thrilling, emotion-packed season as they battled the competition to win yet another national championship.

We are extremely grateful to the many dedicated people who made this book possible. First we would like to thank head coach Tom Osborne and his staff, who showed brilliance both on and off the field.

Special thanks go to Nebraska athletic director Bill Byrne. Also, we thank Chris Anderson, Chris Bahl, Vicki Cartwright, Jonathan Kerr and the entire Nebraska athletic department. Their dedication to this project was immeasurable. Thanks also to Bill Battle and Cory Moss at the Collegiate Licensing Company for their assistance.

Of course, we thank Tom Vint and Mike Babcock, the co-authors of this publication. Tom Vint was selected to write the game stories because of his seasoned and unwavering dedication to covering Nebraska football year after year. Mike Babcock, who for the past several years has reported on Husker games and especially their bowl appearances, provides a personal glimpse at the players, coaches and athletic director, as well as an exciting recap of the Fiesta Bowl.

We are especially proud of the coverage provided by the photographers Joe Mixan, John Williamson and Dennis Hubbard. Each game of the season is brought instantly back to life with their pictures. Thanks also to contributing photographers Tim Benko, Jeff Jacobsen and Chris Wildrick for their fine work, and to Alan Jackson of ACTON Shooting Gallery for supplying us with the photograph of Nebraska's back-to-back National Championship Trophies. We are especially thankful to Nebraska Sports Information and to Richard Voges and Tom Slocum of UNL Photo Services for supplying many of the photographs, without which this book would not be complete.

Special thanks to Fiesta Bowl President Purd Thomas and the Fiesta Bowl's 2,500 volunteers for their assistance in providing materials for this book and allowing us to reprint the cover of the Fiesta Bowl Game Program. We are equally grateful to USA Today for providing us with page 1C from the January 3, 1996 edition. (Copyright 1996, USA Today. Reprinted with permission.) Special thanks also to Bob Bennett and Huskers Illustrated for providing and granting us permission to reprint their cover and special thanks to Chris Anderson, Nebraska SID for allowing us to reprint the cover of the Nebraska Fiesta Bowl Guide.

And, finally, we thank the players. Your talent on the field and dedication to each other, your coaches and your school are truly the marks of champions. We are honored to have been involved in producing this book, which is for and about you.

Please enjoy.

The University of Nebraska 1995 National Championship book is officially licensed by the University of Nebraska through the Collegiate Licensing Co.

University of Nebraska National Champions 1995 Staff: Publisher: Ivan Mothershead; Associate Publisher: Charlie Keiger; Controller: Lewis Patton; Managing Editor: Ward Woodbury; Editors: Betty Alfred Mackinson and Mark Stefanik; Layout and Design: Paul Bond, Michael McBride and Brett Shippy; Administrative Staff: Henry Boardman, Mark Cantey, Mary Cartee, Lisa Clark, Mary Costner and Carla Greene.

ISBN 0-943860-11-3

Table of Contents

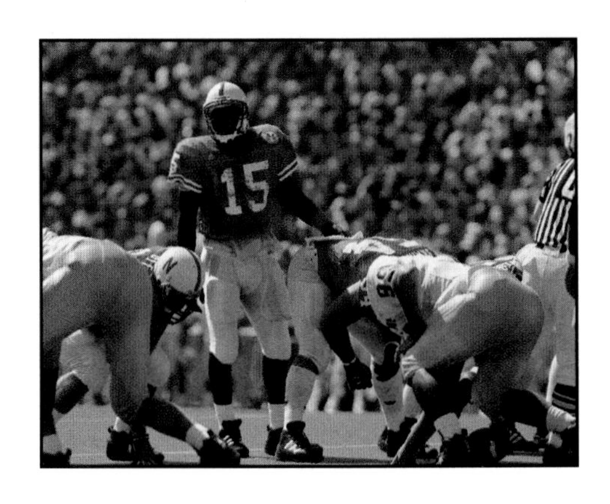

Foreword

Dear Friends:

Winning the 1995 national football championship was a tremendous tribute to Coach Tom Osborne, his staff and the student-athletes who came together in brilliant fashion to add another sensational chapter in the history of Husker football.

Credit, too, can be shared with the thousands of Husker fans who week-after-week and year-after-year rally in support of the University of Nebraska and its athletic program. No other institution can match the enthusiasm, dedication, interest, attendance and support demonstrated by generations of Nebraska fans.

Winning a national championship in college football is always a difficult task because of the competition, poll system and the bowl alliance plan, but winning the No. 1 spot in successive years is an especially tremendous accomplishment. Coach Osborne and the 1995 Huskers, like the 1994 champions, faced difficult moments, considerable adversity and national media pressures that would have decimated a lesser group of dedicated young men.

But the 1995 Huskers never faltered in the wake of distractions and stayed the course they set for themselves prior to the 1995 season. No strangers to pressure, Coach Osborne and the 1993 Huskers were ridiculed prior to the Orange Bowl game as no match for Florida State and a paper tiger in the hunt for No. 1. A stunned nation watched the Huskers come within a whisker of defeating the Seminoles in a game clearly dominated by Nebraska.

Few teams ever faced more adversity than the 1994 team when injuries struck with a vengeance. Top defensive back Mike Minter went down early with a knee injury. Then, quarterback Tommie Frazier suffered life-threatening blood clots and back-up quarterback Brook Berringer was sidelined with a collapsed lung. But the Huskers never missed a beat as reserves stepped in to the breach to ensure an undefeated season. Then, in an emotional bowl game, the Huskers knocked off Miami on the Hurricanes' home Orange Bowl turf to complete the Tom Osborne national championship odyssey.

But could Osborne and the Huskers do it again? The Huskers said yes in the off-season and made it come true in the fall, handily defeating every opponent en route to a fifth-consecutive Big Eight title, a No. 1 ranking and a spot in the Fiesta Bowl against undefeated No. 2-ranked Florida for a national championship decision.

All that was accomplished despite the off-the-field problems that prompted unprecedented media distractions. But it was a unified, dedicated and determined Nebraska team that met Florida on January 2nd in the Tostitos Fiesta Bowl and administered one of the most impressive victories in bowl history, a devastating 62-24 margin over the vaunted Gators of the Southeastern Conference.

Thus, with two consecutive national championship trophies, Coach Tom Osborne once again reinforced his long-standing reputation as one of the most successful and respected leaders in college football. Nebraska fans everywhere and football fans nationwide recognize the Nebraska program as the pace-setter in competition, academics, graduation and success.

This book, which chronicles the wonderful 1995 season, is dedicated to Coach Tom Osborne, his staff, the players and all the many Nebraska fans who have made it all possible. I join in thanking them and all the many people who make Nebraska's athletic program so successful.

All of us at the University of Nebraska hope you enjoy this exciting book as much as you have enjoyed another championship season. As you read through this book, it will once again remind you that "There is No Place Like Nebraska."

Bill Byrne
Director of Athletics
University of Nebraska

Nebraska

Athletic Director - Bill Byrne

Bill Byrne wasted no time in making his presence felt at Nebraska. During his three years as athletic director, the Cornhuskers have won three national championships: two in football and one in women's volleyball. Coach Terry Pettit's Huskers were the NCAA women's volleyball champions in 1995.

Nebraska athletic teams won nine of 20 Big Eight Conference titles in 1994-95. They finished in the first division of the conference in four other sports. In addition, Nebraska won a 16th-consecutive Big Eight all-sports championship in 1994-95 and almost certainly will win a 17th in 1995-96.

Such remarkable success depends not only on coaching and athletes but also on strong administration. And Byrne has provided that since replacing Bob Devaney in January of 1993.

Under Byrne's direction, an athletic department budget deficit has been erased, donations have doubled and marketing revenue, driven by the national championships, has skyrocketed.

Nebraska's athletic department operates on a budget of more than $20 million.

Also, Byrne has addressed gender equity, leading the effort to add women's soccer to the Cornhuskers' offerings. Nebraska now sponsors 22 varsity sports, 11 for men and 11 for women.

During his brief tenure, the on-going renovation of Memorial Stadium began. Among other things, the HuskerVision replay boards have been added and the coaches' offices have been remodeled.

Byrne also has spearheaded Nebraska's involvement in the formation of the Big 12 Conference, looking out for the Cornhuskers' interests while working with the new league's other members. Evidence of his vision could be seen during the Big 12's discussions of a football playoff between the champions of the conference's north and south divisions. Nebraska wasn't in favor of such a playoff, believing the Big 12 would be better served by having an opportunity to get two teams in the Bowl Alliance.

When the decision was made to have a playoff, Byrne set about putting together a proposal on behalf of Nebraska to be the host to such a playoff. "If it's just money, we can match or do better than anybody else," Byrne said in discussing the proposal. "If it's anything else, I think we're in better shape to get this thing done right than any of the other places that are bidding for the playoff."

NEBRASKA

Head Coach - Tom Osborne

A somewhat disheveled Tom Osborne met the press following Nebraska's 62-24 victory against Florida in the Tostitos Fiesta Bowl. He had been a victim of the obligatory drenching by his players. "I'm soaking wet and kind of cold, so I'm not going to talk very long," he said.

Late on the night of Jan. 2, 1996, there was little left to be said, by Osborne or by anyone else.

Nebraska had just earned a second national championship in as many seasons, rolling over 12 consecutive opponents and leaving no doubt about its claim to the No. 1 ranking. Osborne's 23rd team was clearly the nation's best — possibly among the best college football teams of all time.

In a season of parity, one in which Northwestern won the Big Ten championship, Nebraska was unchallenged. "This is the most complete team I've coached," Osborne said.

The 1994 national champions were impressive, overcoming, among other things, the loss of quarterback Tommie Frazier on their way to winning 13 games — including the dramatic, come-from-behind, 24-17 victory against Miami on the Hurricanes' home field in the Orange Bowl.

"But the numbers would indicate (the 1995 team) is the best team," said Osborne.

The 1995 champions averaged more points and more yards per game than any team in Nebraska's history, including the "Scoring Explosion" team in 1983. But the only numbers really necessary for supporting Osborne's assertion were the scores of the Huskers' 12 games. No opponent came close.

(Above) Senior Phil Ellis gets a pregame handshake from the coach.

Signals from the sideline.

Even the most cynical critics would have difficulty finding a more dominant team throughout college football history. In 1944, an Army team that included Glenn Davis and Doc Blanchard outscored nine opponents, on average, by an NCAA-record 52.1 points. Nebraska was such a team.

The Huskers were so strong in 1995 there was an element of the matter-of-fact following their demolition of Florida, which had come to Tempe, Ariz., with a 12-0 record and No. 2 ranking. "There's not nearly as much emotion," Osborne said. "We were supposed to do this. People expected it."

When Nebraska returned to Lincoln on the day after the Fiesta Bowl game, a crowd estimated at 8,000 came to the Bob Devaney Sports Center to cheer the champions. The crowd wasn't as large as the one the year before, in part because January 3, 1996, was a workday, whereas January 2, 1995, (the day after last year's Orange Bowl) was not. Also, "there's not the newness of (the national title) this year," said Osborne. Even so, fans braved frigid temperatures and began arriving for the celebration some six hours before the doors opened. "We had a lot of people come out, and some of them probably took off from work to be here. We appreciate the support."

The support Nebraska enjoyed, as evidenced by a continuing NCAA-record 208 consecutive sellouts at Memorial Stadium, was undiminished in 1995.

The adversity the Huskers overcame to win the 1994 national championship paled by comparison to the challenge of repeating in 1995.

"I learned a lot this year," Osborne said. "There were some times I was running on empty. I take my spiritual life very seriously. And frankly, I relied on my faith more than I ever have.

"I was grateful for the sustaining strength that was there."

Nearly every week, it seemed, some national news gathering organization was in Lincoln to question Osborne. He constantly was forced to defend himself and his program, while, at the same time, prepare for the next opponent. Nevertheless, Osborne remained optimistic about his team's chances for success.

He expected his team to be sustained by the kind of character demonstrated the previous season. "This has been a good team as far as attitude," he said. "They like to play. They are physical. They are talented. However, I can't dictate their attitude. It will have to come from them." It did.

The cumulative effect of the season couldn't be hidden in the celebration following the Fiesta Bowl victory, however. "It was a terrible year. And it was a great year," Osborne said at a news conference on the morning after the game. "It was taxing. On the other hand, it was very gratifying to work with a group of players who had the focus and drive to carry them through. That was the redeeming factor."

If winning were all that mattered to Osborne, the national championship would have been its own reward. Since the Associated Press began its ratings in 1936, only eight other teams have repeated as national champions. The most recent was Alabama, which won titles in 1978 and 1979. They also won national championships in 1964-65. Oklahoma won titles in 1955-56 and 1974-75. Notre Dame won in 1946-47, following Army's championships in 1944-45. Minnesota was the national champion in 1940-41. And, of course, Bob Devaney coached Nebraska to the first two of its four national championships in 1970 and 1971 — with Osborne coordinating the offense.

The 1995 Huskers were the first to go undefeated and untied in earning consensus national championships back-to-back since Bud Wilkinson's Oklahoma teams in 1955 and 1956.

Wilkinson's Sooners dominated college football during the 1950s, posting an NCAA-record 47 consecutive victories from 1953 to 1957. Nebraska would be setting its sights on that record now if a 45-yard field goal with one second remaining in the 1994 Orange Bowl game had been successful.

The Huskers' winning streak stands at 25. They have lost only once in three seasons and 37 games. No other team in college football history has won 36 games in three seasons. Only two others have won 35 games in three seasons. "I'm very proud of this stretch of three years," Osborne said.

The Huskers' mini-dynasty, which could continue in 1996, will take its place in college football history along with Miami in the 1980s, Alabama, Oklahoma and Southern Cal in the 1970s, Alabama in the 1960s, Oklahoma in the 1950s, Notre Dame and Army in the 1940s and Minnesota in the 1930s. And it will enhance Osborne's place among the great coaches such as Amos Alonzo Stagg, Pop Warner, Knute Rockne, Bernie Bierman, Bud Wilkinson and Bear Bryant.

That place of honor is already assured for the 59-year-old Osborne, who has the nation's best winning percentage among active major college football coaches. Osborne's record is remarkable: 231-47-3 (.827). He is one of only six active football coaches in Division I-A of the NCAA with 200 or more victories. Osborne's teams have won 12 Big Eight championships, including the last five.

Former Southwest Conference schools Texas, Texas A&M, Baylor and Texas Tech will join to form the Big 12 in 1996. Under a threat by Texas that it would withdraw if it didn't get its way, the conference passed a rule that will prohibit academic non-qualifiers from competing in athletics for member institutions. During his post-Fiesta Bowl news conference, Osborne addressed the issue. "I'd like to say this respectfully to the Big 12 presidents. I hope they'll take a look at the fact that we (the Big Eight) have four teams in the Top 10, and we did it with Big Eight rules. We hope very much that they will reconsider and try to let the Big Eight play with Big Eight rules and not change things," he said.

"Our graduation rate is already higher than the general student body, so I'm at a little bit of a loss as to why we would want to tamper with (the entrance requirements)," Osborne said.

Thirty-four of his Huskers have been awarded a combined 43 first-team Academic All-American certificates. Eight of his players have earned the NCAA's highest academic honor — Today's Top Six/Eight Award. Center Aaron Graham was Nebraska's third such winner in as many years. Rob Zatechka received it in 1994 and Trev Alberts in 1993. Zatechka and Alberts both play in the NFL.

Prior to the season, a survey of major college football coaches conducted by *Newsday* identified Osborne as the nation's best "on the field coach." That estimation by his peers was reaffirmed in 1995. The Huskers achieved extraordinary success under extremely difficult circumstances.

"I think the players expected they were going to win it," said Osborne.

Before the season began, he said Nebraska was capable of a repeat championship. On the Monday before the opening victory at Oklahoma State, Osborne told reporters, in power of positive thinking candor: "Somebody has to win the national championship. It might as well be us.

"Saying it and doing it are two different things. Most people in Nebraska probably have it a little bit out of kilter how easy it could be (to repeat as national champions). It's going to be very difficult, but I don't want the players thinking they can't do it. I want them to believe they can and to expect to do it."

Five months later, those expectations were realized, in unthinkable fashion.

"They just won enough, I guess, that it wasn't ho-hum, certainly, but it was more matter-of-fact. I think when they look back on it, five or 10 years from now, they're probably going to appreciate this three-year run," Osborne said as water dripped from the sleeves of his shirt after the Fiesta Bowl game.

Perhaps, he will be better able to appreciate his success then, too.

Prior to the 1993 season, the defining moment in his career as a head coach occurred on the night of January 2, 1984, in the Orange Bowl, where Osborne earned the respect of the nation by playing to win instead of settling for an almost certain tie. He never hesitated in calling for a two-point conversion attempt following a touchdown run with 48 seconds remaining in the game. The score was Miami 31, Nebraska 30. The attempt failed and the score became final. Osborne had to wait 11 more seasons to celebrate his first national championship.

After the 1984 Orange Bowl loss, Milton Richman of the United Press International wrote: "This is as good a time as any to propose Nebraska's Tom Osborne as Everyone's Coach of the Year ... The Nebraska Cornhuskers lost the game, but not their dignity. For that, they can thank their coach."

That same dignity characterized Osborne's behavior in the handling of all the off-the-field obstacles Nebraska overcame in repeating as national champion in 1995.

During a news conference before the team left for the Phoenix area to prepare for the Fiesta Bowl, Osborne expressed the way he felt about the 1995 Huskers — and it didn't depend on the outcome of the championship game. "This year's team will be one I'll always remember. They have been a team in the true sense of the word. I appreciate their attitude and effort," he said.

Despite the off-the-field problems, "I think the character level is among the very top we've had here. Character — and I hate to wear that word out — had to play into it somewhere. I think they care very much about being a good football team. And they care very much about a lot of things."

So does the man who coached them. As he has throughout his 23 seasons as Nebraska's head coach, Osborne proved the simple truth in the title of his autobiography.

What drives him to succeed is *More Than Winning.*

Osborne's game face shows the ever-present concentration that has helped him to become college football's most successful active coach.

The Osborne Record

Year	Won	Lost	Tied	Pct.	Pts.	Opp.	Bowl
1973	9	2	1	.792	306	163	Cotton
1974	9	3	0	.750	373	132	Sugar
1975*	10	2	0	.833	367	137	Fiesta
1976	9	3	1	.731	416	181	Bluebonnet
1977	9	3	0	.750	315	200	Liberty
1978*	9	3	0	.750	444	216	Orange
1979	10	2	0	.833	380	131	Cotton
1980	10	2	0	.833	470	110	Sun
1981**	9	3	0	.750	364	125	Orange
1982**	12	1	0	.923	514	167	Orange
1983**	12	1	0	.923	654	217	Orange
1984*	10	2	0	.833	387	115	Sugar
1985	9	3	0	.750	421	163	Fiesta
1986	10	2	0	.833	446	165	Sugar
1987	10	2	0	.833	451	164	Fiesta
1988**	11	2	0	.846	477	205	Orange
1989	10	2	0	.833	509	215	Fiesta
1990	9	3	0	.750	434	192	Citrus
1991*	9	1	1	.864	454	230	Orange
1992**	9	3	0	.750	441	199	Orange
1993**	11	1	0	.917	437	194	Orange
1994**+	13	0	0	1.000	479	162	Orange
1995**+	12	0	0	1.000	576	150	Fiesta
Totals	**231**	**47**	**3**	**.827**	**10,166**	**3,953**	**23 Consecutive Bowls**
(Bowl Games	**9**	**13**	**0**	**.409**	**433**	**487)**	

**Big Eight co-champions. **Big Eight champions. +National Champions.*

(Above) Coach Osborne and wife Nancy.

(Left) Coach Osborne looks over several of his monster linemen: the "Pipeline" continued in 1995.

Assistant Head Coach / Running Backs Coach

Frank Solich

Frank Solich looks as if he could put on the pads and play the way he did 30 years ago as a fullback on the Nebraska football teams coached by Bob Devaney. Solich remains in good physical condition and he doesn't show his age, even though the 1995 season should have given him a few gray hairs.

The six-game suspension of I-back Lawrence Phillips, a Heisman Trophy candidate going into the season, created considerable stress for Solich and a significant problem for him to solve.

Nevertheless, Nebraska's running game didn't miss a step. The Huskers led the nation in rushing for the eighth time in the 13 seasons Solich has coached the running backs. Somehow, Solich managed not only to replace Phillips but also to keep Nebraska's four other talented I-backs happy.

And, as for fullbacks, even though the top three all came to Nebraska as walk-ons, they combined their skills to make the position as strong as always, if not stronger. You would expect as much of fullbacks coached by a former fullback, particularly one as determined as Solich.

The 5-foot-8 Solich weighed less than 160 pounds when he played at Nebraska. The Huskers recruited him out of Cleveland, Ohio, because they were also interested in a high school teammate. Tom Osborne, then a Nebraska graduate assistant, reportedly thought at the time: "If we're not recruiting guys any bigger than (Solich and his teammate), we're never going to win a game."

It was one of the few times on record that Osborne's judgment proved wrong. Solich was first-team All-Big Eight and a Husker co-captain as a senior in 1965 when Nebraska went 10-0 during the regular season. During Solich's three seasons, the Cornhuskers' combined record was 29-4.

After graduation, Solich began his coaching career at Omaha Holy Name High School. He moved on to Lincoln Southeast High, where he won two Class A state championships; he joined Osborne's staff as head freshman coach in 1979. Solich became Nebraska's running backs coach in 1983 and was given the added responsibilities of assistant head coach in 1991. Solich turned down an offer to become offensive coordinator for Barry Alvarez, another former Husker, at Wisconsin prior to the promotion.

Nebraska has had at least one All-Big Eight running back in 12 of Solich's 13 seasons coaching the position.

Devaney once said of him: "He's quite a football player, for his size." The record shows that Solich has become quite a football coach, as well.

Defensive Coordinator / Defensive Line Coach

Charlie McBride

A smile crossed Charlie McBride's face as he sat in front of reporters in the South Stadium varsity lounge following Nebraska's 35-21 non-conference victory against Washington State.

"You want the blitz? You got the blitz, right?" he said. As a result of a breakdown in a first-quarter blitz by the Cornhuskers, Washington State scored a touchdown on an 87-yard run.

Good things can happen when a defense blitzes. But bad things can happen, too, which is why being a defensive coordinator isn't nearly as easy as it seems to those armchair experts who are quick to offer McBride advice on how to do his job.

McBride, who began as a high school coach in his native Chicago in 1963, has been coaching a long time. He's been at Nebraska for 19 years, including 14 as defensive coordinator. He's heard it all over the years.

During his first 15 or so years of coaching, he used to get sick to his stomach before each game. "Now, I don't do that anymore," he says. He's much more relaxed — outwardly, at least.

McBride, an All-Big Eight end and punter at Colorado in 1962, has fashioned a defense that perennially ranks among the nation's best. The Cornhuskers were No. 2 in rushing defense, No. 4 in scoring defense and No. 13 in total defense in 1995. It was the 10th time in McBride's tenure as defensive coordinator that Nebraska has ranked in the Top 15 nationally in both scoring and total defense.

Although the Cornhuskers' reputation for high-scoring offense is certainly deserved, they have won back-to-back national championships by playing rugged defense, as well.

Nebraska has changed its defensive philosophy in recent seasons, scrapping its 5-2 alignment and replacing it with a 4-3 base. Officially, the change came in the spring of 1993. But the changeover began before that, as the Cornhuskers looked for a way to deal more effectively with the warm-weather, pass-oriented offenses with which they were confronted annually in bowl games.

The switch has been popular, as well as successful. "The kids love to play the 4-3," says McBride. "I don't want to say it's a less disciplined defense, but it's freer and less complicated."

In addition to coordinating the defense, McBride coaches the interior defensive line. In 1992, *The Sporting News* named him the nation's best defensive line coach. Even so, he still gets an occasional suggestion. Fans are particularly enamored with blitzes. They only see the ones that work.

Linebackers Coach

Craig Bohl

Craig Bohl got off to a good start at Nebraska. He celebrated his first season as a full-time assistant by sharing in a national championship. It doesn't get any better than that.

Bohl, a graduate of Lincoln East High School, jumped at the opportunity to return to Nebraska last spring. In the late 1970s, he played for the Cornhuskers as a walk-on defensive back. He also served as a Nebraska graduate assistant for three seasons after calling it quits as a player.

"This is close to a dream come true," he said after replacing Kevin Steele, who left for a job with the Carolina Panthers, the National Football League's expansion team, following the 1994 season.

Bohl is one of four former Nebraska players on Coach Tom Osborne's staff. The others are Frank Solich, Tony Samuel and Turner Gill. That makes the job special, according to Bohl.

"The guys who played here and come back, you cut their arms and Nebraska blood runs out. It's hard to describe. There's a tremendous amount of loyalty," Bohl says.

"That's a big advantage. It makes you feel good."

Bohl, who suffered a broken leg and six shoulder separations as a player, made five coaching moves in 10 years after leaving Nebraska in 1984. He began his sojourn at North Dakota State. After that, he went to Tulsa, Wisconsin, Rice and Duke.

He was the Blue Devils' defensive coordinator, earning the nickname "Blitzin' Bohl" because of his aggressive, attacking philosophy. Such a philosophy was a good fit for Nebraska, which has dramatically revamped its defense during the 1990s, replacing the 5-2 alignment with a 4-3 base.

It was apparent to him that the Cornhuskers were willing to change with the times. "The days when you could be passive, read and react have gone the way of the white buffalo," he says.

The determination reflected by his walking on at Nebraska in his football-playing days has served Bohl well as a coach. It helps to facilitate communication. He can better empathize with those who play for him.

Being a product of the Cornhuskers' system in football is the equivalent of being a business student who earns an MBA from Harvard University, says Bohl. Coaching in other programs has given him a unique perspective. "I had an opportunity to see what this program is all about," he says.

With apologies to novelist Thomas Wolfe, you can go home again. Bohl has.

Receivers Coach

Ron Brown

Ron Brown could have written this. He is a writer and speaker for the Fellowship of Christian Athletes as well as the author of two books, the latter, based on Nebraska's national championship season in 1994 titled *Unfinished Business*. His abilities are as diverse as the options in Tom Osborne's offense.

Brown has spent nine years at Nebraska, handling an extremely difficult task with good cheer. In addition to teaching those who play for him the skills of their position, he must keep them happy in a run-oriented attack. For Cornhusker receivers, blocking is at least as important as catching passes.

Because of that fact, Brown emphasizes the need to make the most of each opportunity. He carefully organizes practices so receivers learn to handle every conceivable circumstance.

On "sun ball day," for example, he has players catch passes looking into the sun. And, on "tough catch day," he has them diving onto mats in order to catch passes that would otherwise have been out of reach. Sometimes, he even has "wet ball day," a self-explanatory description.

"When they drop a ball in a game, I have to ask myself if I put them in that situation (during practice)," Brown says. "With the offense we have, there is tremendous pressure (on receivers)."

Brown is a participant, not just an observer. He is a familiar sight at practice, firing passes with his strong left arm. "I can't throw as much as I used to," he says. "But I still like to throw some."

He also is an active participant in the lives of those who play for him. At a weekly meeting of the Extra Point Club last season, Brown explained that role to a group of Cornhusker boosters.

"We treat these young men like they're our children. They are our family," he said. "These aren't just gladiators on a Saturday afternoon who perform to the delight of 76,000 people. These are young men who are so impressionable, and we feel like perhaps we're the last line of defense they have."

On the football field, those who play for Brown regularly nullify the opposing team's last line of defense. They have earned a reputation for being tenacious downfield blockers.

Nebraska's running game is designed in such a way that even the most basic play can produce a long gain if blocked properly. And the receivers are an important element of the blocking scheme. "(Tampa Bay Buccaneers head coach Tony Dungy) told me that if receivers in the NFL blocked like we did, it would change the way defensive coordinators approached the game," Brown has said.

Defensive Backs Coach

George Darlington

A coach for whom George Darlington played at Rutgers University once asked him how he ended up with the responsibility of handling Nebraska's defensive backfield. "He asked what they had caught me doing to make me coach the secondary," Darlington said with a smile.

"He told me there was no logical reason that a person with a (bachelor's) degree from Rutgers and a master's degree from Stanford would be coaching the secondary."

A defensive backs coach, like those who play for him, is rarely noticed unless the context is negative, such as pass coverage breaking down. "There's pressure on every position, but coaching the secondary is one of the most stressful," said Darlington. "It's a great challenge. You're on the edge."

Darlington has been on that edge for 10 years after spending 13 seasons coaching the Cornhusker defensive ends. He is the only carry-over from Tom Osborne's original staff in 1973.

Darlington's 23 years are evidence of his loyalty, not only to Osborne but also to the program that gave him a job when he had none. He had been fired by San Jose State, along with head coach Dewey King and the rest of the staff, following a 5-6 season. Darlington, a West Virginia native, was recommended to Osborne by King while they were attending a meeting of the Fellowship of Christian Athletes.

Osborne didn't have to do much persuading to get Darlington to move to Lincoln.

"When you're out of a job, you don't need a great sales pitch," Darlington has said.

Darlington didn't need much persuasion to move from coaching the defensive ends to handling the secondary, either. His only request was that defensive backs would be as much of a scholarship recruiting priority as any other position. "I said I wasn't going to play with just walk-ons," he said.

The Cornhuskers' change from a 5-2 base defense to a 4-3 has meant finding defensive backs who can cover receivers man-to-man, which, in turn, means defensive backs with exceptional speed. The back-to-back national championships are evidence Nebraska has been successful in that search.

"I think we can run with a lot of people," Darlington said after the Fiesta Bowl victory. "You've got to be able to match up when you're playing teams like Florida, Miami and Florida State.

"Our kids have played pretty well against a lot of talented people (wide receivers)."

If they hadn't, they would have drawn a lot of attention. And their coach would have, too.

Quarterbacks Coach

Turner Gill

Just a short time ago, Turner Gill was the standard by which Nebraska quarterbacks were measured. During the last four seasons, he has been the coach of a new standard: Tommie Frazier.

Gill's Cornhusker coaching career also has spanned four seasons. He returned to Nebraska to coach full-time (he was a graduate assistant at Nebraska in 1990) at the same time Frazier arrived in Lincoln for his freshman season. Both have benefited from their association, and so has Nebraska.

Gill's recruitment out of Fort Worth, Texas, was a crucial step in the development of the Cornhuskers' option offense, which Frazier has elevated to another level.

Gill's choice of schools came down to Nebraska and Big Eight-rival Oklahoma.

"It was tough," Gill has said. "I grew up thinking if Oklahoma ever offered me a scholarship, that's where I was going to go. I didn't really know a whole lot about Nebraska. I basically saw the Nebraska-Oklahoma game on television. That's all. Oklahoma definitely recruited me hard. But I guess there was a little doubt I would play quarterback. The other big issue was my playing both football and baseball. I was going to go to a school that would let me play both, and I didn't believe for sure that Oklahoma would.

"I trusted Coach Osborne more than I felt I could trust Coach (Barry) Switzer. It was very close to me going to Oklahoma. I really felt comfortable with Coach Osborne. He was the main reason for my decision. Coach Switzer still kids around about it. I'm glad I chose Nebraska."

Being comfortable with Osborne, and thinking like him, is essential for Cornhusker quarterbacks, according to Gill. "Basically, you have to think like Coach Osborne thinks," he said. "You've got to get into the head of Tom Osborne. Every quarterback (who plays at Nebraska) does."

The demands placed on Nebraska's quarterbacks because of the option are unique.

"We ask an awful lot," said Gill. "We're pretty exacting because we're reading the defense, all 11 guys. Most people will read the secondary, but we also read the defensive fronts. We're asking our quarterbacks to read the defense, run the option and pass. No other team in the country asks their quarterback to do all of that, not that I can think of, anyway. I might be wrong. But most do only two of the three."

When quarterbacks are recruited, "you hope they can do all three," he said.

Of course, "some of that is my responsibility, too." Gill now teaches what he once did.

Outside Linebackers Coach

Tony Samuel

Jared Tomich and Grant Wistrom? They're simply the best, according to Tony Samuel. "As a twosome, productivity-wise, they're as good as I've had so far," Samuel has said.

To appreciate the significance of that estimation, consider that Samuel has coached Nebraska's outside linebackers for 10 years, during which seven of his players have been selected in the National Football League draft, including three in the first round: Broderick Thomas, Mike Croel and Trev Alberts, who also was the Cornhuskers' first Butkus Award winner as the nation's best linebacker.

Four of those seven, plus another who wasn't drafted but signed as a free agent, played in the NFL this season. A fifth played in Canada and a sixth was on the NFL's injured reserve list.

Outside linebacker (formerly called defensive end) is a showcase position on the Cornhusker defense. It has been that way almost from the time the NCAA reinstated two-platoon football.

Among those who played there before Samuel became the position coach were All-Americans Willie Harper, Bob Martin, George Andrews, Derrie Nelson and Jimmy Williams. Samuel, himself, earned three letters playing the position for Nebraska from 1975 through 1977. His position coach was George Darlington, who now has responsibility for the Cornhusker defensive backs.

Outside linebacker has become even more of a high profile position in Nebraska's defense since the Cornhuskers scrapped the 5-2 base alignment in favor of the 4-3. The attack philosophy on which the 4-3 depends allows the outside linebackers to be aggressive. That, in turn, puts them in position to make big, highly visible plays, such as quarterback sacks. In order for Nebraska to be successful defensively, "the position has to dominate," Samuel said.

That's what it did this season, even though both starters were new. Tomich, a junior, earned All-America honors this season. He and Wistrom, a sophomore, both were chosen on All-Big Eight teams.

There were solid players behind Tomich and Wistrom on the depth chart, as well, including steady senior Luther Hardin, redshirted freshman Mike Rucker and true freshman Chad Kelsay.

"If you get enough of those kids and they're willing to work, they've got a pretty good chance at the pros," said Samuel, who lets the players he coaches be themselves, within the system. "They're coming to a school that highlights the position. They know they have an opportunity to be an elite."

Offensive Line Coach

Milt Tenopir

Prior to the start of spring practice, Milt Tenopir predicted success for the 1995 version of Nebraska's offensive line. By the end of spring drills, "I think we'll have enough improvement to where we can be better than average," he said, in typically optimistic fashion.

At the time, Tenopir's prediction might have been dismissed simply as evidence of his can-do attitude. Only one starter, center Aaron Graham, was returning from an offensive line ranked by some as one of the best in college football history. The interior offensive line that opened the way to Coach Tom Osborne's first national championship in 1994 included three players who are now in the National Football League: Zach Wiegert, the 1994 Outland Trophy winner, Brenden Stai and Rob Zatechka.

Nebraska's 1994 offensive line was featured in Sports Illustrated. At least one newspaper columnist suggested the line as a unit should be considered a candidate for the Heisman Trophy. Rarely has an offensive line, at any level, attracted so much attention. Nevertheless, Tenopir remained enthusiastic.

In retrospect, his enthusiasm wasn't misplaced. Tenopir and Dan Young, who also works with the Cornhuskers' offensive line, put together another line of comparable ability. Steve Ott, who was sidelined by injury a year ago, Aaron Taylor, Chris Dishman and Eric Anderson joined Graham as the starters, with Adam Treu, Jon Zatechka and Steve Volin among the top back-ups. Together, they opened a path to Nebraska's sixth NCAA rushing title in the last eight seasons and its 12th all-time.

Behind their blocks, Nebraska averaged 399.8 rushing yards per game, the second-highest average in school history. They were rarely penalized. And they didn't allow a single quarterback sack.

Tenopir has been at Nebraska for 22 seasons. He has coached five Cornhusker Outland Trophy winners. In addition to Wiegert, that select group includes Will Shields, Dean Steinkhuhler and Dave Rimington, who won the award as the nation's best down lineman in back-to-back seasons.

Tenopir's coaching imprint is firmly affixed to the prestigious award. Nebraska's only other Outland Trophy winners were defensive linemen: Larry Jacobson and Rich Glover.

Nebraska set school records for points and yards per game in 1995, surpassing standards established by the "Scoring Explosion" team in 1983. The offensive line played a key role — further evidence that under Tenopir's direction, the Cornhuskers don't rebuild in the offensive line, they reload.

Offensive Line / Kickers Coach

Dan Young

Because of Nebraska's offensive dominance in 1995, it might be easy to overlook the importance of the kicking game to the Cornhuskers' success. They only punted 29 times, for example.

But Coach Tom Osborne has always emphasized kicking and the play of special teams. And, given his remarkable record, it is impossible to argue the point.

Dan Young, who also helps Milt Tenopir coach the offensive line, has been responsible for Nebraska's kicking game for 10 of his 13 years as a Cornhusker assistant. He coached Nebraska's freshman-junior varsity team his first three seasons, compiling a 14-1 record.

Such success came as no surprise. Young was the head football coach at Omaha Westside High School for six seasons before coming to Nebraska. During those six seasons, his teams had a combined record of 55-11 and won two Class A state championships.

Young's responsibility in the kicking game was never greater than this season, when he had to find a capable replacement for versatile Darin Erstad, who did the punting and shared the place-kicking duties in 1994. The problem Young had to solve following Erstad's departure as the No. 1 pick in the major league baseball draft was two-fold. Nebraska needed a new punter and a new place-kicker, and there were no experienced players with whom to begin. Even so, the Cornhuskers were typically successful.

Jesse Kosch, a redshirted sophomore, stepped in as the punter, averaging 40.3 yards on 27 punts, as Nebraska ranked 17th nationally in net punting. Opponents returned only five punts, a school record, for a net of 12 yards. Eleven times they were forced to begin inside their own 20-yard line following a punt.

Kris Brown, a true freshman, emerged as the Cornhuskers' place-kicker. He was the first true freshman in the modern era, in fact, to handle the place-kicking and kickoff duties for Nebraska.

Brown was successful on 13 of 16 field goal attempts, including 7-of-9 of 30 yards or longer. He also kicked 58 extra points, to establish a Cornhusker record for points by kicking in a season.

During one stretch, he kicked 31 consecutive extra points.

"It's kind of amazing how well it has all come around," Young said of the kicking game during the week before the Fiesta Bowl game. Amazing, maybe. But it is certainly no accident.

"I believe there is no substitute for hard work," says Young, who does as he says.

Associate Athletic Director / Football Operations

Steve Pederson

Nebraska will attempt to win a third-consecutive national championship in 1996 — a feat no college program has been able to accomplish since the Associated Press established its rankings in 1936.

The Cornhuskers will have to replace many important players from the 1995 national champions, among them quarterback Tommie Frazier. And that won't be easy.

But they won't rebuild. They will reload, as they always have, on the field as well as off.

If it were any other way, Nebraska wouldn't have achieved such extraordinary success, not only in winning back-to-back national championships but also throughout Tom Osborne's 23 seasons as head coach. Osborne's program has succeeded because it is solid from top to bottom.

Steve Pederson is a case in point. He arrived in the spring of 1994 to replace Dave Gillespie, who left the job as Nebraska's recruiting coordinator to become an on-the-field coach at Kansas. At the same time, the NCAA passed legislation limiting the duties of recruiting coordinators.

The change in rules was significant, particularly for Nebraska, which has been forced, by geographical considerations, to outwork other programs during recruiting. Enter Pederson, an energetic Nebraska graduate who once worked in the Cornhusker sports information office.

After spending a year as public relations director at Ak-Sar-Ben in Omaha, Pederson was hired by Osborne to be Nebraska's recruiting coordinator in 1982. Pederson held the job for four years, producing recruiting classes that were ranked among the nation's best by prominent recruiting analysts.

The Cornhuskers' 1985 scholarship class was ranked No. 1 nationally by at least one expert.

Pederson left Nebraska to enter private business, then returned to football as recruiting coordinator at Ohio State. He moved on to Tennessee, where he was an assistant athletic director for recruiting and football operations. During his three years in Knoxville, Tennessee's recruiting classes ranked among the best in the nation. The Volunteers' success in recent seasons is evidence of the accuracy of those rankings. And when Gillespie left Nebraska, Pederson returned to his home state to handle the considerable responsibilities of organizing and supervising Osborne's program off the field.

Pederson works closely with Cornhusker athletic director Bill Byrne as a liaison for football and a link to the NCAA. He handles the myriad details that comprise a quality program.

Athletic Director Emeritus

Bob Devaney

In 1961, Nebraska posted a 3-6-1 record. In 1962, Bob Devaney arrived at Nebraska from Wyoming to become head football coach and forever change the course of Cornhusker history.

During Devaney's 11 seasons as coach, Nebraska's record was 101-20-2. His Cornhuskers won eight Big Eight titles and played in nine bowl games. And, of course, they won national championships in 1970 and 1971, back-to-back success reproduced by Tom Osborne in 1994 and 1995.

Devaney's skill as an administrator was comparable to his skill as a coach. During his tenure as athletic director, which began while he was still coaching, Nebraska's athletic program excelled and expanded, as did its facilities, including Memorial Stadium. The multi-purpose Bob Devaney Sports Center stands in tribute not only to his administrative skills but also to his personal popularity in the state.

However, when listing Devaney's achievements, one of his most significant decisions is often forgotten. Devaney selected Osborne to succeed him in 1973. As a result, Cornhusker football has never missed a beat.

Director of Athletic Performance

Boyd Epley

Nebraska's back-to-back national championships are a function of many factors, not the least of which include the strength and conditioning program designed by Boyd Epley and his staff.

Nebraska has been a national leader in strength and conditioning under Epley, whose 26-year association with the Cornhuskers began as an athlete — specifically, a pole vaulter.

Epley was a visionary, becoming the first strength coach in the Big Eight Conference.

Under his direction, the system by which the Cornhuskers train and develop has been constantly revised and updated. It remains on the cutting edge. In 1990, however, the program lost some focus, according to Epley, who told an Omaha newspaper reporter: "It was the low point of my involvement with Nebraska. I wasn't doing the best job because that was the time we were opening our new facility, and I was spending so much time with that."

It was then that he set about correcting the problem. The results have been obvious.

Graduate Assistant Coaches

Clayton Carlin

Mike Grant

Clayton Carlin certainly has been in the right place at the right time.

The Philadelphia, Pa., native has served as a Nebraska graduate assistant for two seasons and the Cornhuskers have won national championships both of those seasons.

Carlin has assisted George Darlington in coaching the secondary, while working on a master's degree in educational administration. Prior to coming to Nebraska, he spent two years as the defensive backs coach at Delaware Valley College in Doylestown, Pa.

Mike Grant, like Clayton Carlin, is two-for-two as a Cornhusker graduate assistant: two national championships in two seasons on Coach Tom Osborne's staff.

Grant also played for Osborne, earning three letters as a quarterback from 1989-1992. After finishing a degree in communications studies, he worked for two years as an assistant in the recruiting office. The Tampa, Fla., native has worked with Ron Brown, coaching the receivers.

Grant is working on a master's degree in mass communications.

The Players

Awards and Honors

HUSKER FIRST TEAM ALL-AMERICANS

Tommie Frazier
Quarterback

Aaron Graham
Center

Jared Tomich
Outside Linebacker

ATHLETIC HONORS

National Honors:

Quarterback Tommie Frazier:
*Heisman Trophy Runner-up
**The Sporting News* Offensive Player-of-the-Year
*Johnny Unitas Golden Arm Award Winner
*UPI Player-of-the-Year
*UPI Player-of-the-Year Runner-up
*Davey O'Brien Finalist (1 of 3)
**Football News* Offensive Player-of-the-Year Finalist (1 of 7)
*TD Club of Columbus Quarterback-of-the-Year
*Maxwell Award Finalist (1 of 3)
*Walter Camp Offensive Player-of-the-Year Finalist (1 of 5)
*ESPY Awards College Football Player-of-the-Year

*Football News Defensive Player-of-the-Year Semifinalist:
Jared Tomich, OLB
*Butkus Watch List: Phil Ellis, LB
*Chevrolet Coach-of-the-Year: Tom Osborne
*UPI Coach-of-the-Year Runner-up: Coach Tom Osborne
*TD Club of Washington, Team-of-the-Year: Nebraska
*TD Club of Washington, Offensive Lineman-of-the-Year:
The Entire Nebraska Offensive Line

All-America Honors:

*First-Team All-Americans:
Tommie Frazier, QB (Football Writers, Walter Camp, AP, AFCA, UPI, American Football Quarterly, College Sports)
Aaron Graham, C (Football News, AP, American Football Quarterly)
Jared Tomich, OLB (AP, American Football Quarterly)
*Second-Team All-Americans:
Jared Tomich, OLB (Football News, Athlon)
Terrell Farley, LB (UPI, AP)
*Third-Team All-Americans:
Aaron Taylor, OG (Football News)
Grant Wistrom, OLB (AP)
*Honorable-Mention All-Americans:
Tommie Frazier, QB (Football News)
Christian Peter, DT (Football News, UPI)
Ahman Green, IB (UPI)
Chris Dishman, OT (UPI)
Aaron Graham, C (UPI)

All-Big Eight Honors:

*Offensive Player-of-the-Year: Tommie Frazier, QB (AP, Coaches)
*Defensive Newcomer-of-the-Year: Terrell Farley, LB (AP, Coaches)
*Offensive Freshman-of-the-Year: Ahman Green, IB (AP, Coaches)
*Offensive Newcomer-of-the-Year: Ahman Green, IB (AP)

(AP–Associated Press; Coaches–Big Eight Coaches)

***First-Team All-Big Eight:**

Eric Anderson, OT (Coaches)
Chris Dishman, OT (FB News, Coaches)
Terrell Farley, LB (AP)
Tommie Frazier, QB (AP, FB News, Coaches)
Aaron Graham, C (AP, FB News)
Ahman Green, IB (Coaches)
Christian Peter, DT (AP, FB News, Coaches)
Aaron Taylor, OG (AP, FB News)
Jared Tomich, OLB (AP, FB News)
Tyrone Williams, CB (AP, Coaches)
Grant Wistrom, OLB (Coaches)

***Second-Team All-Big Eight:**

Reggie Baul, Returns (Coaches)
Chris Dishman, OT (AP)
Terrell Farley, LB (Coaches)
Aaron Graham, C (Coaches)
Ahman Green, IB (AP)
Mike Minter, Rover (AP, Coaches)
Aaron Taylor, OG (Coaches)
Jared Tomich, OLB (Coaches)
Tony Veland, FS (AP, Coaches)
Grant Wistrom, OLB (AP)

***Honorable-Mention All-Big Eight:**

Eric Anderson, OT (AP)
Reggie Baul, SE (Coaches)
Kris Brown, PK (AP, Coaches)
Phil Ellis, LB (AP, Coaches)
Brendan Holbein, SE (Coaches)
Clester Johnson, WB (Coaches)
Jeff Makovicka, FB (Coaches)
Jason Peter, DT (Coaches)

Big Eight Player-of-the-Week Nominations:

Opponent:	Offense:	Defense:
Oklahoma State	Tommie Frazier,QB	Jared Tomich, OLB
Michigan State	Eric Anderson, OT	**Phil Ellis, LB**
Arizona State	Tommie Frazier, QB	Michael Booker, CB
Pacific	Damon Benning, IB	Terrell Farley, LB
Washington State	Tommie Frazier, QB	Grant Wistrom,OLB
Missouri	**Tommie Frazier, QB**	Terrell Farley, LB
Kansas State	Tommie Frazier, QB	Grant Wistrom, OLB
Colorado	**Tommie Frazier, QB**	Terrell Farley, LB
Iowa State	Ahman Green, IB	Mike Minter, Rov.
Kansas	Tommie Frazier, QB	Jared Tomich, OLB
Oklahoma	Tommie Frazier, QB	**Jared Tomich, OLB**

Bold indicates winning conference award.

National Player-of-the-Week/Game Honors

Honda/ESPN Scholar-Athlete vs. OSU: Aaron Graham, C
Wrangler/ESPN NU Player-of-the-Game vs. OSU: Lawrence Phillips, I-Back
Chevrolet Player-of-the-Game vs. MSU: Lawrence Phillips, I-Back
AT&T Long Distance Run From Scrimmage: 80 yards (TD), James Sims vs. Michigan State
AT&T Long Punt: 73 yards, Jesse Kosch vs. ASU
CNN Player-of-the-Week–Tommie Frazier vs. MU
Chevrolet Player-of-the-Game (CU, KSU, KU, Fla.)–Tommie Frazier, QB
Chevrolet Player-of-the-Game (OU)–Grant Wistrom, OLB

ACADEMIC HONORS

National Honors:

*CFA/Hitachi Good Works Team: Aaron Graham, C
*CFA/Hitachi Scholar-Athlete: Aaron Graham, C
($1,000 to Graham's high school in Denton, Texas)
*Burger King Scholar-Athlete Award Winner: Aaron Graham, C, Dec. 2, 1995 ($25,000 to UNL general scholarship fund)

GTE/CoSIDA Academic All-American:

*First-Team:
Aaron Graham, C, 3.33, cum., animal science
*Second-Team:
Steve Ott, OG, 3.49, cum., biological sciences
Brian Schuster, FB, 3.71, year, pre-education
Steve Volin, OG, 3.86, cum., biological sciences
*All-District VII:
Aaron Graham, C, 3.33, cum., animal science
Steve Ott, OT, 3.49, cum., biological sciences
Brian Schuster, FB, 3.71, year, pre-education
Ryan Terwilliger, LB, 3.23, cum., pre-education
Steve Volin, OG, 3.86, cum., biological sciences
Grant Wistrom, OLB, 3.58, cum., pre-pharmacy

Phillips 66 Academic All-Big Eight:

***First-Team All-Big Eight:**

Aaron Graham, C, 3.33, cum., animal science
Mark Gilman, TE, 3.15, cum., pre-education
Grant Wistrom, OLB, 3.58, cum., pre-pharmacy
Eric Stokes, FS, 3.17, year, sociology
Ryan Terwilliger, LB, 3.23, cum., pre-education
Steve Ott, OG, 3.49, cum., biological sciences
Brook Berringer, QB, 3.00, year, business administration
Jesse Kosch, P, 3.06, year, meteorology/climatology

***Honor Roll:**

Lance Brown, WB, 3.78, cum., business administration
Tim Carpenter, TE, 3.00, year, pre-education
Jon Hesse, LB, 3.49, cum., psychology
Jason Jenkins, DT, 3.18, year, graduate studies
Jeff Lake, SE, 3.68, cum., consumer science and education
Joel Makovicka, FB, 3.88, cum., undecided
Kory Mikos, OT, 3.30, year, pre-education
Aaron Penland, LB, 3.18, cum., business administration
Ted Retzlaff, PK, 3.42, cum., agribusiness
Scott Saltsman, DT, 3.17, cum., marketing
Brian Schuster, FB, 3.71, year, pre-education
Matt Turman, QB, 3.68, cum., pre-education
Steve Volin, OG, 3.86, cum., biological sciences
Matt Vrzal, C, 3.02, cum., business administration
Jon Zatechka, OG, 3.82, cum., fisheries and wildlife

AP All-Time Big Eight Conference Football Team (1995)

Nebraska Players:

Johnny Rodgers, WR (1970-72)
Dean Steinkuhler, OT (1981-83)
Zach Wiegert, OT (1991-94)
Dave Rimington, C (1979-82)
Rich Glover, DT (1970-72)
Willie Harper, DT (1970-72)
Best Offensive Player: Johnny Rodgers, WB (1970-72)
Best Coach: Tom Osborne (1973-95)
Best Game: Nebraska 35, Oklahoma 31 (Nov. 25, 1971)

91
10

Eric Anderson #70

Nebraska's motto this season was: Business As Usual. And that's how it was, right through the Tostitos Fiesta Bowl game. According to Eric Anderson, Coach Tom Osborne said the same thing before the championship game he always says before a game: "Play hard, and if we go hard on every play, we'll get the victory."

Anderson, one of 13 players from Lincoln on this year's team, grew up listening to Husker games on the radio. He was among four new starters in the offensive line, stepping up to replace Outland Trophy winner Zach Wiegert (now playing in the NFL) at right tackle.

The newcomers wasted little time settling in. They opened the way for 671 total yards, including 513 rushing, in a 64-21 opening-game victory at Oklahoma State.

After the first play from scrimmage, they were no longer rookies. "Physically, everyone here can play," Anderson said. "But the mental part of the game is where you separate people."

Anderson, who started every game, averaged nearly seven "pancake" blocks per game in helping Nebraska win its second-consecutive NCAA rushing title and its 10th during Osborne's 23 seasons as head coach. The Huskers rushed for an average of 399.8 yards per game, the second-best average in school history and 60 yards per game more than the much-publicized "Pipeline" of the 1994 season.

Despite being slowed by an ankle injury late in the season, Anderson earned first-team All-Big Eight recognition from the conference coaches. He received all-conference honorable mention from the Associated Press. His best individual performance was against Michigan State, when he was selected as the Huskers' offensive Player of the Week after achieving a rare perfect 2.0 grade.

The next week, Anderson invited his coach at Lincoln Southeast High School, Chuck Mizerski, to be his guest for the Arizona State game at Memorial Stadium, his first start at home. His grade that afternoon was 1.94. Offensive line coach Milt Tenopir considers 1.85 winning football.

Reggie Baul #7

Reggie Baul was Nebraska's second-leading receiver with 17 catches for 304 yards. In dramatic contrast, Ike Hilliard was Florida's second-leading receiver with 57 catches.

"Florida is the ideal place for receivers," Baul explained before the Fiesta Bowl game. "But we feel we can make what we do count more here. We're winning as a team, and that's why we're here."

Baul arrived at Nebraska from Papillion-LaVista High School as a walk-on. "I could catch anything thrown my way," he said. "(But) as receivers, we have to block and catch. I just couldn't block."

Receivers who don't block, don't play. That's how the Huskers have led the NCAA in rushing offense for the second season in a row. Everyone has to get into the blocking act. "I sat a lot," Baul recalls.

Learning to block became not only a priority but also a point of pride for Baul, who was awarded a scholarship prior to the 1993 season. "What's really impressive is when people tell me they saw us blocking downfield," said Baul. "We know we may go a whole game without catching a pass.

"But when guys tell you what you did is important, it makes you feel good."

Baul also returned 10 punts for 96 yards in 1995.

His contributions to the Huskers' second national championship didn't go unnoticed. The conference coaches named him to the All-Big Eight second team.

Baul didn't catch a pass in the Fiesta Bowl victory. Even so, he contributed to Nebraska's remarkable offensive totals against the Gators, who threw 38 passes. The Huskers attempted only 15 passes, six of which were complete. "I honestly believe that we probably concentrate and treasure our passes more than they do," said Baul, who caught 41 passes during his three-year career, 16 fewer than Hilliard's total passes during the 1995 regular season alone. Hilliard caught six passes for 100 yards and one touchdown in the Fiesta Bowl. Baul wasn't envious, however.

After all, he has two national championship rings to Hilliard's none.

Damon Benning #21

Damon Benning began fall practice at No. 2 on the depth chart, behind Heisman Trophy candidate Lawrence Phillips and essentially tied with Clinton Childs, the third I-back listed. Highly-regarded freshman Ahman Green had arrived on campus and sophomore walk-on James Sims had achieved remarkably high scores in pre-fall strength and conditioning tests.

Given the talent of these five young players, the competition for playing time at I-back was bound to be spirited. Unfortunately, Benning was slowed by a hamstring pull that caused him to miss the second and third games. Someone less determined might easily have become discouraged. But Benning remained upbeat. "I know where I stand," he said at the time.

"The coaches know I can play. I can't stress enough how much I like to compete. If I know I've got a guy who's going to step in and do what I do, then that's going to make me work harder." Which, of course, is what he did. As a result, he was prepared to take advantage of his opportunity when it came.

Childs was moved up to No. 1 on the depth chart after the Michigan State game. He started the game with Arizona State, but suffered a severe knee strain, which gave Benning the opportunity to start the next week's game against Pacific.

Benning, who had started two games as a freshman, responded to the challenge, rushing for 173 yards and three touchdowns on only 10 carries in the 49-7 victory against Pacific.

"It's not like we're throwing people into the fire," said assistant head coach and running backs coach Frank Solich. "Not only do I have a lot of confidence in them (the back-up I-backs), but the rest of the team does, too." With good reason.

Despite a severe ankle sprain, Benning also started the Washington State game before giving way to the talented Green. He continued to contribute on special teams and as a reserve I-back.

Benning is philosophical about competing for playing time in a program such as Nebraska's. "One day you can wake up a superstar. But you miss a class or two, or things don't go right in your personal life, and the next thing you know, you're on the outside looking in," he said.

Brook Berringer #18

From a personal standpoint, the 1995 season was difficult for Brook Berringer. In 1994, he led the Huskers to seven victories and the Big Eight championship after coming off the bench when Tommie Frazier was sidelined by bloodclots. He was a second-team all-conference pick by the Associated Press after completing 94 of 151 passes for 1,295 yards and 10 touchdowns.

One of his most memorable performances was against upset-minded Wyoming. He came on for Frazier and directed a 42-32 victory, scoring three touchdowns and completing 15 of 22 passes.

In 1995, with Frazier healthy, he played sparingly, completing 26 of 51 passes for 252 yards, earning him the distinction of becoming the best back-up quarterback in the Big Eight, and possibly the country.

He was sidelined for two games with bursitis in his right knee.

"(The season) obviously hasn't turned out like I had hoped," Berringer said.

Prior to the season, when he was competing with Frazier for the starting job, Berringer expressed a philosophy on which team success depends. "Our team goal is to win a national championship," he said. "My personal goal is to do whatever I can to help the team achieve that goal."

He set an example for his teammates by his quiet resolve. "I'm not a big rah-rah, talk-a-lot kind of leader. I just try to go out and play hard ... practice hard and lead by example," he said.

It was fitting that Berringer scored Nebraska's final touchdown in the Fiesta Bowl victory.

Despite seeing limited action, Berringer was invited to play in the Hula Bowl All-Star game and demonstrate his skills for National Football League scouts. "I want to play pro football, but I don't know if that's going to happen," he said. "I feel like I'm a good player, and I'm going to give it a shot."

His experience at Nebraska has prepared him well. "Perseverance is definitely one of the things I've learned here. No matter what you're up against, if you really think you can do it and believe in yourself and your abilities, you can accomplish almost anything you want," Berringer said.

Michael Booker #20

Immediately after the Huskers' 62-24 victory against Florida in the Tostitos Fiesta Bowl, CBS television sideline reporter Michele Tafoya presented trophies near mid-field.

Amid the cheers of the fans who had given Nebraska a decided home-field advantage at Sun Devil Stadium, Tafoya announced that Michael Booker had been chosen the defensive Player of the Year. Actually, Michael had been chosen as the CBS defensive Player of the Game."

Given the situation, her misstatement was understandable. The way Booker had played, he must have seemed like the defensive Player of the Year to the Gators.

The Fiesta Bowl game was, quite likely, Booker's finest hour as a Husker. Not only did he break open the game by intercepting a Danny Wuerffel pass and returning it 42 yards for a touchdown with 2:40 remaining in the first half, but also he was a constant source of frustration for Florida receivers.

During pre-game warm-ups, the second-ranked Gators were talking some trash. "After the game started, they stopped the trash talking," said Booker, who had a hand in silencing them.

Booker started all but the first two games of the season at left cornerback, joining Tyrone Williams in providing the Nebraska secondary with exceptional man-to-man cover speed.

Booker has been timed at :04.47 in the 40-yard dash. He's among the fastest players on the team, a fact that might have come as a surprise to Florida's fleet receivers. "It's very unusual to see a cornerback at any level of football the size of Michael," said George Darlington, his position coach.

Florida's offensive game plan involved picking on him, Booker said afterward. The plan was ill-conceived. Nebraska had a defensive plan to counteract it. "Our base defense is man-to-man (coverage)," said Booker, who shared the team lead in pass interceptions and pass breakups this season.

"We ran basic coverages we've been running all year."

The Huskers' speed in the secondary enabled them to do that.

"We've got speed just as well as power," Booker said.

Kris Brown #35

In the first quarter of the season-opener at Oklahoma State, Kris Brown missed the first extra-point kick of his Husker career. But he didn't lose his confidence.

"I don't let things like that bother me," he said after the 64-21 victory. "I figured I wouldn't have been the starting kicker if somebody hadn't had at least a little confidence in me.

"You just have to trust yourself and keep going."

That's exactly what Brown did. He went on to make 31 consecutive extra-point kicks before missing again. He finished the regular season with 58 of 61 extra points and 13 field goals in 16 attempts. His 97 points broke Husker single-season records for points by kicking and points by a freshman.

Brown, who earned All-Big Eight honorable mention from both the Associated Press and the conference coaches, was successful on seven of nine field goal attempts of 30 yards or more. His longest was a 47-yarder against Michigan State, one of four games in which he kicked three field goals.

And his .813 field goal percentage was the best in school history.

Among Nebraska's concerns going into the season was finding a replacement for place-kicker and punter Darin Erstad, the first player chosen in the major league baseball draft.

Brown, a high school quarterback, proved to be more than capable, becoming Nebraska's first true freshman place-kicker in the modern era. "We've always had pretty good kickers, but they've never stepped up to the plate like Kris has," said Dan Young, the Huskers' kicking coach. "If he continues at the pace he's going, he'll go down as the all-time kick scorer in Nebraska history."

Brown's performance in the Fiesta Bowl reflected the success he had had all season. After his first extra-point kick was blocked, he made the next five. He also kicked field goals of 26 and 24 yards late in the first half. The second field goal came with just eight seconds remaining in the first half. "It wasn't until I was watching last year's win for the national title that I knew I was going to be a Husker," Brown said. Little did he know he would play such an important role in helping Nebraska win a second championship in a row.

Tim Carpenter #90

Probably there were those who expected Tim Carpenter to follow in the footsteps of Cory Schlesinger. Carpenter came to Nebraska as a fullback from Columbus High School, as Schlesinger did, and displayed a similar toughness, but as a tight end rather than a fullback.

The Huskers were looking for tight ends to step up and join senior co-captain Mark Gilman this season, following the departure of Eric Alford and Matt Shaw. The success of Coach Tom Osborne's run-oriented offensive system depends on the contributions of more than one tight end.

Carpenter made the biggest step, earning the No. 2 spot during spring practice and holding it for all but two games. He missed the Iowa State and Kansas games because of a knee injury.

The pain of the injury to his right knee was such that Carpenter had to take himself out of the Colorado game. The next day, he had arthroscopic surgery to remove damaged cartilage. Less than a month later, he was back in action — evidence that you can't keep a good man down.

While he was recovering, Sheldon Jackson and Vershan Jackson (also a converted fullback) filled in, quite capably. "It's always good knowing that you have backups that can do just as good," Carpenter said. "It keeps you on your feet." Or gets you back onto your feet, as was the situation with him.

Carpenter caught only one pass during the 1995 season (for a 15-yard gain against Pacific). But the contributions of tight ends to Nebraska's offense can't always be measured by the number of their receptions.

"I think the ability I have is to block," he said. "If I can enhance my ability as a receiver, I'm going to try. But I think my main ability is to block."

That was Schlesinger's main ability, as well. Carpenter is following in some big footsteps, just at another position.

Clinton Childs #26

Clinton Childs ran off-tackle on the first play from scrimmage in the Arizona State game. He didn't stop until he was in the end zone. The play covered 65 yards. Only 11 seconds elapsed.

It was an auspicious start to Childs' season at Nebraska. Before he left the game for good after suffering a knee strain early in the second quarter, he scored another touchdown on a 38-yard run. He limped to the sideline with 143 rushing yards on just 12 carries.

Convincing Arizona State's defense that Childs was the Huskers' No. 2 I-back would have been difficult on that particular afternoon. It was Lawrence Phillips' departure after the second game of the season that gave Childs his chance. "I'm sorry that I got the start like that," said Childs, who is Phillips' friend as well as his teammate.

"But I knew I had to pick up the pace." And obviously, he did.

Like many Huskers, Childs succeeded because of persistence and determination. He agreed to learn the fullback's responsibilities when it appeared the team might be thin at that position.

Childs made no excuses for missing the opening game against Oklahoma State after being suspended for an unexcused, missed practice. His absence was a result of the personal pain that followed the death of a grandmother who helped raise him.

"I failed to (notify the coaches) and suffered the consequences," he said.

Once back with the team, he had to re-establish himself. But he never considered giving up. "I've never given up on anything. I'm way too far along in the ballgame to quit," Childs said. "I'll never quit."

Even though the knee strain caused him to miss the Pacific and Washington State games, Childs finished as the Huskers' fourth-leading rusher, gaining 431 yards on 55 carries.

He also returned 10 kickoffs and contributed on kick coverage teams.

"You've got to have some kind of dreams to make it somewhere," said Childs, who was selected to play in the Hula Bowl All-Star game. "I followed them."

Doug Colman #46

In college football lore, "Mr. Inside" and "Mr. Outside" refers to Glenn Davis and Doc Blanchard, Army's Heisman Trophy-winning running backs of the mid-1940s. But Nebraska has had its own "Mr. Inside" and "Mr. Outside" at middle linebacker throughout its back-to-back national championship seasons.

Doug Colman has been "Mr. Inside" and Phil Ellis "Mr. Outside."

Going into the 1995 season, first-year linebackers coach Craig Bohl said of Colman: "Doug is awful good if we encounter a power football team with an inside rushing game."

Ellis, on the other hand, "has been a pleasant surprise to me as far as his acceleration and the way he covers the field. He makes a lot of plays sideline to sideline," said Bohl.

For the past two seasons, the two have alternated as starters. In 1995, Ellis started the first four games. When he suffered a broken foot during practice the week before the Washington State game, Colman became the starter for the next six games. In 1994, Colman started the first eight games, before giving way to Ellis for the last four. They even had lockers side-by-side.

Their competition was good-natured throughout, according to Colman. "I know his family and he knows mine. We just seem to leave it at that and not worry about who is starting and who is playing," he said. Colman finished the season with 46 tackles (his jersey number), including 19 unassisted tackles and two quarterback sacks. He also had four quarterback hurries and one of Nebraska's two pass interceptions against Colorado.

The media tends to focus on the high-profile offensive, quarterback and I-back positions. "The quarterbacks are always in the paper," Colman said. "They have good and bad days. I think we hear about everything they do. We have the same kind of competition at middle linebacker and some other positions. But you don't have to hear about every little thing. Nobody looks at us much."

To some extent, that probably was because Husker fans felt comfortable with either "Mr. Outside" or "Mr. Inside" playing the middle, or "Mike," linebacker position.

Chris Dishman #75

During spring practice, Coach Tom Osborne said he was "fairly sure" Nebraska's rebuilt offensive line would be "decent." By fall camp, however, he expected the line to be "relatively good." Once the season began, Osborne up-graded his estimation again. By season's end, he, and just about everyone else, said the 1995 version of the offensive line was comparable to the one in 1994.

Chris Dishman, the heaviest of the linemen at 310 pounds, was among the reasons for that. "Dishman is a big fellow out there, and he gets the job done," said the Huskers' veteran offensive line coach Milt Tenopir.

"I like being compared to last year's offensive line and being compared to last year's national championship team," Dishman said before the Oklahoma game. "Those guys (last season) were great and I don't compare what we do to what they did. But it's kind of nice when other people do."

Dishman replaced Rob Zatechka at left tackle and made his presence felt, averaging 4.27 "pancake" blocks per game. He was credited with six of the noteworthy, knockdown blocks in each of three crucial conference games: Kansas State, Colorado and Oklahoma.

For his efforts, he was chosen first-team All-Big Eight by the conference coaches and received All-America honorable mention from the United Press International, despite the fact he wasn't always at his best because of personal distractions.

"When you have a lot on your mind outside of football, it's hard to play your best on every down," Dishman told a newspaper reporter before the final regular-season game against Oklahoma. By then, he had worked out solutions to his off-the-field problems and was playing at maximum efficiency.

Dishman and junior split end Brendan Holbein have been football teammates since they were seventh-graders in Cozad. They also were roommates during their first year at Nebraska.

Phil Ellis #41

College football success demands an extraordinary personal commitment.

Phil Ellis will tell you that. He speaks with five years of experience.

"You learn a lot about yourself, what you're capable of doing," he said. "You don't know how far you can push your body. It's mind over matter. Your body will do whatever you want it to do."

Ellis alternated with Doug Colman in the middle of the defense on the Huskers' back-to-back national championship teams. He was chosen by his teammates as a co-captain in 1995.

He handled his responsibilities with a quiet determination that belied his frustration at being sidelined by a broken right foot suffered during practice in late September. He was the only starter on offense or defense to miss more than one game because of an injury. He had to sit out three games.

Even so, he finished with 27 tackles, including 11 unassisted, and earned All-Big Eight honorable mention from both the conference coaches and the Associated Press. Prior to the injury, he was included on the "watch list" for the Butkus Award, presented to the nation's top collegiate linebacker.

Ellis returned for Nebraska's stretch run toward a second national championship. He was a source of constant concern for Florida quarterback Danny Wuerffel in the Fiesta Bowl game. He moved in and out of the line as the Huskers disguised their defenses and was credited with six tackles.

While he and his teammates were achieving extraordinary success he focused on one game at a time.

"It wasn't until somebody asked me what I thought about all those win streaks and stuff that I knew we had them," Ellis said before the Fiesta Bowl game. "It's nice to know. But the only reason we got this far three years in a row is because we took each game separately. It's pretty neat what we've done."

Terrell Farley #43

Terrell Farley started for the first time against Kansas State. "(Husker linebackers coach Craig Bohl) told me I would be starting (and) my heart dropped. I was nervous all day," Farley said.

You wouldn't have known it, however. The transfer from Independence, Kan., Community College was credited with 10 tackles, including six solo, in the 49-25 victory over Kansas State.

He also sacked Wildcat quarterback Matt Miller twice for 22 yards in losses.

Such a performance was business as usual for Farley, who shared playing time at the "Will" or weakside linebacker position with junior Ryan Terwilliger. In his first game as a Husker against Oklahoma State, Farley intercepted a pass and returned it 29 yards for a touchdown.

Farley never let up, proving his reputation for making big plays was deserved. He also returned an interception for a touchdown in the Arizona State game and blocked a punt for a safety in the Missouri game. He led the Huskers in tackles with 62, including 27 unassisted.

Throughout the remainder of the season, Farley had a third interception and a second blocked punt. By season's end, he had had five quarterback sacks for losses totaling 45 yards, 12 quarterback hurries and broke up five passes.

It came as no surprise that he was chosen by the Associated Press as the Big Eight's "Defensive Newcomer of the Year" or that he was a first-team all-conference selection. He even received second-team All-America recognition from the Associated Press and the United Press International.

"We have liked his athleticism since Day No. 1," Coach Tom Osborne said. "He makes plays. Somehow he gets in the right place at the right time and covers a lot of field in doing it."

Those who still doubted Farley's prowess by the time Nebraska played the Gators in the Fiesta Bowl were set straight on the matter by his performance that day. He made eight tackles and sacked quarterback Danny Wuerffel twice for nine yards in losses.

Jay Foreman #56

Jay Foreman, the son of former Minnesota Vikings running back Chuck Foreman, started every game at the strongside linebacker or "Sam" position for the Huskers this season. He played with remarkable consistency, especially considering the demands of the position.

Foreman was a redshirted freshman, which makes his performance even more remarkable. "Playing at the 'Sam' demands a lot of a guy physically," said Tony Samuel, Nebraska's outside linebackers coach. "You're asking him to be very good against the run, a man-to-man pass cover guy against what often is a great receiver and also a great blitzer. That's a tall order for a lot of guys.

"Plus, it's a fairly complicated position from a learning standpoint."

Foreman learned the intricacies of the position as a redshirt, then established himself at the top of the depth chart during spring practice, succeeding Troy Dumas, a four-year letterman. He eliminated any remaining doubt about his qualifications for the position in the spring intrasquad game. He made 12 tackles, including six unassisted and two for losses totaling 12 yards, and broke up two passes, despite the fact he wasn't completely healthy. He was bothered by a sprained left shoulder.

After the spring game, Samuel said: "He was a pleasant surprise. Everybody was saying Jay Foreman came out of nowhere. But we knew he had talent. So he didn't really come out of nowhere. He just showed a lot of improvement. He's a student of the game. He's a reliable kid, very dependable.

Foreman, an outstanding high school running back, picked up in the fall where he left off in the spring, sharing time with junior Jamel Williams and playing with a quiet consistency that belied his age. He made 32 tackles, including 10 solo, and had two quarterback hurries during the season.

Foreman finished his first season as a Husker in characteristic fashion, making three tackles, two of them unassisted, in the Fiesta Bowl victory against Florida.

Tommie Frazier #15

Tommie Frazier was simply the best in 1995.

"We won some big games last year when he was hurt. But he has been a big factor," Coach Tom Osborne said at a news conference before Nebraska left Lincoln for the Fiesta Bowl. "I would say if I were to choose one player who has had the most impact on the outcome of the greatest number of games over the longest period of time since I've been at Nebraska, it would be Tommie Frazier."

Frazier was the first true freshman to start at quarterback for Nebraska in the modern era. His record as a starter was 33-3. He is the Husker career total offense leader, surpassing Jerry Tagge with 5,476 yards. He accounted for a school-record 79 touchdowns rushing and passing during his career. He established school records for rushing touchdowns by a quarterback in a career (36) and in a season (14). He threw more touchdown passes (43) during his career than anyone in Nebraska history.

No Husker quarterback has done it better. Frazier finished second to Ohio State's Eddie George in voting for the Heisman Trophy. After Frazier earned the award as the outstanding offensive player in the Fiesta Bowl, teammate Jason Peter said: "People should take their Heisman Trophy votes back and do it over. Without a doubt, Tommie Frazier is the best player in college football."

Anyone associated with Nebraska would agree. But the respect Frazier earned went far beyond provincialism. He was chosen as a first-team All-American by the Associated Press, the Football Writers, the Walter Camp Foundation, the United Press International and the American Football Coaches Association. That's as much of a consensus pick as is possible.

He won the Johnny Unitas Golden Arm Award. He was the Big Eight offensive Player of the Year. And he was the outstanding offensive player in the East-West Shrine Game, running for one touchdown and throwing for another in leading the West to a 34-18 victory.

Afterward, Terry Donahue, former UCLA coach and coach of the West team, said of Frazier: "He can raise havoc on a football field. He's magical."

Mike Fullman #12

Mike Fullman, the Husker's smallest player, wasn't included in Nebraska's comprehensive football media and recruiting guide. Not only was he excluded from the biographical capsules, but also his name wasn't among the nearly 180 names listed on the roster. But he wasn't overlooked because of his size. Rather, it was because he hadn't established himself at the time the guide was published.

Fullman began his college career at Rutgers, where he started 10 games as a redshirted freshman. He transferred to Nebraska at the urging of former Husker Barron Miles. The two played at the same high school in New Jersey.

Because Mike was small like Miles and played cornerback like Miles, people assumed he was adept at blocking punts like Miles. Fullman, however, preferred returning punts to blocking them. The problem was, he had never been given the opportunity.

When he did get the chance against Michigan State, he muffed a punt. As a result, his confidence was down. Down, that is, until the Kansas State game.

Early in the first quarter, Fullman fielded a punt and, with the help of a highlight-film block by redshirted freshman outside linebacker Mike Rucker, returned it 79 yards for a touchdown. It was Nebraska's first punt return for a touchdown since 1988.

Fullman, who also backed up Michael Booker at cornerback, was anonymous no more. So, when he returned a pass interception 86 yards for a touchdown against Kansas, it was no surprise.

"Mike just has a nice knack of running with the football," Husker defensive backs coach George Darlington said. "He's taking (the ball) with the intention of scoring every time."

Fullman averaged 13.6 yards per punt return to rank first in the Big Eight and 10th in the nation.

A walk-on, he was awarded a scholarship for the second semester.

Mark Gilman #87

Mark Gilman was recruited by Nebraska as a tight end, even though in high school he played quarterback for one season and wide receiver for two. His qualifications for playing tight end for the Huskers left something to be desired; there was little evidence he could block.

"In high school, I had never blocked," Gilman once told a newspaper reporter.

"You know how much blocking high school wide receivers do. You just go out and bump a guy. And at quarterback, (my high school coaches) always took me out of the contact drills. If you think about it, if I was going to play tight end, this was the worst place I could go."

Nebraska's wide receivers don't play if they don't block. So you can imagine the blocking demands placed on tight ends, who are as much extensions of the offensive line as anything.

Despite his lack of qualifications for the position, Gilman worked his way into the rotation as a junior and became the starter as a senior. The respect he earned by his commitment in the weight room and on the field was such that his teammates chose him to be a co-captain in 1995.

Gilman set an example during the off-season and over the summer, when the Huskers laid the physical foundation for their repeat national championship. He emphasized the importance of individual commitment during an interview prior to the season. "This would have to be a summer not only of hard work but also of confidence-building in all of us," Gilman said.

Gilman, a two-time Academic All-Big Eight honoree, started five games, as Coach Tom Osborne varied his offensive alignments throughout the season. He finished the season third on the team in pass receptions with 16, one fewer than his total as a junior. He got more out of his receptions, however, gaining 256 yards.

Aaron Graham #54

Aaron Graham was asked to comment on Nebraska's back-to-back national championships and three consecutive undefeated seasons after the Tostitos Fiesta Bowl game.

"Historical significance as a group? Well, I think we did a lot," he said. "I mean, to go three years and lose one game, that one being almost a controversial one, one that maybe we should have won, I don't really know how you describe that. I mean, it's just been a total team effort. We just keep getting guys in here who like to compete, like to work hard and like playing in national championship games, I guess."

Graham possesses those qualities, though he is too self-effacing to focus on himself. The praise has come from others. "Aaron is probably the best center I've had around here in 22 years and the best center I've seen playing today," said Milt Tenopir, Nebraska's offensive line coach. Among the centers Tenopir coached was Dave Rimington, a two-time Outland Trophy winner. That pretty much says it all.

Graham was a three-year starter. He was a first-team All-American in 1995 and two-time first-team All-Big Eight selection. He also was a three-time Academic All-Big Eight honoree and received the NCAA Today's Top Eight Award, the highest honor bestowed on student-athletes.

He approached football and academics with similar resolve. "When I came in as a freshman, I saw seniors who had done four and a half years of work who weren't getting on the field," he said.

"I thought if I was going to be here four or five years, I was going to play as much as I could. I've always been that way. If I'm doing something and not giving it 100 percent, I stop doing it."

When they were redshirt freshmen, Graham and several other Huskers vowed to win five Big Eight championships and two national championships before they were finished. They made the vow in Miami Beach, where Nebraska's headquarters for the 1992 Orange Bowl game were located.

Four years later, their mission was accomplished.

Ahman Green #30

Ahman Green was exactly as advertised when he arrived at Nebraska from Omaha Central High School. He was supposed to be an extraordinary player, and he was.

Among the many things Green accomplished in his first collegiate season was a rushing total of 1,086 yards. No Nebraska freshman, true (like Green) or redshirted, had ever run for 1,000 yards. Furthermore, only one freshman running back in Big Eight history had ever rushed for more yards than Green.

"When you look at the (running) backs we've had here and the fact that it hadn't happened before, that speaks volumes about Ahman," said Frank Solich, Green's position coach. Green also caught 12 passes for 102 yards and scored 16 touchdowns — 13 by rushing. He had at least one touchdown in all but three games, including the Fiesta Bowl, in which he gained 68 yards on nine carries and scored Nebraska's third touchdown. That's not bad for someone who began the season at No. 5 on the depth chart.

Green's starting place on the depth chart was little more than a formality. Solich and Coach Tom Osborne had indicated that he almost certainly would not be redshirted.

"When you come out of your junior year of high school and test better than 90 percent of our guys, you've got to figure he's a pretty good talent," Osborne said. Green had achieved outstanding test scores at Nebraska's Big Red Football Camp the summer before his senior year at Central High.

He scored similarly well in pre-season strength and conditioning tests at Nebraska. "There has never been a freshman to compare to Ahman Green's test scores," said Boyd Epley, assistant athletic director for athletic performance. Among other things, Green ran the 40-yard dash in 4.47 seconds.

Against Washington State, his first of six games as a starter, Green rushed for 176 yards and one touchdown on only 13 carries. He also ran for 176 yards (and three touchdowns) against Iowa State.

He was named the Big Eight's offensive Newcomer of the Year and offensive Freshman of the Year, and he was chosen to the All-Big Eight first team by the conference coaches.

Luther Hardin #58

Even though he was a back-up to All-American Jared Tomich, Luther Hardin considered himself a leader. "I'm an emotional center of the team," said Hardin. "I'm always there to help the team, (to) keep spirits high and (to) tell the younger guys to be ready to play."

In regard to his Husker career as a player, he said: "I know I've been a factor for five years."

At times, those five years were difficult. Hardin, whose nickname was "B.L." or "Big Lu," was recruited as a defensive tackle. But he weighed only 205 pounds when he arrived at Nebraska.

In his first season as a Husker, Hardin struggled to compensate for his lack of size at the inside linebacker position. He was moved to outside linebacker in the spring of 1993 after the Huskers changed to a 4-3 base defense.

"I've paid a big price, playing with pain, getting knocked down and getting back up," Hardin said. Even though it was discouraging, he persevered. "I'm not a quitter," he said. "Once I start something, I finish it. I could have (transferred) to Missouri or Illinois. But I started here, and I was going to finish here."

He finished strong, playing in every game and starting one when Tomich was injured.

The personal highlight of Hardin's senior season came in the Kansas State game when he caught a Wildcat shovel pass that had been deflected by teammate Chad Kelsay and scored a touchdown. He had two other quarterback hurries in that game, as well. He had recorded the first quarterback sack of his Husker career the week before against Missouri.

Hardin was among the most up-beat players on the team, always smiling and offering encouragement to his teammates. "In college, it's not a commitment; it's a task," he said of football. "You have to concentrate on every play. You have to have the right strength level. It shocked me. You have to pay your dues.

Jon Hesse #44

Just seven semesters after enrolling at Nebraska, Jon Hesse, a psychology major, received a bachelor's degree. In addition, he made the Phillips 66 Big Eight Academic Honor Roll for the second-consecutive season with a 3.49 cumulative grade-point average. Hesse downplayed his achievement. "It's not like I did anything stupendous," he said.

Most others wouldn't share that opinion.

"It's an unusual thing to be able to do in major college football," said Tom Osborne, who couldn't recall another player finishing that quickly during his 23 seasons as head coach.

On the field, Hesse again backed up Phil Ellis and Doug Colman at middle linebacker, finishing with 37 tackles, 20 of them unassisted and six for losses totaling seven yards. He also forced a fumble.

Hesse is among the many talented athletes whose playing time has been limited not by his lack of ability but rather by an abundance of talented players at his position. "I thought I might never play," he said. "You have to get in the back of the line."

The situation was aggravated by his own introspection. "You can put so much pressure on yourself, thinking: 'I've got to get there.' I worried about where this guy and that guy were compared to where I was. I don't think I really improved my first year or year-and-a-half here," he said.

"There were times I used to get really worried about not playing. But my life always seems to kind of take care of itself, if I keep doing the right thing."

Hesse has contributed any way he can. During the second half of spring practice, he switched from middle linebacker to rushing end, providing the versatility so important with limited travel rosters.

He also has been an important contributor on special teams.

But middle linebacker has remained his position of choice and, when Ellis was sidelined by a broken bone in his right foot, Hesse joined Colman to pick up the slack in the middle.

Hesse was prepared. "I feel like I'm ready," he said at the time. "This whole season I've felt ready."

Brendan Holbein #5

Brendan Holbein was one of 15 native Nebraskans on the Huskers' offensive two-deeps for the Tostitos Fiesta Bowl game. That so many came from in-state was significant, he said.

Homegrown players provide a special quality. "In terms of attitude, I think it's like Jeff Makovicka says: Nebraska guys are 'blue-collar' workers," said Holbein. "I'm not saying guys from outside the state don't work hard. But Nebraska guys want to work extremely hard to play here."

Holbein is a case in point. He was an outstanding running back at Cozad High School, rushing for 2,740 yards and 38 touchdowns. He led his team to the Class B state championship as a senior. The Omaha World-Herald chose him as the state's prep offensive player of the year.

Even though he had the credentials of a scholarship athlete, he was willing to walk on at Nebraska and make his way not as a running back but rather as a wide receiver. That meant paying his own way — and learning to block. When he arrived, he wondered how good a blocker he could be. "Coach (Ron) Brown kept stressing the fact that you've got to block (as a wide receiver)," Holbein said. "Either you do and play or you don't and sit."

Holbein hasn't done much sitting the last two seasons.

Brown has described him as the best blocking wide receiver in college football, and he still has another season to play.

Holbein caught 14 passes for 151 yards and one touchdown in 1995. The touchdown came against Missouri with time running out in the first half on a pass tipped by teammate Jon Vedral.

Holbein also caught a pass late in the first half of the Fiesta Bowl game for a 33-yard gain to the Florida 12-yard line, setting up Kris Brown's second field goal with 8 seconds remaining.

It was for such opportunities that Holbein turned down Iowa State's scholarship offer to become a Husker walk-on. He now has a scholarship. "What motivated me the most was pride," he said. "This was a big-time program. They play on television and for national championships.

"It would have killed me not to give it a try. My gut instinct was to come here."

Sheldon Jackson #88

During the celebration that followed the Fiesta Bowl game, Sheldon Jackson took a large red flag emblazoned with a white "N" and made a victory lap around the field at Sun Devil Stadium. Actually, he didn't make a complete lap. It was more like half a lap. But you get the idea.

Jackson was excited about celebrating a national championship in his first collegiate season.

A highly-regarded recruit who has been compared to former Husker tight end Johnny Mitchell, Jackson joined sophomore Vershan Jackson (no relation) in backing up Mark Gilman and Tim Carpenter. Sheldon caught six passes for 52 yards and two touchdowns in 10 games. The touchdowns came on consecutive Saturdays: a 6-yarder against Missouri and an 11-yarder against Kansas State.

Sheldon Jackson redshirted his first season at Nebraska. He gained 20 pounds (and lowered his speed). Receivers coach Ron Brown was prompted to say: "He looks like the real deal."

As is the case with every young player, however, there were some doubts.

"It looked like he had marginal hands in high school," Brown said. "I thought he'd be an excellent line of scrimmage player, a very large-framed player who had tremendous explosion coming off the football."

In Nebraska's offensive system, being explosive off the ball is usually a greater asset for tight ends than having good hands. Their first (and sometimes their only) responsibility is blocking. For example, Matt Shaw, one of the tight ends in the rotation on the Huskers' 1994 national championship team, made a significant contribution for three seasons without catching a single pass.

To ensure that Sheldon Jackson would have sufficient time to develop his skills, Vershan Jackson was moved from fullback to tight end during spring practice.

As it turned out, however, Sheldon didn't need the time. He was already on his way to making a name for himself.

Clester Johnson #33

Clester Johnson arrived at Nebraska as a quarterback and immediately was moved to cornerback. But it was at the wingback position where he finally found an opportunity to play. "Clester was like a doorstep baby," said Ron Brown, the Husker receivers coach. "I'm glad he landed on my doorstep."

Johnson, however, encountered considerable frustration resulting from the many changes that first season. But, he persevered. "I'm proud that I can look back and say that I wasn't one of those guys who folded the tent when things didn't go my way here," he said. "Things didn't always work out the way I would have liked them to. But I never quit working hard. That's an attitude I've always had."

The 1995 season was Johnson's most productive, although statistically, it didn't start out that way. Johnson caught only one pass in the first two games. He was the forgotten receiver.

In the third game against Arizona State, that changed. Johnson caught four passes for 129 yards and the first of two touchdowns of the season. Early in the second quarter of the 77-28 victory at Memorial Stadium, he teamed with quarterback Tommie Frazier on a 28-yarder.

He also had a 61-yard pass reception against the Sun Devils. His second touchdown pass came on a 52-yard play at Colorado to complete the Huskers' 21-point first quarter.

Johnson finished the season as Nebraska's leader in pass receptions (22) and receiving yards (367). He also rushed for 35 yards on three carries. But, like the other Husker wide receivers, his most significant contribution was as a downfield blocker. He did that with great tenacity.

Johnson learned to take pride in his blocking. "When the offense is making those 60- and 70-yard runs, people don't see the receivers knocking down the safeties," he said. Florida's defensive backs could attest to that. Johnson also caught two passes for 43 yards against the Gators.

Johnson's strong play belied his tendency toward introspection off the field. "Clester is very serious about life," said Brown. "But he also has a gentleness about him. I just love the kid."

Chad Kelsay #57

Chad Kelsay described his first collegiate season as "picture perfect."

"I was hoping at the beginning of the year to see a little time on special teams and a little bit at outside linebacker," he said. "And that's exactly what happened."

Kelsay makes his freshman season seem matter-of-fact. But it wasn't, not when you consider that only two other true freshmen played for the Huskers' national championship team: I-back Ahman Green and place-kicker Kris Brown.

Kelsay played in every game. He made 20 tackles, including 13 unassisted and three for losses totaling 13 yards. He broke up three passes, the most notable against Kansas State when he deflected a shovel pass to teammate Luther Hardin for a touchdown.

Kelsay backed up sophomore Grant Wistrom on the right side. Wistrom, who played as a true freshman on the 1994 national championship team, encouraged Kelsay.

"He told me there would be times when I wanted to quit," Kelsay said. "But he said: 'You do anything you can, anything it takes to get on the field, because once you get there, you won't regret it.'"

Once he got there, it was a dream come true for someone who grew up in Nebraska. The first time a player runs onto the field at Memorial Stadium, "you can't really describe it," he said.

Kelsay was still in high school when he watched the Huskers defeat Miami 24-17 in the Orange Bowl game to give Coach Tom Osborne his first national championship. "Ever since I was a little kid, I've been watching Nebraska on television. When you see those guys, they seem so much bigger and faster. It almost seemed like they weren't human," said Kelsay.

A year later, Kelsay played in the 62-24 victory against Florida for the second national title. "I didn't know how realistic a goal it was to play (as a true freshman). You grow up watching (Nebraska football), and you feel like you want to work harder, give a little bit more."

Kelsay couldn't have painted a more perfect picture.

Jesse Kosch #19

Jesse Kosch got a kick out of the 1995 season. He got several kicks, in fact.

But he didn't get enough to qualify for the official Big Eight Conference statistics. That's the fate of the punter on a team as offensively potent as Nebraska. More often than not, the Huskers turned their possessions into points and Kosch's services weren't needed.

In order to qualify for the conference statistics, Kosch would have had to average 3.6 punts per game. He averaged fewer than three, however. He punted only once in the season-opener at Oklahoma State, a 53-yarder, and didn't punt at all against Iowa State.

You might think he'd lose the knack, but he didn't. He averaged 40.3 yards per punt and achieved a net punting average of 39.9. Nebraska ranked 17th nationally in that category. Kosch pinned the opposition inside its own 20-yard line 11 times. And he had four punts of 50 yards or longer, including a career-best 74-yarder against Arizona State.

His 27 punts in 1995 comprise his collegiate career. Kosch was Darin Erstad's backup in 1994 and, as a redshirted freshman, he had only one opportunity to punt. He got in the game near the end of a 70-21 victory against Pacific. He punted the ball but was roughed, and the play was nullified by a penalty.

He did get a chance to punt in the Fiesta Bowl game: a 36-yarder early in the fourth quarter.

Kosch has a punter's personality. "(He) seems calm about things," said Coach Dan Young, who coaches the Husker kickers. He also has an appropriate major for a kicker: meteorology.

"All I care about is the wind," said Kosch, an Academic All-Big Eight honoree.

His career goal is to be a "behind the scenes weatherman."

Kosch walked on at Nebraska, following in his father's footsteps. Bill Kosch was a starting defensive back for Coach Bob Devaney's national championship teams in 1970 and 1971.

Now, Jesse also has been a member of back-to-back national championship teams.

Jeff Makovicka #22

Jeff Makovicka walked on at Nebraska after playing eight-man football in his final three seasons at East Butler High School. Originally, the Huskers were skeptical of his chances for success.

"Nebraska didn't even want me to walk on," he said. Makovicka was persistent, however, sending letters and film of his games to Nebraska. "On the day of (high school) graduation, Coach (Frank) Solich called my dad. Maybe they decided to let me walk on just so I would quit bugging them.

"For a while, I wanted to go somewhere that I could come back and play against Nebraska," he said. He wouldn't have been happy playing college football somewhere else, though. Makovicka grew up a Husker fan and took Nebraska's 45-21 loss to Georgia Tech in the 1991 Citrus Bowl game to heart. "I didn't want people ever to talk about Nebraska that way again," he said.

After sitting out his first season as a redshirt, Makovicka began his career as an I-back. He played both I-back and fullback as a sophomore, and contributed on special teams. In 1994, he became a fullback full-time, alternating with Cory Schlesinger and making a significant contribution to the national title campaign.

In 1995, he became the starter, rushing for 371 yards and one touchdown (on a 13-yard run against Arizona State). He received All-Big Eight honorable mention from the conference coaches.

He carried six times for 32 yards in the Tostitos Fiesta Bowl game.

His brother, Joel, a redshirted freshman who also walked on, was Nebraska's No. 3 fullback. Joel carried 22 times for 185 yards and two touchdowns in his first season as a Husker.

His small-town, eight-man background has been the subject of regular discussion throughout his career, said Jeff, who shakes his head. "I've done like five or six stories a year (about that). It's not like I'm an alien being. I just needed a chance. It's not where you're from; it's where you're at."

He and his brother were well-prepared to compete at the major college level, Jeff said. "My dad was an All-American (football player) at Kearney State. He was a coach, too. He was a coach and a student of the game. We'd go back of the house and have hitting drills. He'd show us what to do."

Mike Minter #10

Mike Minter was forced to watch from the sideline while Nebraska won its first national championship by defeating Miami 24-17 in the 1995 Orange Bowl game. He had suffered a torn anterior cruciate ligament very early in the season.

That's why he pushed himself and his teammates during the 1995 season. Before spring practice, he said: "I've got to play in one (national championship game). It was exciting when games were going on, but I didn't feel like I was a part of the team otherwise. I'm going to be pushing everyone.

"I know the fellas want to do it again, and that makes me feel good."

Minter was so determined, he stayed in Lincoln over spring break to work out in preparation for spring practice. His commitment paid off, but not before he experienced even more frustration.

Minter continued to show the effects of his reconstructive knee surgery early in the season. After the Washington State game, in fact, Husker defensive coordinator Charlie McBride expressed serious doubts about Minter's future as a player. "I don't know if he'll play again," McBride said.

So, Minter altered his training routine and, as a result, not only did he play again, but he also played at a level comparable to that before his injury. Minter finished second on the team in tackles with 53 (including 27 solo), caused one fumble and intercepted two passes.

Prior to his injury, he earned second-team All-Big Eight recognition from conference coaches as a redshirted freshman. In 1995, when he returned to his pre-injury form, he was included on the all-conference second teams of both the coaches and the Associated Press.

Before the Tostitos Fiesta Bowl game, Minter couldn't hide his excitement about being able to play instead of watch. "Last year, I got to watch," he said. "This year, I get to play. It's like a dream come true. I've just had this dream every day, about every five minutes for the last two years."

Jeff Ogard #97

To quote the classic poet John Milton: "They also serve who only stand and wait."

So it was for Jeff Ogard, who found himself in the unenviable position of being a backup to Christian Peter. There was little opportunity to play. Mostly, Ogard had to watch from the sideline.

"When you get the opportunity to play, you've got to make the best of it," said Charlie McBride, the Huskers' defensive coordinator and Ogard's position coach.

By all accounts, Ogard did ... from the get-go.

Midway through the fourth quarter of Nebraska's 64-21 opening-game victory against Oklahoma State, a game televised nationally by the ESPN cable network, Ogard got some prime-time exposure.

On a fourth-down-and-2 at the Husker 26-yard line, the Cowboys attempted a pass to gain a first down and keep their drive alive. Ogard, who was pressuring the quarterback, tipped the ball, then caught it before it hit the ground. "I was running a 'swap play.' That's where I loop outside the outside linebacker, and I was just wide out in the field, wide-open, and he decided to throw the ball," Ogard said.

The ball sailed over his head. "It wasn't very high," said the 6-foot-6 Ogard.

"I got my hand up and tipped it," Ogard continued. "It went straight up."

He lost sight of the ball for a split second. "(When) it got about right to my head level, (it) fell right in my arms. It was like a miracle."

The "miraculous" interception was among the individual highlights of Ogard's season. The two-time Nebraska Class B high school heavyweight wrestling champion played in every game. He made seven tackles, two of them unassisted, and provided the depth on which championship teams depend.

Steve Ott #69

Like Mike Minter, Steve Ott had to watch Nebraska win the first of its back-to-back national championships from the sideline. Ott was in the Huskers' offensive line rotation as one of the top backups through the first seven games of 1994. But he suffered a broken bone in his left foot and was sidelined for six games, including the Orange Bowl.

"It was really hard to watch the (Orange Bowl) game from the sideline, in street clothes," Ott said. "When you play for Nebraska, you always dream of playing in a national championship game."

Ott eventually got his chance to play in such a game. He not only played in the Tostitos Fiesta Bowl, but also made a significant contribution to the Huskers' getting there, joining three other first-team starters in the offensive interior.

Going into the season, there was concern that Nebraska might not be able to rebuild a sufficiently solid offensive line to make a serious run at a second-consecutive national championship.

That concern was quickly dispelled. "We kind of looked at it as a challenge," said Ott. "We wanted to prove people wrong, that we were going to keep up the Nebraska tradition."

He and his linemates accomplished the task so well that, early on, they spent more time on the sideline watching their backups mop up than they did playing. "Last year, the first-team guys got 60 to 70 snaps (per game). This year, the most I've got is 50 snaps," Ott said during the non-conference season.

That changed some when the Huskers got into the Big Eight schedule.

Ott started every game and was credited with 99 "pancake" blocks — 14 of those against Michigan State and 12 against Kansas State. A biological studies major, he made the Phillips 66 All-Big Eight Academic Honor Roll for a third-straight year and was a second-team Academic All-American.

Ott spent three years preparing to play. Then, when he got an opportunity last season, the injury occurred. He was undaunted, however, and things worked out well. "At Nebraska, there is so much talent that each player has to be patient and wait for the opportunity to come along," he said. "When the opportunity does come, the years of work as a backup player make it all worthwhile."

Aaron Penland #52

On a kickoff during the Tostitos Fiesta Bowl game, Aaron Penland raced downfield and collided with a Florida blocker. Both players were knocked to the ground by the force of the collision. The Florida player struggled to his feet and tried to insult Penland, to little effect.

Penland managed to get up without assistance, though obviously shaken, and hustled to the sideline without so much as acknowledging the taunt. You can't keep a good man down.

For the second year in a row, Penland was a wedge-breaker on the Huskers' kickoff team, racing down the field without concern for his personal well-being and generally making life miserable for would-be blockers and ball carriers. I-back Damon Benning, himself a regular contributor to Nebraska's special teams, once described a wedge-breaker. "It's no place for the meek-hearted, I'll tell you that. It's smash-mouth football at its best, where you can make something happen," he said.

Penland followed his brother, Matt, in assuming that responsibility. Like Matt, Aaron Penland walked on. Though never a starter, he made a significant contribution to the national titles on special teams and as a backup to weakside linebackers Terrell Farley and Ryan Terwilliger. Penland made 17 tackles during the season, including six solo, with a single-game high of five against Michigan State.

Not only was Penland a walk-on, he walked on from out-of-state: Penland hails from Jacksonville, Fla. He was one of four Floridians on the Huskers' roster for the Fiesta Bowl game.

Even though the intelligence of those willing to be wedge-breakers is occasionally questioned, Penland made the Phillips 66 Academic Honor Roll twice. He has a 3.18 grade-point average in business administration.

Still, it takes a special individual to put life and limb on the line to break wedges on kickoffs. Penland qualifies. "He's out there," Benning said. "He looks for wedges. He goes out of his way."

Christian Peter #55

After scoring what would be its final touchdown in the Tostitos Fiesta Bowl game, Florida went for a two-point conversion with backup quarterback Eric Kresser looking to pass before being buried by the rush of Husker outside linebacker Jared Tomich. At some point during the tackle, the ball came loose.

Christian Peter picked it up and rumbled the length of the field, then sprawled on his back in the Gators' end zone. Had the play stood, Nebraska would have added two more points to its total. But, the officials ruled Kresser was down before the fumble occurred.

"Can you believe that?" Peter asked rhetorically, during the post-game interview session.

"For crying out loud. I go 90 yards (actually closer to 98) and they call it back. I about had a heart attack on the 10 (yard line). I turned around and they called it back. I was so upset."

Christian had 46 tackles, including 12 unassisted, and nine quarterback hurries in 1995. But his importance to the team went far beyond what could be measured by statistics.

Peter was a team leader. He led by example and by emotion, which is why his teammates chose him as a co-captain. Before the Fiesta Bowl, the Huskers watched a video presentation prepared by Jack Stark, an Omaha sports psychologist who works with Nebraska athletes. The presentation included comments from Peter and the other four captains. His remarks were last, for good reason.

Peter followed in a tradition of New Jersey Huskers, among them Outland Trophy winner Rich Glover, from Jersey City, and Heisman Trophy winner Mike Rozier, from Camden.

He was a consensus first-team All-Big Eight selection and received All-America honorable mention from the Football News and the United Press International. "In my opinion, he's the best defensive lineman in college football today," said his brother Jason, who played alongside him.

Jason Peter #95

There was a time when Jason Peter didn't get along all that well with his brother Christian.

"It was a big brother-younger brother thing," said Jason, the younger brother. "I wanted to hang out with him and he didn't want me to. (Christian) would either yell at me or beat me up."

But that was a long time ago. The brothers are close now. In fact, that's one of the reasons why Jason, a highly regarded high school recruit, accepted Nebraska's scholarship offer. "In the long run, the opportunity to play side-by-side (with Christian) overtook all the other reasons," Jason said.

In 1995, they did so for the first time on a regular basis. Jason stepped in for 1994 starter Terry Connealy and the Husker defense never missed a beat, ranking second nationally against the rush and fourth nationally in scoring. Jason was credited with 30 tackles, including five for losses totaling 13 yards. He forced one fumble and hurried opposing quarterbacks seven times.

He received All-Big Eight honorable mention from the conference coaches.

But the awards and statistics paled in comparison to the pride of playing alongside his older brother. Jason and Christian were nearly inseparable. They even resembled each other, right down to the distinctive tattoos of the "Peterbilt" truck logo on their massive biceps.

They got the tattoos at the suggestion of former Husker defensive tackle Kevin Ramaekers. "We didn't want a skull and crossbones, something we'd get tired of when we were older," Jason said. "We wanted tattoos that meant something. We thought that would be good."

A highlight of Jason's first season as a starter were the two tackles he made in the Tostitos Fiesta Bowl. Another came in the season-opener against Oklahoma State. After the game, Christian told his "little" brother he was proud of the way he had played.

"It meant a lot to me," Jason said.

Lawrence Phillips #1

Lawrence Phillips is likely to be a first-round National Football League draft choice. Under ordinary circumstances, Phillips' performance in the Tostitos Fiesta Bowl would have earned him CBS television's offensive Player of the Game Award. But the extraordinary circumstance in this case was the play of quarterback Tommie Frazier.

Even so, Phillips was impressive, scoring Nebraska's first two touchdowns, one on a 42-yard run and the other on a 16-yard pass play. In response to Florida's opening field goal, Phillips caught a screen pass from Frazier and hurled himself over a blocker and a defender into the end zone.

"I saw somebody blocking," said Phillips, who had to stretch to catch the pass. "I didn't want to take a chance of (the would-be tackler) sliding off the block, so I tried to get over him."

Phillips finished the game with 165 rushing yards on 25 carries and three touchdowns — a performance that reflected the way he began what might have been a Heisman Trophy season.

In the first two games of the season, Phillips rushed for 359 yards and seven touchdowns on only 34 carries (an average of more than 10 yards per carry). He was playing at a level comparable to the best running backs of Tom Osborne's 23 seasons as head coach.

After the Fiesta Bowl game, Frank Solich, Phillips' position coach, praised his play.

"He's got the whole package: the size, the strength, the speed, the ability to make the big play and get the tough yardage," Solich said. "He makes catches coming out of the backfield. He can block."

Phillips was understandably low-key after what would be his final game as a Husker. "It's great to be with my team and win a national championship," he said.

The first week in January, he announced he would submit his name for the NFL draft. In a prepared statement, he said: "The chance to play in the NFL ... wouldn't be happening without the Nebraska football program." He thanked Osborne and Solich for their coaching, teaching, advice and friendship.

Scott Saltsman #74

Scott Saltsman has said that even if his scholarship was taken away, he would pay his own way to play football at Nebraska. It means that much to him.

Saltsman's comeback from arthroscopic knee surgery in mid-October certainly underscores his determination. He missed only one game while recovering. Less than a week after the surgery, he was back on the practice field. His comeback was described in Nebraska's Fiesta Bowl media guide as the fastest in Husker football history.

Saltsman's determination was apparent long before then, however. His football-related ailments have been numerous: In addition to having his right knee scoped, Saltsman has undergone three surgeries on his left knee and one shoulder surgery. His father has even suggested he consider quitting.

Typically, trainers spend the better part of a half hour taping him for practice. "I feel like a mummy, sometimes," said Saltsman, who considers it a small price to pay.

Saltsman, a teammate of Husker offensive guard Aaron Taylor at Rider High School in Wichita Falls, Texas, could have given up long ago. He was sidelined for two games during his high school senior season because of a severe knee strain. "I said when I accepted a football scholarship, they (the Nebraska coaches) were putting their faith in me, so I was going to put my faith in them," he said.

He was Jason Peter's backup in 1995, making 13 tackles, including five unassisted and one quarterback sack, and he had two quarterback hurries. "He's not a big guy in there," Charlie McBride, his position coach, told a newspaper reporter. "But he plays hard on every snap, and we don't feel like we take a step back when he comes in. I just hope he doesn't fall apart one of these days."

Saltsman, a marketing major, has a 3.17 cumulative grade-point average and has made the Phillips 66 Academic Honor Roll twice.

Brian Schuster #28

Brian Schuster and Jeff Makovicka were sitting together at Cory Schlesinger's wedding after the Huskers had won the 1994 national championship. Schlesinger was the No. 1 fullback in 1994; Makovicka and Schuster were his back-ups. All three are from small Nebraska towns.

Frank Solich, Nebraska's assistant head coach and running backs coach, also attended the wedding. While they were waiting for the ceremony to begin, Solich noted similarities in the backgrounds of his top three fullbacks. "He wanted to know if it was something in the water," Makovicka said.

A similar situation existed at fullback in 1995. Jeff Makovicka was the starter. Schuster was No. 2 on the depth chart followed by redshirted freshman Joel Makovicka, Jeff's brother.

All three came to Nebraska as walk-ons. Jeff Makovicka offered an explanation for that unique situation. "Fullback is a position where (the Nebraska coaches) don't recruit as many high-profile players. It's a blue-collar position. Some guys might not want to work at it," he said.

"I think a lot of it has to do with hard work ... but once you get here, you see what you can make out of it. You're like an offensive lineman. But you get the luxury of carrying the ball every once in a while."

Schuster certainly made the most of his opportunities to carry the ball. He finished the regular season with 246 rushing yards on only 28 carries. He also showed breakaway ability, gaining 55 yards on a carry against Iowa State. He was always moving forward: He didn't lose so much as a yard in 1995.

Schuster's background recommends him. He is a cousin of former Husker quarterback Gerry Gdowski and a nephew of former Husker defensive tackle Tom Gdowski. His high school coach, Pat Larsen, earned letters as a Nebraska defensive back in 1980, 1981 and 1982 as a walk-on.

Schuster has made the Phillips 66 Academic All-Big Eight Honor Roll twice and was a second-team Academic All-American in 1995, with a 3.37 grade-point average in pre-education.

Eric Stokes #16

Late in the third quarter of the Fiesta Bowl game, Florida quarterback Danny Wuerffel threw a pass on a second-down-and-10 from the Husker 32-yard line. Although Nebraska led 35-10 by then, there was still a flicker of hope for Florida given the Gators' reputation for quick scores.

Eric Stokes extinguished it, however, intercepting Wuerffel's pass and returning the ball 11 yards to the Husker 30-yard line. Six plays later, after a 35-yard run on a draw play by quarterback Tommie Frazier and an extra-point kick by Kris Brown, Nebraska had extended its lead to 42-10.

The interception provided an upbeat finish to the season for Stokes, who began as a starting cornerback and finished as the No. 2 free safety behind Tony Veland.

The 1995 season was a microcosm of Stokes' Husker career to this point. He has alternated between cornerback and both safety positions when injuries have depleted them. He has accepted being shuffled back and forth without complaint, even though it has meant not being able to settle in.

"The secret to our defense is, everybody plays with a lot of heart," Stokes said.

That was evident in the Fiesta Bowl game. Even though Florida scored first and regained the lead after the Huskers responded, there was no panic on the Nebraska sideline, said Stokes. "Like us, I'm sure their first 15 plays were scripted, so we were going to see their best and then ..."

Stokes knows what it means to hang tough. He was plagued by injuries early on at Nebraska. First, it was a severe hamstring pull. Then it was a pelvic injury that threatened his career.

"It was a crazy road. I went from top to bottom," said Stokes, an Academic All-Big Eight honoree. "I don't take anything for granted because it was almost taken away from me."

But it was Stokes who did the taking away in the Fiesta Bowl. "This is probably the most watched game in the history of college football, and I made a big play," he said afterward. "What more could I ask for?"

Aaron Taylor #67

During a news conference before the Tostitos Fiesta Bowl game, Aaron Taylor was asked how he had changed since arriving at Nebraska as a freshman.

"I was 300 pounds," he said. "But not the 300 pounds I am now."

Taylor reshaped himself in the Husker weight room following an outstanding career at Rider High School in Wichita Falls, Texas. His dedication in the weight room has made him into one of the most powerful offensive linemen. He's also among the most athletic, holding a performance index record for offensive linemen.

"If you grow up in this system and work hard, you know you're going to be successful when your turn comes," said Taylor, a rare sophomore starter in Nebraska's offensive line.

With center and co-captain Aaron Graham as the only returning starter from the Huskers' 1994 offensive line, "people were wondering how much of a drop-off there would be," Taylor said.

"We felt there wasn't going to be any. We knew we were going to be a good line."

Nebraska's 1994 offensive line, which included current National Football League players Brenden Stai, Rob Zatechka and Zach Wiegert (the 1994 Outland Trophy winner), was nicknamed the "Pipeline." Taylor and his linemates played so well, they earned the nickname "Pipeline."

In some ways, the sequel was better than the original version. The Huskers averaged 60 rushing yards more per game behind the 1995 offensive line, eventually breaking single-season school records for average total offense and points per game. They were even more productive than the famed "Scoring Explosion" team of 1983. And a key to their success was what was up front.

Taylor led the linemen in "pancake" knockdown blocks with a remarkable total of 128. He had 17 "pancakes" three times in games against Michigan State, Arizona State and Oklahoma.

He was chosen first-team All-Big Eight by the Associated Press and was included on the conference coaches' second team. The Football News picked him as a third-team All-American.

Ryan Terwilliger #91

Ryan Terwilliger achieved a longtime goal this season: He earned the black practice jersey of a first-team Husker defensive player. In short, he became a Blackshirt. "It was a huge thrill," he said.

Terwilliger was Ed Stewart's backup last season. But when Stewart was sidelined by injury, Terwilliger got a baptism under fire during Nebraska's 24-17 victory against Miami in the 1995 Orange Bowl.

With that experience and a solid spring, Terwilliger began the 1995 season as the starter at the weakside linebacker or "Will" position. He started the first six games, while highly regarded junior college transfer Terrell Farley became accustomed to the position. They shared playing time over the second half of the season, giving the Huskers the kind of depth that has characterized their back-to-back national championship seasons. (Nebraska's attacking style of defense requires regular rotation of players.)

Terwilliger made 35 tackles during the season, including 18 unassisted. His busiest games were against Arizona State and Missouri. He made seven tackles in each. He also forced a fumble and had four quarterback hurries. Despite his size, he has 4.71 speed in the 40-yard dash and has a vertical jump of 37.5 inches.

Terwilliger has balanced brawn with brains. He has made the Phillips 66 Academic Honor Roll twice, was first-team Academic All-Big Eight this season and was a GTE/CoSIDA Academic All-District VII selection for the second-consecutive year. He has a 3.23 grade-point average in pre-education.

Like every recruit, Terwilliger had doubts when he arrived at Nebraska as a freshman. "You wonder if you'll ever fit in," he said. But, he shouldn't have been concerned. Terwilliger's coach at Grant High School was his father, Marlin. "I've been around the game most of my life," he said.

Jared Tomich #93

Jared Tomich had an outstanding junior season. He earned first-team All-America recognition from the Associated Press, joining a long line of outstanding Husker outside linebackers.

His portrait will hang in the Hall of Americans. And he has another season to play.

"Tomich is going to be a great player," said Tony Samuel, his position coach. "He's already there. But he's not finished improving." That's bad news for Nebraska's future opponents.

Tomich was expected to be a solid player in 1995. But he was exceptional, making 27 tackles, including 18 unassisted and 12 for losses totaling 79 yards. He led the team in quarterback sacks (10), fumbles caused (3), fumbles recovered (2) and quarterback hurries (24).

"I do whatever I have to do to get there," said Tomich.

He and sophomore Grant Wistrom were a two-man wrecking crew, overwhelming blockers with speed, strength and study. Tomich watches films of opponents by the hour. "I've never been around a guy who wants to step in and understand the opponent as much as he does," Samuel said.

Ironically, Nebraska was Tomich's only choice if he wanted to play major college football, in part because he didn't meet the NCAA's freshman eligibility requirements.

He walked on and earned a scholarship prior to his sophomore season.

Tomich's success on the field and in the classroom support those who argue against the newly-formed Big 12's decision to prohibit academic non-qualifiers from competing, even if they prove they can do college work. Tomich wouldn't have been able to play under such a system.

"I have a big opinion about that," he said after the Tostitos Fiesta Bowl. "I hope that (the Big 12 administrators) will keep that just the way it is because if they change things like that, a player like myself and many other players on our teams wouldn't get a chance to do what we can do."

Adam Treu #77

Changes in attitude, changes in latitude, to borrow an image from singer and songwriter Jimmy Buffett. That's how Adam Treu emerged as a force in Nebraska's offensive line.

It wasn't until the walk-on from Lincoln's Pius X High School changed his attitude that his latitude — or, more specifically, his position on the depth chart — changed for the better.

"I never knew if I was going to play, and I let that bother me," Treu said. "Even my grades were going down. But the last year and a half, I've been more optimistic about everything in my life. It just came from within myself. I decided I wasn't going to let things bother me anymore."

He has benefited from the attitude adjustment. And so have the Huskers, who needed some offensive linemen to step forward after four of the starting five interior lineman from a year ago departed. With last season's backups moving up, there were opportunities for players such as Treu.

Not only did he step up, he stepped up in a big way, literally. He's 6'-6" tall and weighs 295 pounds. His height and athletic ability enabled him to be a successful multi-sport athlete in high school. Nebraska asked him to walk on after watching him play basketball.

"I heard Coach (Tom) Osborne mention on television how I was a good basketball player with good feet. Then he said my football skills were OK. I'm like: 'Thanks a lot.'"

Treu admits his work habits early on left something to be desired. But after he began working out with former Husker tight end Matt Shaw, he realized the value of personal commitment.

"Maybe (the coaches) didn't care if I left or not. That's probably what I thought then," said Treu, who was Nebraska's sixth man in the offensive line, rotating with Eric Anderson and Chris Dishman as a third tackle. "I just needed to make up my mind that I was going to get a chance to play."

When offensive line coach Milt Tenopir told him before the opening game at Oklahoma State that he would be alternating, "I'm sure my eyes got a little bigger," Treu said.

Matt Turman #11

Just about everything Nebraska touched this season turned to gold. The Huskers succeeded even when they weren't trying. Consider the touchdown pass from Matt Turman to Lance Brown.

Nebraska faced a third-down-and-13 in the final minute of the Arizona State game. The Huskers were at the Arizona State 39-yard line. The score was 70-28 and the reserves were mopping up.

Coach Tom Osborne called a hook pass, hoping to pick up a first down so that he could send in more lower-unit reserves to reward them for their dedication with a few seconds of playing time.

Brown, a reserve wingback, started to run the hook pattern, but when the Sun Devil defensive back moved up, he adjusted — as he had been taught — and went deep. Turman's pass was perfect. Six points.

"I felt terrible about that last play," Osborne told reporters afterward. "It was a bush league thing to do. That was my mistake. We should have just run a draw play and ran out the clock."

In retrospect, Osborne was being too hard on himself. The responsibility was Arizona State's, not his.

The touchdown pass was one of 14 passes Turman threw in 1995. He played in nine games as the No. 3 quarterback behind Tommie Frazier and Brook Berringer.

Like Berringer, Turman had to accept limited playing time in 1995. He had stepped in and delivered when the Huskers needed him in their 1994 national championship drive. During that season, Turman became the first walk-on to start at quarterback since Travis Turner in 1985. And his start was a memorable one, coming at nationally ranked Kansas State. Turman played the first half, directing a six-play, 28-yard drive for the only touchdown Nebraska really needed in the 17-6 victory.

Turman had the honor of wrapping up the Tostitos Fiesta Bowl victory against Florida. He took the final snap on a first-and-goal at the Gator 1-yard line and knelt for a 2-yard loss.

Steve Volin #68

Steve Volin saw limited action during his five years at Nebraska. But he never complained about his situation and never considered quitting. "I've been lucky," he said.

Volin, a walk-on from Wahoo High School, grew up wanting to be a Husker. "There was nothing else but Nebraska football," he said. "I remember coming with my dad to games.

"Being the chunky kid I was, people told me I would be a Nebraska football player. No way was I going to turn down an opportunity to come here." Even if it meant paying his own way.

Volin was a credit to the program, and not just as a backup to Aaron Taylor. He was an Academic All-Big Eight honoree with a 3.86 cumulative grade-point average in biological sciences and was a volunteer in Coach Tom Osborne's Teammates Program, working with at-risk youngsters.

"There are times when you think that (quitting) is the choice you should make," said Volin. "But I couldn't picture myself doing that. I worked hard and was able to learn things quickly. That helped me."

Five years in a program such as Nebraska's demands a unique commitment from scholarship and walk-on players alike. "You really don't know what it's like until you experience it. You go back (home) and have people pat you on the back. Maybe they understand. But I don't think so," Volin said.

Mike Tranmer, a former Husker co-captain, coached Volin in high school. Tranmer also walked on and was able to provide some insight into what it would be like at Nebraska.

Even so, "You still don't realize how hard it hits you," Volin said. "You come in with the freshmen and then the varsity shows up. Bam! It hits you square in the face, literally and figuratively."

Volin was among a dozen walk-ons on Nebraska's two-deeps in the Tostitos Fiesta Bowl game — evidence of their contribution to the Huskers' success. "That's one of the true saving factors of our program, that we've had players like this," Osborne said.

Jon Vedral #25

Jon Vedral, another of Nebraska's walk-ons, always seemed to be in the right place at the right time. Either that or there was more than one offensive player wearing a No. 25 jersey.

In the Missouri game, Vedral tipped a pass that was caught by teammate Brendan Holbein for a touchdown. In the Kansas State game, Vedral recovered a fumble by Husker I-back Clinton Childs in the end zone for a touchdown. And in the Kansas game, Vedral recovered a fumble by Jayhawk punt returner Isaac Byrd for the touchdown that put Nebraska on the scoreboard in a 41-3 victory.

In addition, Vedral caught 14 passes for 272 yards and five touchdowns.

Hard work during the off-season paid off for the younger brother of former Husker tight end Mike Vedral, who also walked on. "When I first came here, I didn't know if I'd ever play ... you have to have a certain level of self-confidence. You have to think you can get it done," said Vedral, who received a scholarship in the fall. "The toughest part for me was telling myself I could get it done."

His commitment was apparent by his scores in strength and conditioning tests. "Test scores, you can be the best athlete in the world, but if you don't have football sense, it doesn't mean anything," he said.

Not only does he have football sense, Vedral has enough common sense to know that the more things you're willing to do, the better your chances of getting on the field. Besides alternating at wingback with Clester Johnson, he was on the kickoff team and held on extra-point kicks and field goal attempts.

In the Oklahoma State game at Memorial Stadium two seasons ago, Vedral completed a pass to place-kicker Darin Erstad for a two-point conversion. Later in the game, he completed a pass to fullback Jeff Makovicka on a fake field goal attempt. With those completions, his career as a passer was over, Vedral said.

In some cases, walk-ons "may not be difference-makers, but they're people who are very solid, and if you get an injury or two, you just don't run out of players," Osborne said.

Vedral, however, was more than a fill-in. He made a big difference.

Tony Veland #9

Tony Veland went out in style. In the final regular-season game, Nebraska's free safety and co-captain scooped up a James Allen fumble and returned it 57 yards for a touchdown. And early in the fourth quarter of the Tostitos Fiesta Bowl game, he intercepted a Danny Wuerffel pass.

It was a fitting finish to a stellar career that had a difficult beginning. Veland arrived at Nebraska as a quarterback and had it not been for a torn patellar tendon, he might have remained a quarterback. "When I first came here, I was told if things didn't work out, I could switch to defensive back," said Veland, who was determined to play quarterback.

But his attitude changed after he underwent knee surgery. "It didn't take all that long," he said. "It was a spur-of-the-moment decision once I got off the surgery table. I went to Coach (Tom) Osborne and Coach (George) Darlington and they pretty much said they were fine with my decision.

"I think Coach Darlington wanted me to play in the secondary when I got here."

Darlington, the Huskers' defensive backs coach, knows a good player when he sees one. He described Veland as a "prototype NFL safety."

Veland played his junior season at less than full speed. But he needed that time to completely learn the position and the results of his learning experience were obvious. He had an outstanding game against Miami in the 1995 Orange Bowl — a performance that provided a good lead-in to Veland's senior season.

In 1995, he made 38 tackles, including 22 solo. He recovered two fumbles and forced one. And he intercepted a pass (which he returned 43 yards against Missouri) and broke up two others to earn second-team All-Big Eight recognition from both the Associated Press and the conference coaches.

Jamel Williams #28

With 8:36 left in the first quarter of the Oklahoma game, Jamel Williams intercepted a pass and returned it 36 yards for a touchdown that gave Nebraska a 10-0 lead. The play obviously pleased Coach Tom Osborne.

It also made him want to "wring" Williams' neck. Jamel not only crossed the goal line, he almost crossed the line on excessive celebration, an area in which NCAA rules have become more stringent than they once were. Osborne told an official who indicated he almost threw a penalty flag after the play: "I wouldn't have blamed you if you had."

"You really don't think about what you're doing. I didn't think I did anything that bad to get penalized," Williams said later. "Coaches talk to us all the time: 'Don't get penalties.'"

Williams smiled. "I kept my part of the bargain," he said. But just barely.

The junior strongside linebacker probably could have been forgiven for his exuberance, even if he had been penalized. "Jamel is a guy willing to do anything he can to help," said Tony Samuel, his position coach. "One thing we really liked about Jamel is his ability to turn a potential touchdown for an opponent into a short-gainer. When he stops an opponent from making a big play, it's a big play for us."

Williams, who alternated with redshirted freshman Jay Foreman, finished third on the team in tackles with 47, including 22 unassisted, even though he never started. He also forced a fumble. And in the Fiesta Bowl game, he tackled Florida quarterback Danny Wuerffel for a safety early in the second quarter.

Getting to Wuerffel, after it appeared Terrell Farley had already sacked him for the safety, was typical of Williams' play in big games. He made 10 tackles in the Colorado and Kansas games.

Nebraska has gone to slightly smaller but faster linebackers in its 4-3 base defense, and Williams fits in perfectly. "We wanted to get him on the field because of his speed," Samuel said. Williams has run the 40-yard dash (about the length of the Oklahoma interception return) in 4.61 seconds.

Tyrone Williams #8

Tyrone Williams has been a model of consistency in the Huskers' secondary for three seasons. He has gone about his business with quiet determination and the equilibrium necessary to play cornerback. Few notice when a cornerback does his job. But when he doesn't, everyone knows.

"You have to be able to block things out immediately, right when they happen," said Williams, who earned first-team All-Big Eight recognition from both the Associated Press and the conference coaches in 1995, after receiving the same respect from the coaches last season as a junior.

Williams made 28 tackles, 19 of them solo, during the 1995 season. He also recovered a fumble, broke up three passes, hurried the quarterback once and intercepted a pass in the Kansas game.

"The bigger the game, the bigger I seem to play," Williams said.

Williams was a teammate of quarterback Tommie Frazier at Manatee High School. He was among four Floridians on Nebraska's roster for the Tostitos Fiesta Bowl game.

Prior to the Fiesta Bowl, Williams said he was determined to help the Huskers repeat as national champions. "Last year, my roommate (Barron Miles) was a senior, and he often talked about leaving Nebraska No. 1 in the nation. Now I'm a senior and I'm looking forward to getting that job done.

"It's something nobody could ever take away from me."

Williams' speed (4.45 in the 40-yard dash) and his ability to cover receivers man-to-man were significant factors in Nebraska's ability to check Florida's offense in the Fiesta Bowl. Afterward, Williams couldn't hide his excitement about winning a second-consecutive national championship.

"This may be the biggest game of all time, and we were huge," he said.

It was a good way to finish a career that had ups and downs off the field. "Coach Osborne has been a father figure to me," said Williams. "He helped me to express myself. He's been there for me, which is something I wasn't used to. I'll never forget Coach Osborne and the things he did for me."

Grant Wistrom #98

Grant Wistrom earned first-team All-Big Eight honors from the conference coaches and third-team All-America recognition from the Associated Press after starting the 1995 season slowly.

However, Wistrom's slow start was probably more perceived than real. His freshman season was so extraordinary that expectations for his sophomore season were unrealistic given the fact that opposing teams were more aware of his presence than they had been in 1994. As a result, they were less inclined to challenge him.

Wistrom was the Big Eight's defensive Newcomer of the Year in 1994. He played as a true freshman and earned the highest praise from Coach Tom Osborne. "We've had some good freshmen, but I can't ever remember a true freshman who had so much impact in so many ways," Osborne said. "He's playing at a level commensurate with a lot of our seniors. Grant's been at that level almost from the first day."

Wistrom was compared to former Husker Trev Alberts when he was recruited. Alberts, Nebraska's only Butkus Award winner, now plays for the Indianapolis Colts of the National Football League. Tony Samuel, Wistrom's position coach, says Wistrom is further along than Alberts was at the same stage of his career.

The comparison to Alberts also extends beyond the playing field. Wistrom is an outstanding student. He was a first-team Academic All-Big Eight selection and earned GTE/CoSIDA Academic All-District VII recognition with a 3.58 cumulative grade-point average as a pharmacy major.

Wistrom was sixth on the team in tackles in 1995 with 44, including 21 unassisted. He led the Huskers in tackles for loss with 15, totaling 55 yards; four of those 15 were quarterback sacks (for 23 yards in losses). And he was second on the team in quarterback hurries with 13.

Wistrom and Jared Tomich (who led the team in quarterback hurries with 24) were the Huskers' version of Scylla (the rock) and Charybdis (the whirlpool) of classical mythology. If one didn't make the play, the odds were, the other did.

"As a twosome, productivity-wise, they're as good as I've had so far," Samuel said.

Jon Zatechka #64

Jon Zatechka was a ninth-grader when his brother Rob signed a letter of intent to accept a football scholarship from Nebraska. Jon stood in the doorway of the athletic director's office at Lincoln East High School and watched the signing. "He had stars in his eyes," one observer recalled.

Now, Rob has moved on to the National Football League and Jon is a Husker scholarship player. He backed up Steve Ott at right guard in 1995, playing in every game for the "Pipeline."

Zatechka not only bolstered the offensive line, he also bolstered the team grade-point average. He was named to the Phillips 66 Academic Honor Roll with a 3.82 cumulative grade-point average in fisheries and wildlife.

Such success in the classroom is expected in the Zatechka household. Rob made straight A's at Nebraska, and older brother Steve (who didn't play football) was an exceptional student. All three were valedictorians of their high school graduating classes. Jon might have made a run at straight A's at Nebraska, but he earned only a B-plus in a theater class as a freshman. "Only" a B-plus?

Coach Tom Osborne emphasizes the importance of academics and encourages his players to complete undergraduate degrees. "Parents will say academics are important (in the recruiting process), but they pick schools based on football," Osborne said. In the last five years or so, however, that has begun to change.

"Not everybody, but probably 90 percent have bought into the importance of education."

Zatechka bought into the importance. It runs in the family.

Seniors

27 Jacques Allen
Wingback
Kansas City, Mo.

7 Reggie Baul
Split End
Bellevue, Neb.

18 Brook Berringer
Quarterback
Goodland, Kan.

26 Clinton Childs
I-Back
Omaha, Neb.

46 Doug Colman
Mike Linebacker
Ventnor, N.J.

41 Phil Ellis
Mike Linebacker
Grand Island, Neb.

15 Tommie Frazier
Quarterback
Palmetto, Fla.

87 Mark Gilman
Tight End
Kalispell, Mont.

54 Aaron Graham
Center
Denton, Texas

58 Luther Hardin
Outside Linebacker
O'Fallon, Ill.

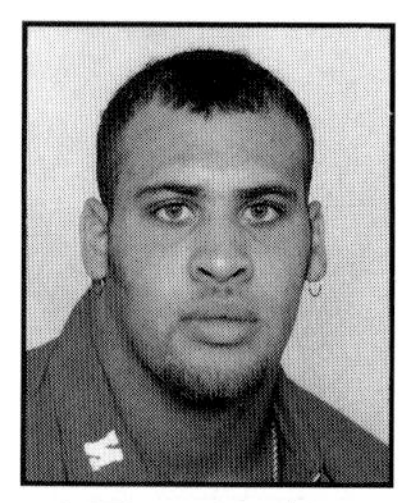
96 Jason Jenkins
Defensive Tackle
Hammonton, N.J.

33 Clester Johnson
Wingback
Bellevue, Neb.

22 Jeff Makovicka
Fullback
Brainard, Neb.

Chris Norris
Fullback
Papillion, Neb.

63 Brian Nunns
Offensive Tackle
Lincoln, Neb.

69 Steve Ott
Ofensive Guard
Henderson, Neb.

52 Aaron Penland
Will Linebacker
Jacksonville, Fla.

55 Christian Peter
Defensive Tackle
Locust, N.J.

37 Darren Schmadeke
Cornerback
Albion, Neb.

9 Tony Veland
Free Safety
Omaha, Neb.

68 Steve Volin
Offensive Guard
Wahoo, Neb.

8 Tyrone Williams
Cornerback
Palmetto, Fla.

Juniors

48 Dave Alderman
Rover
Omaha, Neb.

21 Damon Benning
I-Back
Omaha, Neb.

17 Chad Blahak
Cornerback
Lincoln, Neb.

20 Michael Booker
Cornerback
Oceanside, Calif.

75 Chris Dishman
Offensive Tackle
Cozad, Neb.

43 Terrell Farley
Will Linebacker
Columbus, Ga.

12 Mike Fullman
Cornerback
Roselle, N.J.

44 Jon Hesse
Outside Linebacker
Lincoln, Neb.

5 Brendan Holbein
Split End
Cozad, Neb.

53 Troy Langan
Center
Columbus, Neb.

78 Kory Mikos
Offensive Tackle
Seward, Neb.

83 Bryce Miller
Outside Linebacker
Elmwood, Neb.

10 Mike Minter
Rover
Lawton, Okla.

97 Jeff Ogard
Defensive Tackle
St. Paul, Neb.

1 Lawrence Phillips
I-Back
West Covina, Calif.

39 Mike Roberts
Rover
Omaha, Neb.

27 Tom Royce
Cornerback
Council Bluffs, Iowa

74 Scott Saltsman
Defensive Tackle
Wichita Falls, Texas

28 Brian Schuster
Fullback
Fullerton, Neb.

16 Eric Stokes
Cornerback
Lincoln, Neb.

91 Ryan Terwilliger
Will Linebacker
Grant, Neb.

93 Jared Tomich
Outside Linebacker
St. John, Ind.

94 Larry Townsend
Defensive Tackle
San Jose, Calif.

77 Adam Treu
Offensive Tackle
Lincoln, Neb.

11 Matt Turman
Quarterback
Wahoo, Neb.

25 Jon Vedral
Wingback
Gregory, S.D.

51 Matt Vrzal
Center
Grand Island, Neb.

3 Riley Washington
Wingback
Chula Vista, Calif.

28 Jamel Williams
Will Linebacker
Merrillville, Ind.

Sophomores

47 Matt Aden
Will Linebacker
Omaha, Neb.

70 Eric Anderson
Offensive Tackle
Lincoln, Neb.

11 Jason Benes
Free Safety
Valparaiso, Neb.

90 Tim Carpenter
Tight End
Columbus, Neb.

9 Monte Christo
Quarterback
Kearney, Neb.

2 Leslie Dennis
Cornerback
Bradenton, Fla.

23 Chad Eicher
I-Back
Seward, Neb.

16 Scott Frost
Quarterback
Wood River, Neb.

80 Sean Gard
Outside Linebacker
Omaha, Neb.

82 Ryan Held
Split End
Overland Park, Kan.

59 Josh Heskew
Center
Yukon, Okla.

50 Michael Hoffman
Defensive Tackle
Spencer, Neb.

66 Joe Horst
Offensive Guard
Wood River, Neb.

62 Matt Hoskinson
Offensive Guard
Battle Creek, Neb.

53 Matt Hunting
Linebacker
Cozad, Neb.

34 Vershan Jackson
Tight End
Omaha, Neb.

19 Jesse Kosch
Punter
Columbus, Neb.

89 Jeff Lake
Split End
Columbus, Neb.

4 Octavious McFarlin
Rover
Bastrop, Texas

95 Jason Peter
Defensive Tackle
Locust N.J.

73 Fred Pollack
Offensive Tackle
Omaha, Neb.

13 Ted Retzlaff
Place-Kicker
Waverly, Neb.

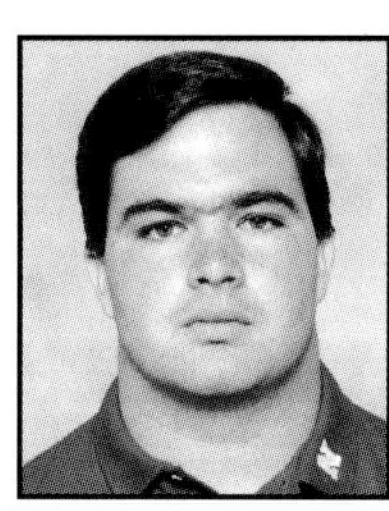
57 Doug Seaman
Center
Bellevue, Neb.

31 James Sims
I-Back
Omaha, Neb.

67 Aaron Taylor
Offensive Guard
Wichita Falls, Texas

24 Todd Uhlir
I-Back
Battle Creek, Neb.

71 Mike Van Cleave
Offensive Guard
Huffman, Texas

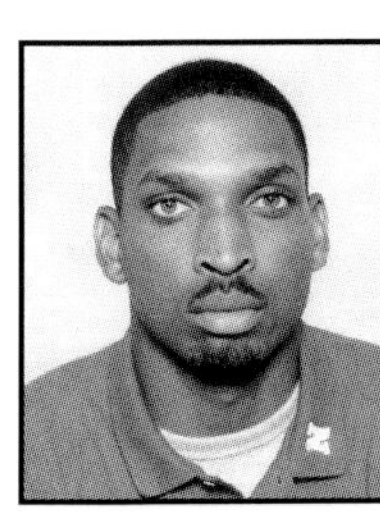
3 Eric Warfield
Free Safety
Texarkana, Ark.

85 Sean Wieting
Wingback
Tulatin, Ore.

29 Shevin Wiggins
Split End
Palmetto, Fla.

98 Grant Wistrom
Outside Linebacker
Webb City, Mo.

86 Brendan Zahl
Outside Linebacker
Stratton, Neb.

64 Jon Zatechka
Offensive Guard
Lincoln, Neb.

Freshmen

61 Derek Allen
Defensive Tackle
Russellville, Ark.

52 Matt Baldwin
Center
Arvada, Colo.

50 Andy Bilanzich
Punter
Salt Lake City, Utah

35 Kris Brown
Place-Kicker
Southlake, Texas

14 Lance Brown
Wingback
Papillion, Neb.

80 Darren Brummond
Outside Linebacker
Englewood, Colo.

6 Kenny Cheatham
Split End
Phoenix, Ariz.

56 Jeff Clausen
Offensive Lineman
Dixon, Ill.

42 Josh Cobb
Fullback
Wallace, Neb.

45 Steve Cook
Middle Linebacker
Blair, Neb.

84 T.J. DeBates
Tight End
Stewartville, Minn.

73 Brandon Drum
Defensive Tackle
Columbus, Neb.

56 Jay Foreman
Sam Linebacker
Eden Prairie, Minn.

35 Russell Froelich
Sam Linebacker
Omaha, Neb.

7 Nate Froeschl
Cornerback
Falls City, Neb.

72 Ben Gessford
Offensive Tackle
Lincoln, Neb.

30 Ahman Green
I-Back
Omaha, Neb.

81 Trent Gumm
Outside Linebacker
Columbus, Neb.

80 Billy Haafke
I-Back
South Sioux City, Neb.

6 Chris Herron
Rover
Scottsbluff, Neb.

49 Quint Hogrefe
Middle Linebacker
Auburn, Neb.

32 Julius Jackson
Sam Linebacker
Gainesville, Texas

88 Sheldon Jackson
Tight End
Diamond Bar, Calif.

58 Marcus Johnson
Offensive Guard
Oceanside, Calif.

76 Adam Julch
Offensive Tackle
Omaha, Neb.

57 Chad Kelsay
Outside Linebacker
Auburn, Neb.

23 Bill Lafleur
Punter
Norfolk, Neb.

31 Charlie Leece
Middle Linebacker
Grand Island, Neb.

40 Billy Legate
Fullback
Elgin, Neb.

12 Frankie London
Quarterback
Lake Charles, La.

58 Casey Macken
Linebacker
Cozad, Neb.

45 Joel Makovicka
Fullback
Brainard, Neb.

5 Karnell Matthews
Rover
St. Peters, Mo.

21 Alex McClymont
Cornerback
Holdrege, Neb.

83 Andy Miller
Split End
Papillion, Neb.

Freshmen

10 Brian Morro
Punter
Middletown, N.J.

65 Erik Nelson
Defensive Tackle
Iowa City, Iowa

33 Tony Ortiz
Sam Linebacker
Waterbury, Conn.

9 Jeff Perino
Quarterback
Durango, Colo.

25 Jerome Peterson
Cornerback
Port Allen, La.

32 David Reddick
Wingback
Camden, N.J.

86 Dorrick Roy
Tight End
Inglewood, Calif.

84 Mike Rucker
Outside Linebacker
St. Joseph, Mo.

66 Anthony Schmode
Offensive Guard
Battle Creek, Neb.

40 Kareem Sears
Middle Linebacker
Enid, Okla.

65 James Sherman
Offensive Guard
LaVerne, Calif.

36 Adam Skoda
Middle Linebacker
Lincoln, Neb.

77 Ross Tessendorf
Defensive Tackle
Columbus, Neb.

92 Travis Toline
Outside Linebacker
Wahoo, Neb.

76 Kyle Tully
Offensive Lineman
Jefferson, Wis.

61 Brandt Wade
Offensive Guard
Springfield, Neb.

29 Eric Walther
Free Safety
Juniata, Neb.

81 Aaron Wills
Tight End
Omaha, Neb.

99 Jason Wiltz
Defensive Tackle
New Orleans, La.

The Games

Season Overview

The 1995 Nebraska Huskers

The pressure was off at the start of the 1995 season. Coach Tom Osborne had finally won the national championship that he had come very close to winning for so many years. He and his 13-0 1994 team had beaten Miami in the Orange Bowl and claimed the top prize.

It was only fitting for the man who built a program other coaches only dream about. In none of his 22 seasons did he have fewer than nine wins. He had a record string of 15-straight New Year's Day bowl games, was ranked in The Associated Press polls for 239 consecutive weeks, had two straight 11-win seasons and had his third 12-win season.

In the spring of 1995, Osborne knew something a lot of other people around the country suspected. He had another pretty good team.

Four starters from the 1994 offensive line, Outland Trophy winner Zach Wiegert, Academic "All-Everything" Rob Zatechka, All-Big Eight guard Brenden Stai and team "pancake" block leader Joel Wilks, had graduated. Those were big shoes to fill, but Osborne had big boys to fill them: 305-pound junior tackle Chris Dishman, 295-pound sophomore guard Aaron Taylor, 275-pound senior Steve Ott and 290-pound sophomore tackle Eric Anderson. They surrounded returning center Aaron Graham with size and more quickness than the "best-ever" line that had departed.

Nebraska's development of linemen had built such a reputation that Dishman was named to at least one preseason All-American team without ever having started a game.

The quarterback position was healthy with returning seniors Tommie Frazier and Brook Berringer in a spirited battle for the starting

(Above) Memorial Stadium, filled by a sea of red. Home for the first time in 1995, Nebraska continued its record of 208 consecutive sellouts.
(Right) Tommie Frazier leads the team onto the field at Memorial Stadium.

N
15

spot. Frazier, who missed eight games with blood clots in his leg in 1994, held a slight edge over Berringer, who won seven 1994 starts and led an unbeaten Husker team to the Orange Bowl.

Frazier won a second Most Valuable Player award by leading the Orange Bowl rally to beat Miami and worked hard over the summer on his passing. He had watched Berringer's touch tosses beat opposing defenses often during the previous season and vowed he could do the same.

Double-trouble for opposing offenses: the Peter brothers — Christian (55) and Jason (95).

Running backs with talent were everywhere. Junior I-back Lawrence Phillips led a stable of I-backs that included junior Damon Benning, senior Clinton Childs, sophomore James Sims and a new kid from Omaha Central High, Ahman Green. Their position coach, assistant head coach Frank Solich, couldn't remember a better group of backs in his 17 years on the staff.

The Makovicka brothers, senior Jeff and freshman Joel, and junior Brian Schuster could run and block at fullback. The tight ends were big and deep, headed by sure-handed senior Mark Gilman.

Seniors Reggie Baul and Clester Johnson led a group of split ends and wingbacks with big-play potential.

Frazier would say often this team had too many weapons for any team to shut down and wouldn't take a back seat to the 1994 group that led the nation in rushing, was fifth in total offense and was sixth in scoring.

The defense lost Big Eight defensive player of the year Ed Stewart at linebacker, outside linebackers Donta Jones and Dwayne Harris, co-captain tackle Terry Connealy, and defensive backs Troy Dumas, Barron Miles and Kareem Moss.

Junior Jared Tomich and sophomore Grant Wistrom, outside linebackers, had plenty of playing experience as backups. Senior Christian Peter was being joined by sophomore brother Jason at tackle and seniors Phil Ellis and Doug Colman were very, very good middle linebackers.

In the secondary, junior Mike Minter returned after missing most of a promising 1994 with a knee injury. Seniors Tyrone Williams and Tony Veland were talented veterans as well.

Also gone was kicking specialist Darin Erstad, who was the No. 1 draft pick in the summer major league baseball draft. Erstad had been one of the nation's top punters in 1994 and had a strong leg for field goals and extra points.

Youngsters Kris Brown and Jesse Kosch were unknown fill-ins who hoped to shine in their first opportunities to kick.

The 1995 season began with a shuffling of the schedule. The Oct. 7 Oklahoma State game was moved to Aug. 31 for an ESPN television date. The earlier date gave the Huskers a chance to try their new faces against a team less likely to be a major challenge than Michigan State (who Nebraska was scheduled to play in a road game on Sept. 9).

Nebraska's offense overwhelmed OSU, under first-year head coach Bob Simmons, the former long-time Colorado assistant. The Huskers ran 55 times for 513 yards and six touchdowns. Frazier and Berringer also combined for 151 yards passing and two more TDs in a 64-21 romp.

The defense displayed big-play potential with an interception return for a touchdown by junior college linebacker recruit Terrell Farley. It would be the first of many big plays for the junior.

"We knew what we were in for," said OSU's Simmons. "We just played a national championship program."

Michigan State on the road was next and again the offensive guns fired often. Phillips ran himself into Heisman Trophy consideration as he stomped and darted through the Spartan defense for 206 yards and four touchdowns. Frazier had five carries for 30 yards but came out limping in the first half.

Berringer came in to direct the offense that would roll up 552 yards rushing and 666 in total offense.

The NU defense also stepped up as it had in 1994 when the NU quarterback ranks suffered injury. Michigan State managed 45 yards rushing and kept Spartan quarterback Tony Banks scrambling all day. The Huskers had three quarterback sacks, forced six fumbles and recovered two of those in the 50-10 victory. There were too many weapons.

After the Michigan State game, the Husker intensity grew and, when a good Arizona State team came to Lincoln, the second-ranked Big Red held back nothing. Childs, who was making his first start, dashed 65 yards for a touchdown on the first play from scrimmage.

Nebraska scored 35 points in the first 15 minutes and added 28 more in the second quarter. The 63-point half broke a school record. Arizona State had given up nine touchdowns and 508 yards of total offense and still had two more quarters to play.

"Coach Osborne said adversity is going to come to every team," Frazier said of the coach's pregame speech. "Only great teams overcome things like (losing Lawrence Phillips)," Osborne said. "So he gave us a challenge," Frazier recalls. "He said, 'Can you be that great team?'"

The Huskers provided the answer. Nebraska walked out of Memorial Stadium that day with a 77-28 win and 686 yards of total offense.

Childs rushed for 143 yards, Green rushed for 111 and Frazier threw for 191. Too many weapons.

Pacific was the next victim, coming in for a second year to meet a team that humbled it 70-21 in 1994. Childs was out with a sprained knee so Benning earned the start. Despite his sore hamstring, he carried 10 times for 173 yards and three touchdowns. Green added 112 yards and two scores.

Only conservative play-calling kept this one from getting out of hand. It ended mercifully, 49-7. Osborne had been nice to old friend Chuck Shelton, Pacific's coach. But Shelton had seen enough to draw comparisons to the 1994 Huskers.

"They're better. I didn't expect that," he said of the 1995 version. "When I started looking at film last week I bawled because I thought they were good enough last year. I thought this year they'd be down because they lost some of those linemen. But they're better."

The Huskers, in game 5 against Washington State, needed another starting I-back. Childs' knee was slow to heal and Benning had sprained an ankle to go with his sore hamstring. As a result, Green was asked to start against one of the top defenses in the nation.

Washington State came to Lincoln fresh from a win over UCLA. The 2-1 Cougars vowed to upset the Huskers — a challenge Frazier took personally.

Washington State surprised the NU Blackshirts with an 87-yard TD run in the first quarter, but their other 23 carries during the day would yield the Cougars a net loss of 15 yards.

Frazier ran for a pair of second-quarter scores and freshman kicker Brown knocked in field goals of 33 and 22 yards. Green smashed through Washington State's prized defense for 176 yards on 13 carries. He also scored a touchdown.

By day's end, the Huskers ran for 428 of their 527 yards of total offense in a 35-21 win against a defense that was ranked No. 4 in the nation against the run. Way too many weapons.

The Huskers missed a few scoring opportunities in that one, according to Osborne, but his team wouldn't miss many the rest of the way.

The Blackshirts threw a shutout at outmanned Missouri, 57-0, after the team had a week off to heal. Frazier also put his name firmly on the Heisman consideration list with three rushing touchdowns and two more passing as he broke the school record for career total offensive touchdowns with 64.

The first of the big conference battles came next. Kansas State under coach Bill Snyder was becoming one of the nation's better teams. The Wildcats were ranked eighth and boasted one of the top defenses in the country.

Big-play Nebraska answered the challenge again. Rutgers transfer Mike Fullman returned a punt 79 yards for a score, the first punt return touchdown for Nebraska in seven years. Wingback Jon Vedral fell on a Childs' fumble in the end zone for another NU touchdown and senior backup outside linebacker Luther Hardin caught a K-State pass batted by NU teammate Chad Kelsay for a 3-yard interception touchdown return.

The race was on. Frazier showed there is more than one

Nebraska's season of success started soon after each opening toss. Rapid starts unsettled even good teams like Kansas State.

dimension to the Nebraska offense. The K-State defense was geared to stop the run and despite Green's 109 yards rushing, the Wildcats did. NU had just 190 yards rushing for the game.

But Frazier's passing touch proved fatal for K-State. Frazier found tight end Sheldon Jackson for an 11-yard score, hit Green for a 10-yard shovel pass TD, threw 32 yards to Vedral for six more points and teamed with Green for a 12-yard game-sealing TD. Frazier ended the day completing 10 of 16 passes for 148 yards and a career-high four TDs.

The Nebraska defense, miffed that the pregame talk focused on the Wildcats, emphasized its own talents. K-State had minus-19 yards rushing and 256 total yards. KSU quarterback Matt Miller was on his back most of the day under an intense Nebraska pass rush that logged nine sacks in the 49-25 win.

"They definitely put their licks on me and put their licks on our offense," Miller said. "They sure hit me hard. That's as much intimidation as I need."

Colorado would fare little better in Boulder the next week. The meeting of teams that had decided the Big Eight championship the past seven seasons was not much of a contest.

The Buffaloes, ranked seventh after a surprising loss to Kansas two weeks before, targeted the Husker rushing game to force Frazier to pass. But Green darted 57 yards for a TD on the first play of the game. He added a 1-yard TD run later in the quarter but it was Frazier's passing that set up the 44-21 win. He threw 52 yards to Clester Johnson for a score, 7 yards to Vedral for another and

Nebraska's fans had lots of opportunity to yell for Husker scores.

Husker yell-squad members offered great support for the national champs.

ended with 14 completions in 23 attempts for a career-high 241 yards.

"We didn't expect him to be able to pass as well as he did," Colorado linebacker Matt Russell said. "We said all week long if we forced him into passing, we'd have the upper hand."

That didn't work. Too many weapons.

The Husker Blackshirts picked off a couple of passes and kept a lid on the high-scoring Colorado offense. The performance was impressive enough to vault the Huskers to No. 1 in the polls over idle Florida State. Even Florida State coach Bobby Bowden wasn't grousing about that. He had been voting Nebraska No. 1 himself.

Nebraska wore the No. 1 label well, romping over outmanned Iowa State 73-14 with 624 yards rushing and 776 of total offense. The game marked the return of Phillips, who was given a warm welcome from the sellout crowd at Memorial Stadium. He played backup to Green, who rushed for 176 yards and three touchdowns.

The Nebraska defense took center stage in the final two regular-season games against 10th- and 12th-ranked Kansas and Oklahoma. The Jayhawks were once-beaten, losing only to K-State, and owned a convincing win over Colorado. It was Glen Mason's best Kansas club and KU's best record and ranking ever heading into a Nebraska game.

But the Blackshirts wouldn't let Kansas come close to the end zone. KU managed just 72 yards rushing and 273 passing. NU had three interceptions, one of which Fullman returned 86 yards for a touchdown.

Vedral again recovered a fumble in the end zone for a touchdown, this one off a fumbled punt. Frazier added to his touchdown totals with two on the ground and one through the air, but his string of 100 consecutive passes without an interception ended in the third quarter. The interception also ended Nebraska's string of 17 quarters without a turnover.

But this team was good enough to win even when it wasn't playing well. In fact, it was good enough to win by a 41-3 margin over a top-10 opponent on the road. More votes for No. 1.

The regular-season finale was built around the farewell to the Big Eight Conference and a traditional rivalry. Beginning in 1996, the league would become the Big 12 with the addition of four schools from Texas. No longer would Nebraska vs. Oklahoma be the premier season finale.

The first meeting between Osborne and Howard Schnellenberger since Schnellenberger's Miami team upset the Huskers in the 1984 Orange Bowl 31-30 would be payback time for Howard.

The 5-4-1 Sooners were struggling offensively and Nebraska showed no mercy. The Blackshirts swarmed Sooner freshman quarterback Eric Moore, who was picked off by Jamel Williams for a 36-yard TD return in the first quarter.

The defense added another TD when safety Tony Veland returned a fumble 57 yards for a score.

It was the eighth defensive touchdown for the Huskers and it was only the second time in Osborne's 23-year career the Blackshirts had scored twice in one game. That unit, too, had plenty of weapons.

The NU offense sputtered and in doing so likely cost Frazier votes in the Heisman race. He would finish second in the Heisman voting to Ohio State's Eddie George despite the impressive, record-setting offense he guided all season.

The rebuilt offensive line. Mountains of men.

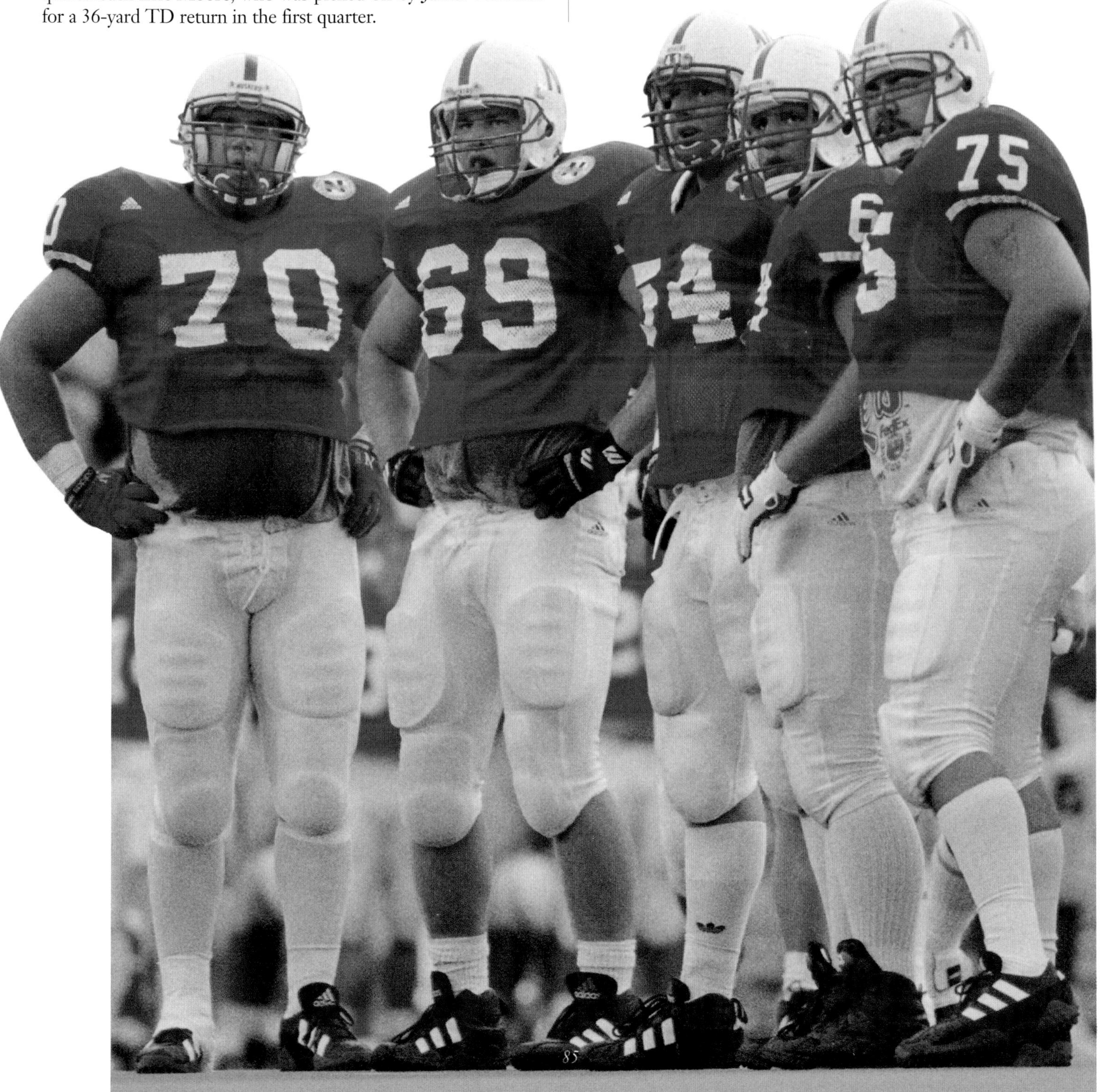

Nebraska ran away with a 37-0 win over OU to break its own Big Eight record for the highest scoring average during a regular season: They scored 52.479 points per game compared to 52.089 averaged by the Huskers over 12 games in 1983.

Frazier finished the season with a completion rate of 56.4 percent, passing for 1,362 yards and 17 touchdowns. On the ground, he ran for a team-leading 14 TDs. During his career at Nebraska, Frazier set school records for total offense with 5,476 yards, passing touchdowns with 43, total offensive touchdowns with 79 and victories as the starting quarterback with 32.

For all the flap he took for not having the traditional All-American quarterback's passing statistics, Frazier was named first-team All-American by the Football Writers, Walter Camp, Associated Press, American Football Coaches Association and United Press International teams. He won the Johnny Unitas Golden Arm Award, was *Sporting News* Offensive Player of the Year, Big Eight Offensive Player of the Year, UPI Player of the Year and a finalist in just about every other award competition for quarterbacks and offensive players.

Osborne labeled him a lot of things over the years, including "great player," "winner" and "difference-maker." Opposing coaches just groused about not being able to find ways to stop him.

I-back depth and talent started with No. 30 Ahman Green and No. 1 Lawrence Phillips, and continued with big-play backups (opposite page) Damon Benning (21) and Clinton Childs (26).

Ahman Green set a school freshman rushing record with 1,086 yards and kicker Kris Brown finished with a school freshman scoring record of 97 points, one point more than Green. The 97 points by Brown also was a season record for kick-scoring at the school.

Center Aaron Graham, who Osborne called Nebraska's best since two-time Outland winner and All-American Dave Rimington, joined Frazier and outside linebacker Tomich on the Associated Press All-American team.

Nebraska led the nation in rushing with 399.8 yards per game, was tops in scoring and No. 2 in total offense (556.3 yards per game). The defense was fourth in scoring, allowing 13.6 points per game, second in rushing (78.4 yards), fifth in turnover margin (+1.18), 13th in total defense (103.0 yards) and 21st in pass efficiency.

The Huskers dominated the All-Big Eight awards and headed to the Fiesta Bowl to fulfill their season's final goal — to win it all again.

Pregame hype was centered around the offenses. Second-ranked Florida was the darling of the passing game, playing coach Steve Spurrier's "Fun 'n Gun" offense that spread speedy receivers all over the field and banked on the arm of quarterback Danny Wuerffel to get them the ball.

Nebraska's running attack — which would feature Lawrence Phillips, the early season Heisman challenger, starting for the first time since the second game of the season — was quite a contrast to Florida's pass-dominated approach.

Quietly in the background sat the Nebraska defense, waiting for a chance to show the nation what the 1995 Huskers were all about — unity, talent and single-mindedness. Wuerffel and company would know they were in a game.

Florida drew first blood with a 23-yard field goal but Nebraska countered with a swing pass from Frazier to Phillips for a 16-yard TD. Wuerffel scored on a 1-yard sneak but NU's Phillips ran 42 yards for the second of his three touchdowns of the night.

Nebraska's defense took control. Jamel Williams sacked Wuerffel in the end zone for a safety that turned the tide and the Gators never looked like competitors from then on. Green scored, Brown kicked a field goal, Michael Booker intercepted a Wuerffel pass for a touchdown, Brown scored another field goal and Frazier had a 35-yard TD run.

Florida didn't know what hit it. It was 35-10 at the half and it didn't get any better after intermission.

Nebraska rolled up 524 yards rushing and 105 passing, while limiting Florida's can't miss offense to minus 28 yards rushing and 297 passing with three interceptions.

Frazier capped the game off with an amazing 75-yard touchdown run, breaking ten tackles as he sprinted to the end zone. He ended with 199 yards rushing and two touchdowns, and threw for another 105 yards and another TD.

Nebraska had become the first unbeaten repeat national champions since Oklahoma in 1955 and 1956, and first back-to-back winner since Alabama in 1978-79.

The win wasn't as surprising as the way it happened. Nobody would have believed a 62-24 blowout, unless it was the Huskers.

"I don't think they were ready for a game like this or a team like ours," Tomich said.

Spurrier agreed. "To be able to match up with them, we've got to be as strong as they are. I don't think we are right now."

It was perhaps Osborne's finest hour. He had withstood the potshots from critics of years gone by when his teams were losing to those of top-ranked Florida State and Miami in the Orange and Fiesta Bowls. He once said that apparently his teams would have to get better if they were going to beat teams like that. Spurrier said after the Fiesta Bowl massacre that his team would have to get a lot better if it hoped to play with a team like Nebraska. How some things change.

Throughout the season, Osborne backed the promising young men to whom he had grown close over the years. Frazier said the team wanted to win this one badly for Osborne. Aaron Graham said the Fiesta Bowl's overwhelming victory was proof of what Osborne built in Lincoln.

"We wanted to come and show everybody we were the best team," he said. "If the program was bad, if the program had flaws in it, then we should have crumbled. We didn't crumble. We stood strong. The program has a strong foundation and we wanted to show that to everybody."

Nebraska 64
Oklahoma State 21

August 31, 1995 - At Stillwater, Okla.

Second-ranked Nebraska opened its national title defense on the road and with the first game of the final Big Eight Conference season at Stillwater, Okla. The Huskers had confidence that the 13-0 season of 1994 and coach Tom Osborne's first national championship would carry over in a successful 1995. But there were several preseason questions that needed answers.

Would quarterback Tommie Frazier rebound from his blood clot problems of 1994 to hold off fellow senior Brook Berringer for the starting spot? Would all the new faces in the offensive line be sufficient to open holes for a fleet of talented backs led by Lawrence Phillips? Would the loss of a handful of defensive starters put the Blackshirts back to square one from a dominating finish in the national championship run?

Heisman Trophy hopefuls Phillips at I-back and Frazier at quarterback claimed most of the attention heading into the fall. They entered the season expecting big things to happen, even behind an offensive line rebuilt around lone returning starter Aaron Graham at center.

The line had to be the big question considering the graduation losses of Outland Trophy winner Zach Wiegert, Academic "All-Everything" tackle Rob Zatechka, All-American guard Brenden Stai and team "pancake" block leader Joel Wilks. Osborne considered the 1994 front the best he had had in 22 years as head coach, and it had helped Nebraska lead the nation in rushing with its overpowering play.

Osborne was hopeful a date swap involving Oklahoma State would be a chance to test his new players in game conditions before a challenging road trip to Michigan State. He also figured playing the Cowboys early in the season on national television (ESPN) could

(Above) Coach Tom Osborne leading the Huskers onto the field is an intimidating view for opposing teams.
(Right) Lawrence Phillips (1) goes airborne for more yards and scores.

Wilson
58

help his second-ranked team in the eyes of poll voters if it played well against an opponent the Cornhuskers had dominated throughout his tenure as head coach.

First-year coach Bob Simmons came to Oklahoma State to take over a 3-7-1 team after seven years as an assistant at Colorado. He was in agreement to the date switch since he figured it might be better to catch the Huskers early than let the Big Red ground machine build momentum through the non-conference schedule prior to the original Oct. 7 date.

The Aug. 31 starting date wasn't set until the spring, however. And it wasn't the only thing that would not iron itself out comfortably for the Huskers. There was a question of whether Phillips could even play. It was learned that Phillips had accepted a ride to lunch and was treated to lunch the previous November by a representative for a sports agent. Both could be violations of NCAA extra benefits restrictions.

Frazier and company dash past the Cowboys on one of the Husker quarterback's 10 rushes against OSU.

But NU officials said Phillips repaid the representative for the lunch and sought an NCAA ruling on the junior back's eligibility. On the Tuesday before the game, NCAA Director of Eligibility Carrie Doyle ruled Phillips could play for the Huskers until the school and NCAA legislative services determined if there were rules violations.

Since the money for lunch with an employee of the California sports agent was repaid, Doyle said, the incident was considered minor and Nebraska was at no risk of forfeiting the game should Phillips play.

And play he did.

Phillips and his teammates made a point early that the rebuilt offensive line, a reloaded defense and the fresh memory of a national championship would be driving forces in 1995.

The Huskers wanted another shot at a national title game, which would be played this season in Tempe, Ariz. The Fiesta Bowl won rights to serve as host for the first Bowl Coalition

I-back Damon Benning breaks a tackle to add to his rushing yardage that would total 62 on eight carries.

(Above) Junior center Matt Vrzal (51) punches a hole in the OSU defensive line.

matchup of the top-ranked teams.

"For the team, our No. 1 goal is to get to Phoenix," Phillips said. "Our goal is to try to get some respect and get in either one of those spots in Phoenix."

Phillips began a three-touchdown, 153-yard rushing night against Oklahoma State with a 6-yard score less than eight minutes into the first quarter.

The Cowboys, who had not beaten Nebraska since 1961, scrapped hard during the first quarter, forcing one Husker turnover and limiting the powerful NU offense to Phillips' TD.

But Oklahoma State soon would know just how good a job Osborne and his assistant coaches had done in rebuilding the defending champs. True freshman kicker Kris Brown, who missed his first career extra point try in the first quarter, booted a 24-yard field goal less than two minutes into the second period.

Transfer linebacker Terrell Farley, the Huskers' only junior college recruit in 1995, then picked off a Tone' Jones pass and ran it back 29 yards for a score just over a minute later.

Oklahoma State's David Thompson darted through the Nebraska defense for 79 yards to set up a 2-yard TD run by Andre Richardson in what would amount to OSU's only big play of the game.

Phillips took away any momentum Oklahoma State might have started to build when he got that six points back on an 80-yard touchdown dash just 12 seconds later.

Phillips added a 27-yard run for another score and Frazier leaped in from the one yard line in the final minute of the first half for a 30-point Husker second quarter and a 36-7 halftime lead.

Phillips had 125 of his rushing yards by intermission and the Nebraska Blackshirts had limited the Cowboys to 95 total yards, most of which came on Thompson's big run.

Nebraska also was well on its way to 671 yards of total offense,

(Below) Tight end Mark Gilman drags the competition downfield.

Freshman Kenny Cheatham showed his big-play potential.

Berringer, whose strength is passing, had led Nebraska to seven wins in his 1994 starts while Frazier was sidelined with blood clots in his leg. Frazier rebounded to return as MVP in the Orange Bowl win over Miami to wrap up the national championship, and opened the 1995 season running and passing like there were no worries about his old injuries.

He hit Reggie Baul for a 76-yard touchdown just over two minutes into the third quarter and came back with a 5-yard TD toss to Jon Vedral about three minutes later.

Frazier ended the game with six-of-10 passing for 88 yards and added 10 carries for 64 yards rushing.

By the end of the third quarter, the Huskers were up 50-14 and the regulars were on the bench. Even Nebraska's three fullbacks — Jeff Makovicka, Brian Schuster and Joel Makovicka — got into the big-play offense with runs of 33, 20 and 39 yards, respectively.

"Our offense has so many weapons that you can't key on one guy," Frazier said. "If a defense takes away one guy, we've got two or three others who can make big plays."

Freshman I-back Ahman Green, in his debut, showed why he was among the nation's top recruiting targets: He got 18 yards on his first career carry and added a 14-yard touchdown run in the final period. Fifth-string I-back James Sims scored from 5 yards out to polish off the Husker romp.

"I don't know quite what to make of a game like that," Osborne said. "We certainly didn't try to embarrass them any. It's a terrible thing, but anymore with the (poll) voting system, you've got to look good on TV a few times. So who knows? If they thought we looked good, we'll be all right."

including 513 rushing for the game. The new linemen were working out very well.

"Our running game was on tonight," Frazier said. "If it's on like that, I don't think too many teams can stop us."

The senior quarterback also was impressed with Phillips, whose sudden stop, then dart to daylight on the 80-yard run, took the air out of OSU in the decisive second quarter.

"Lawrence is one of those rare backs that you just don't find every day," Frazier said. "He can do it all — he has the power, he has the speed, he has the agility, he has the smarts to make a 5-yard loss into a 25-yard gain."

Frazier showed early in the third quarter that he could throw the ball, too. The senior from Palmetto, Fla., had worked hard over the summer to improve his passing and had done it well enough to earn the starting role in a spring practice battle with fellow senior Brook Berringer.

Berringer (18) has room to maneuver behind the big offensive line.

"We knew what we were in for," said OSU's Simmons. "We just played a national championship program. I'm not apologizing for the way we played. They did not do anything that we didn't prepare for. We just didn't execute what we can do."

"We thought it was a gamble, but it worked out," Osborne said of opening on the road against a Big Eight opponent. "We thought if we could come down and win and not have a lot of injuries, it would be a good move. We thought it was good to get a game in before Michigan State."

New offensive line starters Chris Dishman and Eric Anderson at tackles and Aaron Taylor and Steve Ott at guards answered any skeptics with their dominance in the trenches.

"They're a group that's got the potential to be as good as they want," Berringer said. "They're going to get better and better as the year goes on."

Aaron Graham knew how good the line was going to be and how good that would make the overall team.

"We are 110 percent confident this year," he said. "After you've won the whole ball of wax and you know what it's all about, we're shooting for the top. We're not saying we want to be Big Eight champs and we'll be satisfied with that."

The new faces on defense shined as well. Junior Jared Tomich had two sacks in his first start at outside linebacker. Farley had the touchdown return. OSU managed 282 total yards, most coming late in the game against the reserves. Not counting Thompson's big gainer, NU's top unit allowed less than 2 yards per snap.

"We definitely have the capability to go out and play like we did last year," said senior defensive tackle and co-captain Christian Peter. "We have some big, fast guys. I think the school is known for a great big dominant running game, but if you're around the Midwest, you know there's a defense here. A good defense."

Game 1 Statistics

	1st Quarter	2nd Quarter	3rd Quarter	4th Quarter	Final
Nebraska	**6**	**30**	**14**	**14**	**64**
Okla. State	**0**	**7**	**7**	**7**	**21**

FIRST QUARTER
NU-Phillips 3-yard run (kick failed), 6:20.

SECOND QUARTER
NU-Brown 24-yard field goal, 13:09.
NU-Farley 29-yard interception return (Brown kick), 11:54
OSU-Richardson 2-yard run (Vaughn kick), 9:53
NU-Phillips 80-yard run (pass failed), 9:41.
NU-Phillips 27-yard run (Brown kick), 4:18.
NU-Frazier 1-yard run (Brown kick), :59.

THIRD QUARTER
NU-Baul 76-yard pass from Frazier (Brown kick), 12:52.
NU-Vedral 5-yard pass from Frazier (Brown kick), 9:59.
OSU-Thompson 8-yard run (Vaughn kick), 2:56.

FOURTH QUARTER
NU-Green 14-yard run (Brown kick), 14:49.
OSU-Grenier 8-yard pass from Jones (Vaughn kick), 9:10.
NU-Sims 5-yard run (Brown kick), 7:02.

OSU

TEAM STATISTICS	NU	OSU
First downs	28	14
Rushing att.-yards	55-513	38-144
Passes	20-12-1	27-11-3
Passing yards	158	138
Total att.-yards	75-671	65-282
Returns-yards	8-72	2-6
Sacks by	4-35	0
Punts-average	1-53.0	7-43.4
Fumbles-lost	1-1	0-0
Penalties-yards	6-55	5-33
Time of poss.	29:55	30:05

INDIVIDUAL LEADERS

RUSHING:
NU: Phillips 12-153-3; Frazier 10-64-1; Benning 8-62-0; Jo. Makovicka 6-55-0; Green 6-52-1.
OSU: Thompson 16-128-1; Richardson 10-19-1.

PASSING:
NU: Frazier 10-6-0, 88; Berringer 8-5-0, 31.
OSU: Jones 27-11-3, 138.

RECEIVING:
NU: Gilman 3-31-0; Holbein 3-21-0; Baul 1-76-1.
OSU: Mayes 4-72-0; Richardson 2-20-0; Luck 2-16-0.

INTERCEPTIONS:
NU: Farley 1-29-1; Ogard 1-19-0; Dennis 1-0-0.
OSU: Johnson 1-12-0.

TACKLES (UT-AT-TT):
NU: Hesse 4-5-9; McFarlin 4-2-6; Stokes 2-4-6; Rucker 1-4-5.
OSU: Fisher 6-5-11; Johnson 6-4-10; Green 5-3-8.

SACKS:
NU: Tomich 2-22; Saltsman 1-9; Ellis 1-4.
OSU: None.

Nebraska 50
Michigan State 10

September 9, 1995 - At East Lansing, Mich.

The 1995 campaign continued with a second road game and this one was in Big Ten territory. Coach Tom Osborne was happy his Huskers already had a game under their belts before this one, which promised to be a good test on regional television (ABC). Michigan State was starting its season under new coach Nick Saban, a former defensive coordinator for the NFL's Cleveland Browns. But Saban wasn't so certain his team was ready for the likes of Nebraska.

"We don't have enough good players on defense," Saban said. "We probably have five players who are legitimate, and the rest are very average."

Still, Osborne wore his regular game face of concern. Ever wary, he even wondered if having the 64-21 win over Oklahoma State as a warmup was such a good thing.

"They probably know a little better what to expect from Nebraska than we know what to expect from them," he said. "I'm not saying that by way of complaint; that's just the way it is. We hope we've had some repetition (in practice) on what they do, but we won't know until Saturday whether we've guessed right."

Osborne and his staff didn't know what to expect of Michigan State's first game with its new coach, so the preparation had to be more widespread. When in doubt, prepare for everything. They did know that the Spartans had a gifted quarterback in mobile and strong-armed Tony Banks. The senior had completed 61 percent of his passes in 1994 for 2,040 yards and 11 touchdowns.

"Tony has done a good job in developing leadership," Saban said. "That part of our team is the strength of our team."

(Above) Lawrence Phillips vaults over the line for one of his four TDs against Michigan State.
(Right) Clinton Childs cuts back against the outmanned Spartans.

HUSKERS
26
MARTIN
21

(Above) Middle linebacker Phil Ellis calls the set for the Husker defensive unit.
(Right) Outside linebacker Jared Tomich (93) uses his quickness to evade a Michigan State blocker.

And it was Banks who would keep Michigan State in this game for a while.

Nebraska got on the board quickly, getting a 22-yard field goal from freshman kicker Kris Brown, who was proving to be a good replacement for the departed Darin Erstad. Erstad, who also punted for Nebraska during the national championship season, left school early as the No. 1 pick in the June major league baseball draft.

Husker I-back Lawrence Phillips also picked up where he left off after the Oklahoma State game with a 1-yard touchdown run to give Nebraska a 10-0 lead five minutes into the game.

Banks brought Michigan State back with a 16-yard scoring pass to Mushin Muhammad less than four minutes later.

Then Nebraska received a scare it hoped to avoid: Injury to quarterback Tommie Frazier. Frazier came limping off early in the second quarter. He had taken a knee to his thigh while trying to duck inside a tackle.

Frazier had missed most of 1994 with a blood clot in his right leg.

"I thought I could walk it off and be ready in a play or two," he said of the new injury. "If they needed me, I could have come back in. But at the time it happened, I didn't want to go back."

The Husker coaches took no chances. They sent in senior Brook Berringer, who had directed seven victories in 1994 while Frazier sat out with the blood clot problem.

Berringer would hit six-of-11 passes for 106 yards while directing the offense the rest of the way. And Phillips and the Blackshirt defense, like they had done when the Huskers were short of healthy quarterbacks early in the 1994 season, took control.

Phillips added another 1-yard touchdown, Brown booted a 47-yard field goal and the defense pitched a second-quarter shutout for a 20-7 halftime lead.

The Huskers were ahead but it wasn't pretty. They had given up a pair of turnovers, committed four penalties and Banks had picked the secondary apart for 123 yards of passing offense.

"Sometimes it wasn't pretty but it was a pretty good score," said Nebraska senior safety Tony Veland.

"They got to us pretty good in the first quarter," Phillips said. "But I think like our last game, we wore them down."

It was textbook Nebraska football. Hammer, hammer, hammer and eventually something has to give.

Brown kicked his third field goal of the game, a 20-yarder, five minutes into the second half; Michigan State matched that with a 24-yarder of its own. Then Phillips, despite being slowed by a sore ankle, scored on runs of 1 and 50 yards as he piled up 206 yards rushing on 22 carries.

"The line was blocking well and there were a lot of holes. I just had to run the ball," Phillips said. "It shows that no matter who the quarterback is, no matter who the running back is, there are going to be holes to run through and chances to score."

Frazier had been watching the line, too.

"They are a lot faster. And in some areas, they are stronger than last year's line," he said. "This group of guys is a bright bunch. They are young, but they probably know more than last year's line. That's not to put last year's line down, but these guys really focus on what needs to get done because they know a lot of eyes are on them."

The Husker ground game was brutal. Reserve I-backs Clinton Childs, James Sims and Ahman Green added 83, 80 and 74 yards rushing respectively. Green scored on a 57-yard run early in the fourth quarter and Sims, the fastest player on the squad, outran the Spartans from 80 yards away with just over eight minutes left to play.

Nebraska totaled 552 yards on the ground to go with 114 passing. But there also were four fumbles, two of which were lost, and five penalties. Coach Osborne noticed.

"I think sometimes you win 50-10 and you say, 'What are you nit-picking for?' But those things will make a difference later on down the road," Osborne said. "I think we didn't throw the ball as well as we could have or will."

On the other side of the ball, the Blackshirts dominated the second half. Michigan State managed just one field goal and ended the game with 45 yards rushing on 34 carries. The Spartans committed six fumbles, two of which were lost, had 11 penalties for 91 yards, suffered through three sacks and had one of Banks' 35 passes picked off.

Brook Berringer came off the bench and piled up over 100 yards passing.

Defensive speed meant there was no room for the Spartans (top) and no time for Michigan State quarterback Tony Banks (bottom).

"I thought they played really hard," Nebraska defensive coordinator Charlie McBride said of his unit. "And they seemed to react well to adversity and things like that. When Tommie got hurt, it was business as usual. We played very well on both sides of the ball."

Actually it was more than business as usual. Several defenders admitted that when Frazier went out, they kicked it up a notch. They remembered 1994 when Frazier was hurt, Berringer suffered a collapsed lung and the offense had to depend strictly on the run. It was up to the defense to make certain there was no way an opponent was going to win. After all, you can't win if you can't score.

Banks did get 290 yards passing, however, even though he managed to get only one of his throws into the end zone.

"We've had people throw more than that," McBride said.

Still, nobody could convince Banks that the Huskers made things easy.

"There were just a lot of things we couldn't do," Banks said. "We still have some young guys on the offensive side of the ball and I think they learned a lot."

Saban wasn't certain what he saw in his team but he knew he didn't like it.

"We made too many mistakes," he said. "I was disappointed in the way we competed as a team in the second half. I felt our players quit. I don't think we played with the same kind of enthusiasm in the game and the kind of attitude that I would expect

our team to play with for 60 minutes. To me, that point far outweighs anything else that we need to get done in the game — that our players learn to do that."

Saban, whose team eventually would earn a spot in a postseason bowl game, perhaps would learn later that Nebraska does that to a lot of teams. What seems like giving up is more like giving out. Even well-conditioned prize fighters get weak in the knees when they are continually battered. The Huskers were drawing a line in the sand as the biggest, most physical guys on the beach.

With a second road win under its belt, Nebraska headed home with Frazier's health looming as the big question. The senior wasn't as concerned as his coaches about his playing availability.

"If they needed me I could have come in," he said. He thought he would be ready for Arizona State the following week in the home opener at Lincoln. "I'm going to go back and get treated and hopefully I'll be ready."

Osborne wasn't as optimistic.

"This could be a two-week or three-week thing or it could be a two- or three-day thing," he said. "We'll have to wait to see about him."

Berringer turns for a handoff on one of the Huskers' 58 rushes for 552 total yards.

Game 2 Statistics

	1st Quarter	2nd Quarter	3rd Quarter	4th Quarter	Final
Nebraska	**10**	**10**	**16**	**14**	**50**
Mich. State	**7**	**0**	**3**	**0**	**10**

FIRST QUARTER
NU-Brown 22 field goal, 12:21.
NU-Phillips 1 run (Brown kick), 10:09.
MSU-Muhammad 16 pass from Banks (Gardner kick), 6:28.

SECOND QUARTER
NU-Phillips 1 run (Brown kick), 10:52.
NU-Brown 47 field goal, 3:36.

THIRD QUARTER
NU-Brown 20 field goal, 10:18.
MSU-Gardner 24 field goal, 6:27.
NU-Phillips 1 run (run failed), 4:29.
NU-Phillips 50 run (Brown kick), 1:10.

FOURTH QUARTER
NU-Green 57 run (Brown kick), 13:24.
NU-Sims 80 run (Retzlaff kick), 8:23

TEAM STATISTICS

	NU	MSU
First downs	28	17
Rushing att.-yards	58-552	34-45
Passes	14-7-0	35-21-1
Passing yards	114	290
Total att.-yards	72-666	69-335
Returns-yards	3-15	1-2
Sacks by	3-16	0
Punts-average	3-36.0	8-43.0
Fumbles-lost	4-2	6-2
Penalties-yards	5-55	11-91
Time of poss.	28:40	31:20

INDIVIDUAL LEADERS
RUSHING:
NU: Phillips 22-206-4; Childs 8-83-0; Sims 1-80-1; Green 4-74-1.
MSU: Greene 8-34-0; Crenshaw 3-17-0.
PASSING:
NU: Berringer 11-6-0, 106; Frazier 2-1-0, 8.
MSU: Banks 35-21-1, 290.
RECEIVING:
NU: Gilman 2-13-0; Holbein 2-10-0; Baul 1-51-0.
MSU: Greene 4-75-0; Mason 4-55-0; Muhammad 4-85-1.
INTERCEPTIONS:
NU: Minter 1-0-0.
MSU: None
TACKLES (UT-AT-TT):
NU: Ellis 7-2-9; Minter 6-2-8; C.Peter 4-3-7; Terwilliger 4-2-6; Farley 4-2-6; Veland 3-3-6.
MSU: Wright 9-2-11; Shurelds 8-2-10; Martin 6-2-8; Garnett 4-4-8.
SACKS:
NU: Farley 2-10; Tomich 1-6; Ellis 1-5.
MSU: None.

Nebraska 77
Arizona State 28

September 16, 1995 - Memorial Stadium

National media attention had been drawn to Nebraska and it would not ease up the rest of the season. For the Husker program, the public fish bowl that seems to surround national champions of recent years would be made of magnifying glass. Everyone wanted to know what had happened at Nebraska. Questions centered on the loss of star I-back Lawrence Phillips, who had rushed for 359 yards and seven touchdowns in two games.

And there was still the question of Frazier's health. After last season, when a blood clot problem sidelined the star quarterback for most of the fall, the Huskers were taking no chances with the leg bruise the senior quarterback suffered in the second quarter against Michigan State. Frazier missed Monday's practice, but tests found no clotting and he would return.

And how about the team's ability to handle the adversity of such a week? How would the loss of one of the nation's top running backs affect a team that lives by the run?

Fellow Big Eight coaches joined in the discussion. Oklahoma State coach Bob Simmons, who had lost to the Huskers in Week 1, knew how Nebraska would be affected.

"Not much," he said. "You saw Childs and Green play this past weekend. Those two kids are going to come in and do an excellent job. Nebraska never depends on one player, which was very obvious last year when Frazier went down and Berringer came in."

The adversity brought unity to the Nebraska team. The players voted not to do any interviews that week. No outside diversions were tolerated. There were still games to be played and won. The team, if anything, became intensely focused. It was evident on game day.

(Above) ASU's talented Jake Plummer (16), making good use of what little time Jared Tomich (93) allows him, gets rid of a pass.
(Right) Christian Peter (55) closes on a Plummer rollout, but the ASU star bruised Nebraska through the air.

PLUMMER
16

ASU's Lenzie Jackson (83) feels a Husker gang tackle taking him down.

A 1-1 Arizona State team arrived in Lincoln with visions of a bowl-bid season and first-division finish in the Pac 10. Coach Bruce Snyder had a team with talent. Quarterback Jake Plummer was coming off a season in which he completed 54 percent of his passes throwing for 2,179 yards and 15 touchdowns. Receiver Keith Poole was quick and had good hands. He had 669 yards in receptions and six TDs in 1994.

Plummer and his Sun Devil mates had confidence after their 45-20 romp over Texas-El Paso. Nebraska's defensive coaches expected another good test, particularly after Michigan State's Tony Banks threw for 290 yards against the Blackshirts the week before.

But ASU soon would become a victim of Husker frustrations. All of the week's concerns would be blown away in one impressive 30 minutes of Big Red football.

Clinton Childs drew the starting spot at I-back and opened the game with a 65-yard run on Nebraska's first play from scrimmage. Freshman Ahman Green ran 3 yards for a touchdown on the next possession. Frazier scored from 15 yards out on the next. Frazier hit Jon Vedral for a 27-yard TD pass on the fourth, and fullback Jeff Makovicka scored on a 13-yard run the next time Nebraska had the ball.

It was a 35-7 game and just the first quarter.

Frazier credited Osborne's pregame talk for the rapid start.

"Coach Osborne said adversity is going to come to every team," Frazier said. "Only great teams overcome things like that, so he gave us a challenge. He said, 'Can you be that great team?'"

Arizona State's Plummer threw his second touchdown pass of the game: an 80-yarder to Poole to open the second period. But big-play Nebraska had an answer. Childs ran 38 yards for a score. Clester Johnson hauled in a 28-yard pass from Frazier for six more points. Green bolted into the end zone from 26 yards out and Frazier added a 3-yard TD just before the second period came to a close.

Aaron Graham (54) drew Osborne's praise as one of the best centers ever to play for Nebraska.

Poole finished the game with six catches and a career-high 200 yards, including the 80-yard TD catch against cornerback Tyrone Williams in the second quarter.

"I just could not accelerate to the ball," Williams said. "You should never get beat deep, and I did. As a secondary, we have improved. But we still make a lot of busts. It's hard to keep focused and keep your adrenaline pumping when the offense runs up and down the field with ease."

Nebraska's backup players were given the chance to play much of the second half. Plummer and company ran up 461 yards of total offense. The two teams' 105 combined points tied the record for a game at Memorial Stadium. Oklahoma State and Nebraska had scored 105 in a 63-42 NU victory in 1988.

Nebraska newcomer Terrell Farley intercepted a fourth-quarter pass and ran it back 21 yards for his second interception touchdown of the young season. And in the closing minute, third-string quarterback Matt Turman connected with Lance Brown for a 39-yard score that almost disappointed Osborne.

"I felt bad about it," he said, and apologized to Snyder for the touchdown. Osborne explained that he had called for a 12-yard hook pattern but the receiver properly read the defensive back's movement and broke open. Turman and Brown had done what they were taught to do. Still, the perception was bad.

Speedster Riley Washington (3), another of Nebraska's big-play threats, lines up outside.

It was halftime and the Huskers had given the answer to their coach. This was a great team. NU had 508 yards in total offense and a school record for most points in a half with 63. The old mark, set in 1983, was 55 points scored against Colorado in a 69-19 game.

"It was just kind of an avalanche," Snyder said. "I've never been in an avalanche, but that was kind of the feeling ... you have a sense of helplessness."

"We really wanted to win this for coach Osborne," said Frazier. "We all saw he was real hurt at everybody putting him down. We wanted to win, for him and make a statement that it's not fair. This showed that despite everything that happened, this team isn't worried about it. We're focused on one thing — playing football."

The players made a statement that they were solidly behind the coach who had stood behind them. It became an unspoken theme of the season and certainly a unifying factor. This was a team that stood together in the face of any challenge or adversity.

Nebraska failed to score in the third quarter, but the game already was out of reach and the emotional edge had since vanished. Plus, the Arizona State team was not exactly without talent and had not thrown in the towel despite the score.

Terry Battle's 1-yard run for ASU was the only scoring in the third period.

Frazier (15) was proficient at calling the best possible audibles.

"I've very seldom had a situation like that late in the game with that kind of lead where we've thrown a deep touchdown pass," Osborne said. "I apologized because I didn't think in my wildest dreams that they would press us and play tight man-to-man and we would convert it into a deep pattern. I should have just run a draw play and run out the clock."

Snyder, unhappy after the game, refused to shake hands with Osborne and hinted that the last touchdown might indicate Nebraska was poll watching.

"I don't know what's going on over on their sideline — and within their program — but if they felt that they've got to run it up to match what Penn State did today or what Florida State did today or what those other schools did today, I'm saddened for college football ... if that's the reason," he said.

That day, top-ranked Florida State beat North Carolina State 77-17 and No. 7 Penn State beat Temple 66-14.

Osborne said it was not a matter of poll watching. His team simply did everything right. The final scoring total surprised no one as much as the coach.

This was getting to be more and more like the 1984 season, when Osborne had to apologize for one of the best offensive football teams ever assembled. That team was called the "scoring explosion" for its ability to strike quickly. This 1995 team already was showing it had the potential to be every bit as good.

"It's always your game plan to score," he said, "but I can't say we planned to score on 9 of our first 10 possessions."

Childs, the senior from Omaha, finished the game with 143 yards and two touchdowns before leaving in the second quarter with a knee sprain.

"I proved a lot of things to myself," Childs said. "I just wanted to show myself that I'm more than a backup. I wanted to show the people of Nebraska that I could get the job done."

He also was playing for his friend, Phillips.

"He's missed a lot," Childs said. "He's one of my friends and we inspire each other. He's in good spirits. He's doing well. He lifted me up. He said, 'You know what you can do and I know what you can do. Just keep your head up.'"

Green had 111 yards rushing on 13 carries. Frazier completed seven of 10 passes for 191 yards, the third-best throwing day of his career. Johnson caught four passes for 129 yards and helped build on what was rapidly becoming a team with the reputation of striking quick and striking often.

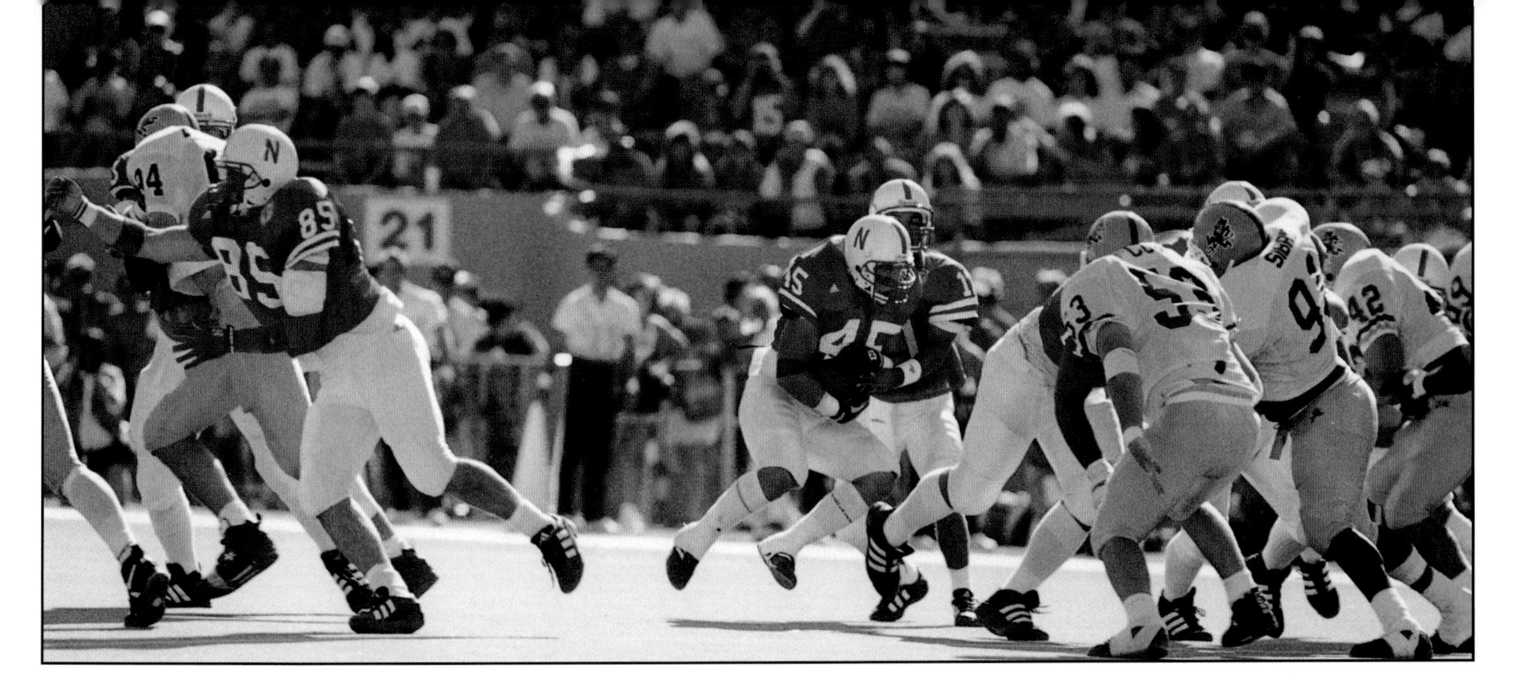

With gaping holes like this one, it was evident that ASU could not handle 394 yards of inspired Nebraska rushing.

Game 3 Statistics

	1st Quarter	2nd Quarter	3rd Quarter	4th Quarter	Final
Ariz. State	**7**	**14**	**7**	**0**	**28**
Nebraska	**35**	**28**	**0**	**14**	**77**

FIRST QUARTER
NU-Childs 65-yard run (Brown kick), 14:49.
NU-Green 3-yard run (Brown kick), 9:53.
NU-Frazier 15-yard run (Brown kick), 7:35.
NU-Vedral 27-yard pass from Frazier (Brown kick), 5:38.
ASU-Poole 2-yard pass from Plummer (Nycz kick), 3:35.
NU-Makovicka 13-yard run (Brown kick), 0:00.

SECOND QUARTER
ASU-Poole 80-yard pass from Plummer (Nycz kick), 14:43.
NU-Childs 38-yard run (Brown kick), 12:35.
NU-Johnson 28-yard pass from Frazier (Brown kick), 10:48.
ASU-Poole 38-yard pass from Plummer (Nycz kick), 9:17.
NU-Green 26-yard run (Retzlaff kick), 3:40.
NU-Frazier 3-yard run (Retzlaff kick), :39.

THIRD QUARTER
ASU-Battle 1-yard run (Nycz kick), 2:02.

FOURTH QUARTER
NU-Farley 21-yard interception return (Retzlaff kick), 12:07.
NU-Brown 39-yard pass from Turman (Retzlaff kick), :38.

TEAM STATISTICS	ASU	NU
First downs	17	30
Rushing att.-yards	45-171	55-394
Passes	33-14-2	20-12-1
Passing yards	290	292
Total att.-yards	78-461	75-686
Returns-yards	1-1	4-58
Sacks by	0	1-4
Punts-average	7-39.4	2-61.0
Fumbles-lost	0-0	1-0
Penalties-yards	8-66	5-30
Time of poss.	30:56	29:04

INDIVIDUAL LEADERS

RUSHING:
ASU: Battle 9-52-1; Martin 11-40-0; Hopkins 12-39-0.
NU: Childs 12-143-2; Green 13-111-2; Sims 7-47-0; Frazier 5-35-2; Makovicka 8-33-1.

PASSING:
ASU: Plummer 26-12-1, 273.
NU: Frazier 10-7-1, 191; Berringer 6-2-0, 16.

RECEIVING:
ASU: Poole 6-200-3; Bush 3-24-0; Boyer 2-17-0.
NU: Johnson 4-129-1; Gilman 3-39-0; Brown 1-39-1.

INTERCEPTIONS:
ASU: Smith 1-1-0.
NU: Farley 1-21-1; Booker 1-6-0.

TACKLES (UT-AT-TT):
ASU: Von der Ahe 4-5-9; Dragoo 3-5-8; Richardson 0-8-8.
NU: Minter 3-5-8; Saltsman 2-5-7; Terwilliger 4-3-7.

SACKS:
ASU: None
NU: Tomich 1-4.

Nebraska 49
Pacific 7

September 23, 1995 - Memorial Stadium

After walloping Arizona State 77-28 the week before, Big West Conference opponent Pacific, a 70-21 loser at Lincoln in 1994, came to Memorial Stadium with little realistic hope of a victory against the nation's second-ranked Huskers. Tiger coach Chuck Shelton, a longtime friend of Nebraska coach Tom Osborne, promised his team would play hard, as it did the year before when Pacific first took the contract to fill in for Utah State, which asked to be let out of its game at NU.

This was labeled the "money game" on the schedule for both teams. Pacific, a Stockton, Calif., school of about 4,000 students, would take home more than $400,000 for playing on the road in Lincoln. Nebraska would get the biggest chunk of more than $1 million in home-game revenue that would help pay the NU Athletic Department's bills for the year.

There really wasn't much more to be said. Everybody knew what this game was about and it wasn't about to be pretty.

Pacific did have a 1,000-yard rusher returning in Joe Abdullah and an accurate passer in Nick Sellers (60-of-110, 54 percent, and three touchdowns in 1994). But the Tigers lacked the depth, the size, the speed and the talent to keep pace with Nebraska, which had scored 77 against Arizona State the week before.

Even Osborne wasn't making more of the game than what it would be, thinking out loud later that he would be glad to get this one over with and move on to a new challenge.

Abdullah said Pacific knew what it had to do. "Pray." But he was part of the team that came to Lincoln the year before and remembered what a benefit it proved to be in a 6-5 season. "The experience of getting to play the best football team in the country is something that helped us as the year went on."

(Above) Berringer (18) reads the defense before taking the snap from center Matt Vrzal (51).
(Right) Frazier (15) initiates the play behind the powerful offensive line.

75
TAYLOR
67
15
54
69
E.ANDERSON
70

Freshman Kenny Cheatham runs through the Tigers on one of his punt returns.

Nebraska, however, was concerned about how much it would help its cause to improve and make a run at a second-straight national title.

Line coach Milt Tenopir admitted that playing time for the starters was getting to be a worry. In each of the season's first three games, they hadn't played for much more than the first two quarters. Since he had four new starters, Tenopir knew they needed the extra work and a challenge to improve.

"He [Tenopir] was really concerned going two or three games in a row and not getting playing time, saying that would hurt us down the road," Osborne said. "It is a concern."

Pacific really didn't have the horses to provide the challenge, either. The school would come to realize it didn't have the resources to get the horses and, at the end of the season, would announce it was dropping the football program.

Quarterback Tommie Frazier said it was difficult to get fired up for the Tigers (1-2) and a quick start didn't make staying fired up any easier. "It's hard when you're expected to beat a team and you go out and you score 14 quick points. The tendency is to drop off."

Damon Benning became the third Husker to start at I-back. He was filling in for Clinton Childs, whose knee sprain from the week before proved tougher to shake than first anticipated.

Just over two minutes into the game, Benning, another of a long line of Omaha high school running backs to play for Nebraska, dashed 26 yards for the Huskers' first score. He ran 17 yards for another touchdown with 10:49 left in the quarter and added a 43-yard TD at the 1:31 mark.

The junior, who had missed two-and-one-half games with a hamstring pull, had performed well enough in practice to earn the start over freshman Ahman Green. James Sims, a sophomore, was backing them up.

However, even as quick as Benning looked in the first quarter, he didn't feel as though his hamstring was 100 percent.

"I was kind of scared to go to the next gear," he said. "I didn't really let loose at all today. The offensive line did a good job of protecting me. I'm sure on paper it looked good, but you saw only 80 percent of me."

Benning romped for a career-high 173 yards in his first career start. But he carried only 10 times before leaving the game early in the third quarter with a sprained ankle.

Damon Benning hurdles into the end zone for one of three touchdowns he scored against Pacific.

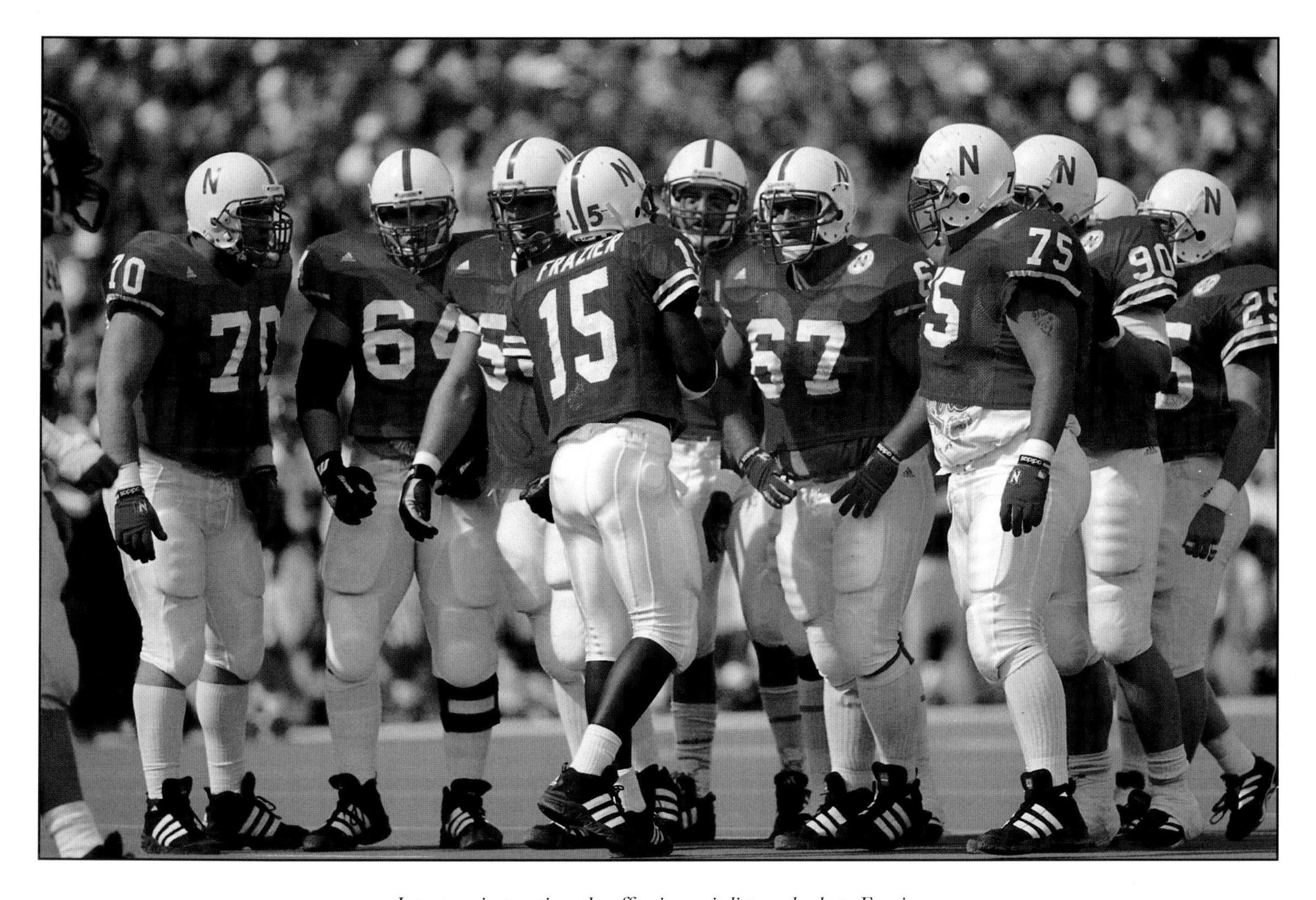

Intent on instruction, the offensive unit listens closely to Frazier.
The offensive line held Pacific to no sacks and gave Nebraska quarterbacks great pass protection.

Green filled in nicely, however. He scored on a 4-yard run in the second quarter, ran the ball in from 13 yards out in the third period and ended the day with 112 yards on 15 carries.

Sims also scored from 9 yards out in the third period but saw limited duty due to a sore back.

"We're very, very thin at a position that looked pretty deep at one time," Osborne said. The coach was ready to work fullback Joel Makovicka at I-back so he could have another backup if the injury woes continued. But even Makovicka wasn't 100 percent.

"He reinjured a toe that has been giving him problems, so that position is depleted pretty badly," Osborne said. "I'm quite certain Clinton Childs will not play next week (Washington State). We'll be very fortunate if he plays against Missouri or even Kansas State."

Even hobbled and hurt, Nebraska's backs rolled up 569 rushing yards against Pacific. Frazier, Brook Berringer and Matt Turman added 162 yards in the air. There were no touchdown passes but the Huskers didn't need a passing game. Fourteen Huskers had carried the football against Pacific.

"Our players responded about as well as they could have under the circumstances," Osborne said. "I don't think they were flat, but I don't think they were quite as excited as they have been or will be. Overall, it went about as well as I could have hoped for. I think we gave everybody a chance to play."

The Huskers took an average of 6.4 plays and 2:31 to score. Tackle Chris Dishman said that speed in scoring might look impressive but it only contributed to the problem of playing time for the first-teamers.

"We have to go out there and think we're going to get better," Dishman said. "If we go out there and think it's nothing, we'll play lazy football. You really have to try and play well for the end of the season."

Osborne also remembered the apology he felt obligated to make to Arizona State coach Bruce Snyder after the 77-28 Nebraska win the previous week. He was worried beforehand that the Pacific game would get out of hand, too.

"I'm glad we got that behind us. I think it was a respectable game, and we got a chance to play a lot of players," Osborne said. "We had 45 to 50 snaps for the starters on offense, but Pacific didn't have a lot of plays so our defensive guys didn't see a lot of snaps."

Osborne, who often is considered conservative in his play calling, really was this time.

"It's sad to say but I think Coach Osborne maybe limited himself on play-calling because of all the talk about running up the

(Left) Realizing an opportunity to exploit the defensive alignment, Frazier calls an audible at the line.

(Below) Brook Berringer unloads one of 17 pass attempts. He completed nine of them for 57 yards.

(Bottom) Junior quarterback Matt Turman (11) gets his chance to lead the high powered offense.

score," said center Aaron Graham. "This week we were a little more conservative. It could have been a lot worse."

Shelton knew that. Despite holding Nebraska to its lowest point total of the first four games, he knew what he had been facing.

"They're better. I didn't expect that," he said of the 1995 version in comparison with the national champs of the year before. "When I started looking at film last week I bawled because I thought they were good enough last year. I thought this year they'd be down because they lost some of those linemen. But they're better."

"I don't know if there's such a thing as a perfect team, but for college football, they're probably the closest to being perfect," Abdullah said.

"We got beat by an awfully good football team," Shelton said, "and I might add, by a class program. This is a class program run by class people."

Pacific managed just 60 yards rushing and 137 passing despite playing much of the game against the Husker reserves.

First-year Husker inside linebackers coach Craig Bohl liked what he saw. After giving up an average of 359 yards per game in the first three outings, the Nebraska defense was in control against Pacific.

"The thing we needed to do was to take steps forward to become a dominating defense," he said. He noted the strength of Pacific's team was its offense and Nebraska shut it down. It was more than halfway through the third quarter before the Tigers managed to cross midfield.

Pacific averaged only 4.1 yards per play and had only six plays of 10 yards or more. The Tigers totaled just 73 yards in total offense against the Blackshirts in the first half.

"It's great blowing these teams out," said NU defensive tackle Christian Peter, who quickly added, "eventually we'll run into a real good team and they'll hang in there for four quarters with us. We're looking forward to a game like that."

Game 4 Statistics

	1st Quarter	2nd Quarter	3rd Quarter	4th Quarter	Final
Pacific	0	0	7	0	7
Nebraska	21	14	14	0	49

FIRST QUARTER
NU-Benning 26 run (Brown kick), 12:59.
NU-Benning 17 run (Brown kick), 10:49.
NU-Benning 43 run (Brown kick), 1:31.

SECOND QUARTER
NU-Green 4 run (Brown kick), 12:03.
NU-Sims 9 run (Brown kick), 7:46.

THIRD QUARTER
NU-Frazier 5 run (Brown kick), 11:49.
NU-Green 13 run (Retzlaff kick), 7:12.
PAC-Watley 12 pass from Sellers (Fleenor kick), 5:24.

TEAM STATISTICS

	Pacific	Nebraska
First downs	7	36
Rushing att.-yards	17-60	70-569
Passes	31-14-1	36-16-2
Passing yards	137	162
Total att.-yards	48-197	106-731
Returns-yards	0-0	11-146
Sacks by	0	1-8
Punts-average	11-43.7	1-33.0
Fumbles-lost	0-0	2-0
Penalties-yards	2-20	3-26
Time of poss.	20:16	39:44

INDIVIDUAL LEADERS

RUSHING:
PAC: Reeder 1-36-0; Abdullah 13-25-0.
NU: Benning 10-173-3; Green 15-112-2; Frazier 7-62-1; Sims 9-55-1.

PASSING:
PAC: Sellers 25-13-0, 132.
NU: Berringer 17-9-0, 57; Frazier 14-6-1, 90.

RECEIVING:
PAC: Atkins 3-63-0; Watley 3-17-1; Abdullah 3-8-0.
NU: Johnson 2-31-0; Holbein 2-24-0; Baul 2-24-0; Vedral 2-23-0.

INTERCEPTIONS:
PAC: Stukes 1-0-0; Burton 1-0-0.
NU: Skoda 1-7-0.

TACKLES (UT-AT-TT):
PAC: Kilgras 10-4-14; Burton 5-8-13; Tatola 2-10-12.
NU: Minter 2-2-4; Farley 2-2-4; Booker 3-0-3; Colman 3-0-3; Terwilliger 2-1-3.

SACKS:
PAC: None.
NU: Farley 1-8.

Nebraska 35
Washington State 21

September 30, 1995 - Memorial Stadium

Finally, Game 5 of the season promised to present Nebraska a challenge. It was something the Huskers were looking forward to: a test to see if they could stand up under pressure, meet a quality opponent and come out on top. Nebraska and coach Tom Osborne never had beaten Washington State. In 1977, the Cougars, with quarterback Jack Thompson under former Husker assistant coach Warren Powers, came to Lincoln and upset the Huskers with a 19-10 win. Current Cougar head coach Mike Price was an assistant to Powers in that game and at Missouri when Powers' Tigers beat Nebraska the following season.

Washington State was 2-0 against the Huskers prior to the Osborne era as well.

The 1995 version of the Cougars was coming off an impressive 24-15 win over UCLA. WSU ranked fourth in the nation against the run, allowing 69 yards per game. Washington State ended its 1994 and 1993 campaigns ranked second nationally in rushing defense — this was no fluke.

Full of confidence, Price said that if his team played a solid 60 minutes in Lincoln it would win. And one of his players boldly predicted the Cougars would come to Lincoln "and shock the world" with a win.

Needless to say, that did not sit well with the Huskers. Quarterback Tommie Frazier took the verbal jab as a slap at what Nebraska had built.

"I took it personally," he said. "If they had won the game, they can make those comments. But not before the game."

(Above) The Huskers show goalline muscle against the talented Cougars, among the nation's leaders against the rush two years straight.
(Right) Fullback Brian Schuster's power game up the middle helps the Huskers roll to 428 total yards rushing.

HUSKERS
adidas
28
WASHINGTON STATE
64
Wilson

The pulling power was too much for Washington State as the Husker line dominated again.

But, when things got started on game day, it appeared Washington State was ready to make good on its threats. Frank Madu put the game's first points on the board with an 87-yard run two plays after the Cougars' Chris Hayes recovered a Jeff Makovicka fumble at the WSU 9 yard line.

The touchdown was the only score of the first quarter. The 7-0 deficit was the first time all season Nebraska had trailed. It served as a wake-up call.

"We didn't need to be behind," Frazier said of the first quarter, "didn't deserve to be behind. We're too good to be behind."

The Huskers made their move. Speedy linebacker Terrell Farley partially blocked a Cougar punt as the quarter drew to a close. The ball went out of bounds 19 yards downfield on the Nebraska 34 yard line. Frazier scored five plays later on a 4-yard run after fullback Brian Schuster broke loose up the middle for gains of 23 and 10 yards, and freshman Ahman Green, in his first start, ran 24 yards to set up Frazier's TD. Kris Brown's extra point kick tied the game moments into the second quarter.

About six minutes later, Frazier ran 20 yards to cap a 66-yard drive. Brown kicked a field goal from 33 yards out. A second field goal was set up by Green's 54-yard run just 27 seconds before intermission. Brown's kick from 22 yards out went through the uprights with 6 seconds left for a 20-6 halftime lead.

Washington State figured its talented run defense would be given a serious test, but it was Frazier who had given Price the most concern coming into the game.

"I don't think you can set up the defense to stop the run because of what Tommie Frazier can do," Price said. "Their offense is too multidimensional. Since I've been here, we've been able to gang up on people's tendencies ... overload sides and double-cover people. We can't do that with these guys."

"We expected a four-quarter game," said defensive end Jared Tomich. "It was a good game. They scored early, and that showed us to get our emotions back up and get in there."

"They came in and issued a lot of challenges," defensive end Grant Wistrom said. "The fans were into it, and it felt different out there than it had all year."

Freshman I-back Ahman Green (30) puts a move on a defender on his way to 176 total yards rushing.

Green was more or less forced into action. Lawrence Phillips was not playing and Clinton Childs sprained a knee in Game 3. Damon Benning sprained an ankle after struggling with a hamstring problem before he had his first start in Game 4. Sophomore James Sims also had a sore back.

It was going to be rookie Green against the toughest defensive challenge of the season to date, but running back coach Frank Solich was comfortable with the decision.

"He's always shown the big-play potential," Solich said of Green. "But today, he showed the toughness and yard-after-contact style you want to see. He played extremely well."

Green would total 176 yards on 13 carries, a 13.5-yard average against the fourth-best rush defense in the nation. On one play he shook through, banged at and dragged five defenders for a 12-yard gain. The state high school sprint champion in track showed he had power to go with his speed.

"Ahman showed a lot today," Osborne said. "He's got that step, that extra step. He played awful well for a freshman. Three or four weeks ago he couldn't have done this. He is getting more confidence and he's growing up with the system. Ahman did some great things."

"I'm a tougher guy mentally now than I was at the start of the season," Green said. "Physically, I was already tough. With the five games I've got under my belt, I'm more mentally tough. And it's getting better and better every game."

Linebacker talent: (Top) Ryan Terwilliger (91) reads the play, while freshman Jay Foreman (56) readies for a stop.

Nebraska fans sensed the challenge, too. They anticipated a battle and were ready to see what the nation's best offense would do against one of the best defenses.

"They were one of the top rush defenses in the nation," Frazier said. "We needed the challenge. There will be some teams in the Big Eight that give us a run for our money. This will help us prepare."

Green added to Nebraska's lead in the third quarter with a 3-yard touchdown run. The youngster, just a year out of Omaha Central High School, was playing well for the nation's top running game. He was backing up junior starter Damon Benning in this game but proved to be more effective than Benning, who was fighting through hamstring and ankle injuries.

"I didn't expect myself to be doing this well as a freshman," Green admitted. "I just expected myself to come on the field when they needed me and do what I had to do to show my ability. It's just a surprise what I'm doing now."

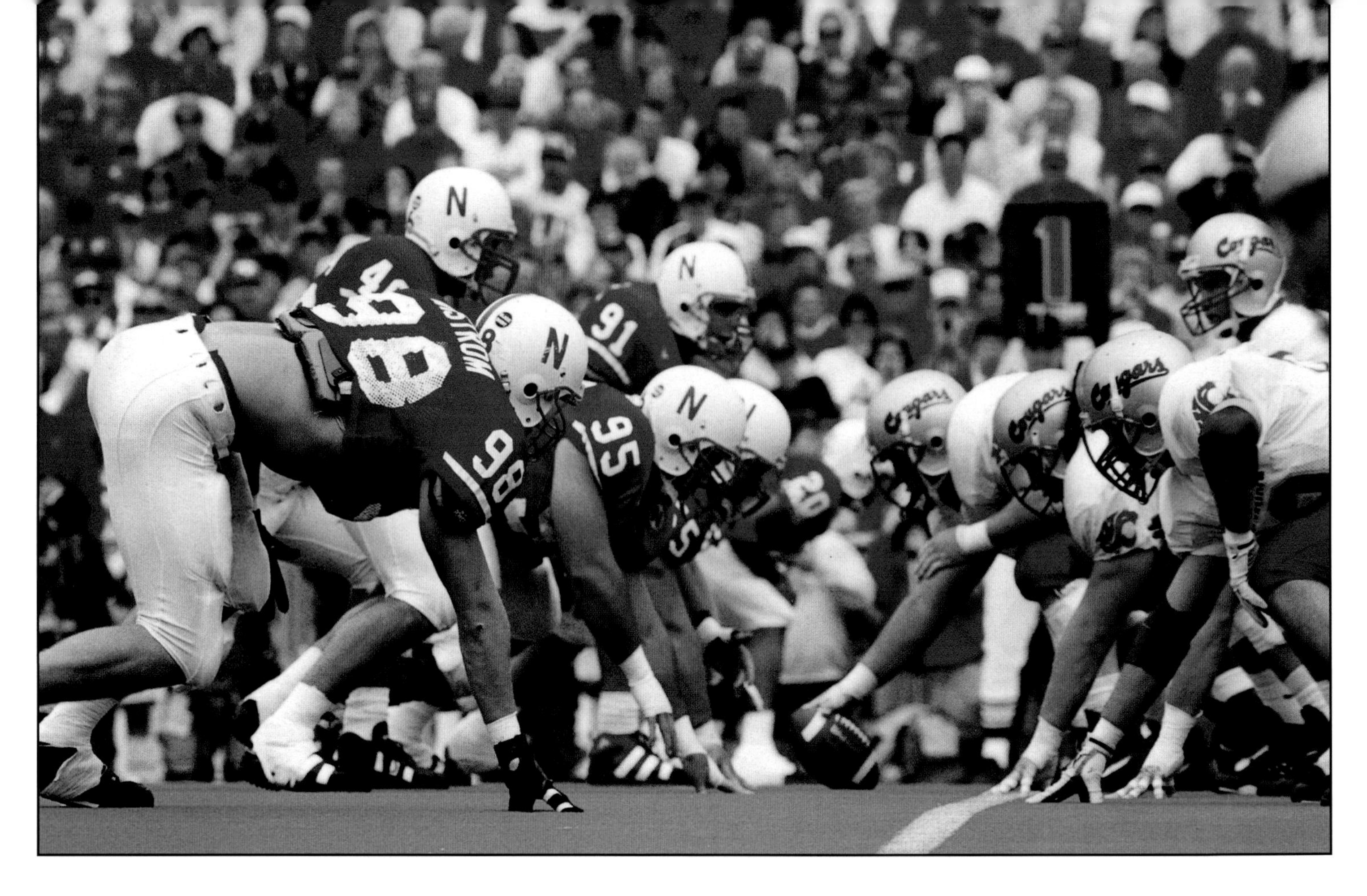

The Blackshirts load the line to challenge the Cougars and win.

Washington State trailed by 21 points going into the fourth quarter, but didn't put its game away just yet. Quarterback Chad Davis hit Shawn Tims for touchdowns of 33 and 30 yards sandwiched around a 35-yard Frazier-to-Mark Gilman touchdown pass for the Huskers.

"Defensively at times we played really well," Osborne said, "and then we let them have those three drives."

Osborne noted that two of Washington State's TDs came against Husker blitzes. But the Cougars weren't able to take advantage of Nebraska's loss of Butkus candidate linebacker Phil Ellis, who broke a foot in practice during the week.

"We thought we would," Price said, "but that didn't work very darn good to be honest with you. I thought we could sweep them like we've been doing. We felt like (Doug Colman) was a little slower than Ellis, but they stopped the sweep cold when we tried it. He (Colman) wasn't a minus factor for Nebraska at all. He's played a lot and he's a good football player."

The Husker defense limited Washington State to 72 yards rushing and 350 total yards. Wistrom and Christian Peter had sacks, Farley, Michael Booker and Peter broke up passes, Farley partially blocked a punt, and Wistrom had four tackles for losses.

Sophomore Jesse Kosch showed talent as a first-year punter and kept opponents deep much of the season.

"It can be very discouraging playing this football team," Price said. "They can get on top of you and break your will.

"I'm very proud of our players. We didn't win. We came here to win, but we didn't win so we're very disappointed about that. But I'm not discouraged at all. We played hard. We have no reason to hang our heads."

Osborne wasn't as thrilled about his team's end results, however. The Huskers did rush for 428 yards against the normally stingy Cougars and had 527 yards of total offense, which was the first time in Osborne's era that an NU team had topped 500 yards in five consecutive games.

"When you get over 500 yards against a team like that, it's pretty good movement," Osborne said. "But the scoring wasn't commensurate with the yards. We missed two or three scoring opportunities. And a couple of times we didn't execute. And a couple of times, maybe I could have called something a little more intelligent."

The Huskers did have to punt a season-high four times, but sophomore Jesse Kosch, who joined freshman place-kicker Brown in providing talented fill-ins for the departed Darin Erstad, had a minus-1-yard in returns. The Huskers were leading the nation in net punting with the first-year kicker who had averaged 42 yards per punt on 11 tries in five games.

But one of the most intelligent things the Husker coaches did against Washington State was to give freshman Green the ball. His tackle-busting runs into the fourth quarter inspired even his own defensive teammates, according to senior co-captain Peter.

"He was intense. He wanted to put some punishment on those guys," Peter said of Green. "When we see things like that, everybody gets fired up."

And the offensive line again was impressive, especially to the defenders who tried to stop Nebraska.

"They time everything perfectly," said Washington State defensive end Dwayne Sanders. "You may see one mistake a game that they make. Other than that, they're right together working in sync and knocking people down."

Nebraska center Aaron Graham was very matter-of-fact in his assessment of the line's game play. Looking at the total yardage against the Cougars (a season low but still impressive), Graham simply said, "I guess that means we're pretty good."

Husker quarterback Frazier (15) scrambles to beat the WSU rush, a talent he polished over four seasons.

Game 5 Statistics

	1st Quarter	2nd Quarter	3rd Quarter	4th Quarter	Final
Wash. State	7	0	0	14	21
Nebraska	0	20	8	7	35

FIRST QUARTER
WSU-Madu 87-yard run (Truant kick), 8:44.

SECOND QUARTER
NU- Frazier 4-yard run (Kris Brown kick), 14:43.
NU-Frazier 20-yard run (Brown kick), 8:29.
NU-Brown 33-yard field goal, 5:08.
NU-Brown 22-yard field goal, :06.

THIRD QUARTER
NU-Green 3-yard run (Schuster pass from Brown), :27.

FOURTH QUARTER
WSU-Tims 33-yard pass from Davis (Truant kick), 12:14.
NU- Gilman 35-yard pass from Frazier (Brown kick), 7:20.
WSU-Tims 30-yard pass from Davis (Truant kick), 3:38.

TEAM STATISTICS

	WSU	NU
First downs	17	27
Rushing att.-yards	24-72	63-428
Passes	37-20-0	20-9-0
Passing yards	278	99
Total att.-yards	61-350	83-527
Returns-yards	1-(-1)	6-47
Sacks by	0	2-17
Punts-average	8-45.0	4-37.0
Fumbles-lost	2-0	5-3
Penalties-yards	5-42	3-35
Time of poss.	24:43	35:17

INDIVIDUAL LEADERS

RUSHING:
WSU: Madu 9-90-1; Sparks 9-1-0.
NU: Green 13-176-1; Frazier 15-70-2; Makovicka 4-64-0; Benning 20-63-0; Schuster 5-42-0.

PASSING:
WSU: Davis 37-20-0, 278.
NU: Frazier 19-9-0, 99.

RECEIVING:
WSU: Dumas 9-100-0; Tims 2-63-2; Thomas 2-31-0.
NU: Gilman 1-35-1; Johnson 4-31-0; Baul 2-19-0; Holbein 1-8-0; Vedral 1-6-0.

INTERCEPTIONS:
WSU: None
NU: None

TACKLES (UT-AT-TT):
WSU: Darling 4-7-11; Glover 7-3-10; Hinchen 4-6-10; Hayes 4-6-10.
NU: Colman 2-4-6; Williams 5-0-5; Tomich 3-2-5; Wistrom 3-2-5.

SACKS:
WSU: None.
NU: C. Peter 1-9; Wistrom 1-8.

Nebraska 57
Missouri 0

October 14, 1995 - Memorial Stadium

The week of rest couldn't have come at a better time for the Huskers. Nebraska picked up the free Saturday when the Oklahoma State game was moved to Aug. 31. It was looking more and more like a brilliant strategy. A badly battered fleet of talented Husker running backs needed time to heal. Tommie Frazier's bruised leg was still sore and his backup, Brook Berringer, suffered a badly swollen knee in the game against Washington State.

Coach Tom Osborne entered the week wondering if junior Damon Benning should get his third-straight start at I-back or if the Huskers should go with freshman Ahman Green, who seemed to be the only truly healthy back in the stable.

Senior I-back Clinton Childs, who started against Arizona State, still was slowed by a knee sprain. Also, Benning was not 100 percent with a sore ankle and hamstring and Green's backup, sophomore James Sims, had a sore back.

The quarterback situation, with only Frazier and No. 3 Matt Turman apparently healthy, was questionable enough that Osborne had true freshman Frankie London working out with the top two offensive units in practice just in case.

Then there was the back sprain of split end Brendan Holbein, the sore hamstring of defensive tackle Jason Peter and the sore knee of backup defensive tackle Larry Townsend. Yes, the time off was badly needed.

"But I've learned one thing over the years," Osborne said, "and that is that it doesn't make any difference. You've still got to perform, and people don't want to hear about injuries. When you have those kinds of situations, other people have to pick it up."

(Above) Senior Luther Hardin (58) gets one of four NU sacks.
(Right) Ahman Green (30) ducks under a tackle to get 90 yards on 15 carries in his first start.

91

The Tigers were in for a long day taking big hits like these (top and right) from junior linebacker Jon Hesse. The backups got some playing time and made the most of it.

As game time approached, it was decided Green would get the starting chance against a 2-3 Missouri Tiger team. Coach Larry Smith's club was coming off a 30-0 loss to Kansas State and he was not happy. The team was in an apparent state of offensive confusion. The Tiger offense was playing poorly and coming to Nebraska just when the Husker defense was showing signs of coming together.

The Missouri defense had shown signs of improving and was playing well. But then, the Tiger defense also hadn't faced the likes of Tommie Frazier and company. There was already speculation in Lincoln that this Osborne offense was as good as the 1983 version led by Heisman Trophy I-back Mike Rozier and All-Americans Turner Gill at quarterback, Irving Fryar at wingback and Dean Steinkuhler at guard.

The statistics for the 1995 team were showing there was potential there to be the best Osborne ever had, and Frazier was about to have one of his golden days, scoring three touchdowns and passing for two more.

The Huskers opened the scoring on a 29-yard Frazier run midway through the first quarter. Frazier added a pair of 1-yard TD runs in the second period and hit Holbein on a 29-yard touchdown pass as time ran out in the first half.

Nebraska was ahead comfortably but was doing it ugly. Even the Holbein touchdown was something less than perfection: he hauled in a deflection off Jon Vedral in the end zone.

Frazier went into the Nebraska record books with his performance that day. The touchdown runs and TD pass gave him 63 career touchdowns, breaking Steve Taylor's old mark of 62 set in his 1985-88 career.

Typically, Frazier downplayed the record and critiqued the game. He wasn't pleased with the performance.

"The passing game is not where it needs to be, but we're going to get better at that," he said. "It's just concentration on my part and on the receivers' part."

Up 28-0 at the half, the Nebraska defense continued its mastery of the Tigers in the third quarter. Terrell Farley blocked a punt for a safety just over five minutes into the second half.

Nebraska drove the ball for a score on Green's 9-yard run. Frazier added to his touchdown total with a 6-yard toss to reserve tight end Sheldon Jackson four minutes later to cap a five-play, 57-yard drive boosted by a 36-yard Frazier-to-Vedral pass.

With Kansas State up next week, Osborne benched Frazier and let Turman, the third-string walk-on from Wahoo, finish up. He drove the team 68 yards and capped another scoring drive with a 1-yard TD before the third quarter ended.

Benning capped Nebraska's scoring with a 16-yard run early in the final quarter.

Nebraska ended the game with a season-low 476 yards of total offense and acted like the world had come to an end. With six fumbles (none were lost), the offense looked a little rusty after its week off between games.

"That's crazy, if you think about the yardage and the rest," center Aaron Graham said. "But it's one of those things where if we were clicking on all cylinders and doing the things we are capable of doing, it could have been a lot better than it was."

Graham, of course, was looking at comparisons with Nebraska's first five games. The Huskers were averaging 491 yards rushing, 656 yards of total offense and 55 points per game. And Missouri was supposed to be another easy warm up to Kansas State and Colorado.

"It was up and down," Frazier said of the offense. "I don't know if it was lack of concentration or maybe doing things differently. We just weren't very consistent."

The Huskers more or less ground it out against Missouri. Green carried 15 times for 90 yards in his first start and Frazier added 71 yards on eight carries.

"For his first time, he did very well," running backs and assistant head coach Frank Solich said of Green. It was a rapid growth process for the first-year college player, Solich said, and Green handled the challenge surprisingly well.

"When he first started it was a little unsettling to him, but he responded well to it," said Solich. "As he went along, he came at a very fast pace. Right now I think he can play football against anybody and do a great job. You don't have a lot of freshmen around the country who you can say that about."

It was 1994 all over again for the Huskers. When the offense

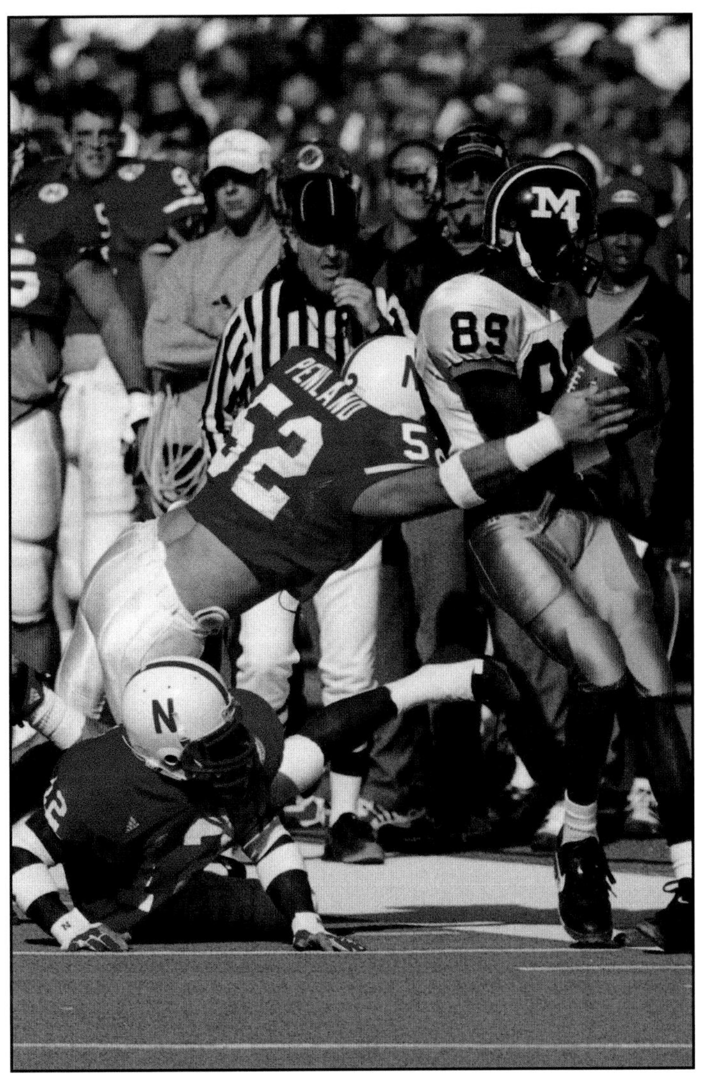

In this Husker shutout, the swarming Nebraska defense came from every direction each time the Tigers touched the ball, which spoke volumes as to where Nebraska was going.

sputtered, the defense rose to the occasion. When injuries sidelined key players, others stepped in and performed. This was another very good, very talented and very deep football team. And adversity only served to bring it closer together.

The defense logged its first shutout of the season against Missouri. The pregame goal of ending its big-play charity seemed to work for the Blackshirts. Missouri totaled only 122 yards in the game.

"Defensively, this was our best performance," Osborne said. "The only disturbing thing was that we did have two or three guys running open, but they couldn't hit them."

Part of that success was the rush the Huskers put on Missouri's quarterbacks. True freshman Chad Kelsay had two of the team's four sacks. The Huskers had eight tackles for losses.

Even Missouri coach Larry Smith's efforts to shake up his offense with secretive practices all week weren't enough to get his Tigers going against Nebraska.

"We really simplified things," Smith said. "But I don't think we ever gave ourselves a chance to get rolling. We'd come up

15

(Left) Tommie Frazier, the Heisman Trophy candidate, breaks a tackle en route to 71 yards total rushing and 204 yards total offense for the game.

with positive yardage and then, boom, we'd jump offsides or take a delay of game penalty. We'd end up going from second-and-five to second-and-10 or a first-and-10 to a first-and-15."

Even Tiger running star Brock Olivo left Memorial Stadium frustrated. He entered the game averaging 101.8 yards per game and managed only 10 yards on 11 carries.

Nebraska defenders didn't think Missouri had shuffled things up too much, at least not from what they saw on pregame film.

"We were kind of antsy early because they had their practices closed all week," outside linebacker Jared Tomich said. "But it wasn't that much different. They tried a little option, but we practice against the best option offense every day. I don't know what they were thinking. This was by far our best defensive game yet."

"We dominated them," said rover Mike Minter. "We've been looking for a shutout all season, and we finally accomplished it. We wanted to prove to the nation that we've got a tough defense."

That was the kind of momentum the Huskers needed heading into what Osborne believed to be the toughest part of the schedule. Up next would be No. 8 Kansas State, sharper mentally after surviving a 23-17 scare at Oklahoma State.

But what concerned Nebraska coaches was getting the Huskers tuned to run better.

"We were not a well-oiled machine," receivers coach Ron Brown said. "Fifty-seven points is a lot no matter who you play, but we look at execution. We put the ball on the ground six times even though we got them all back. It wasn't clicking all the time. Part of that was our excellent field position and how well their defense played. They were good. But we also weren't in sync."

Game 6 Statistics

	1st Quarter	2nd Quarter	3rd Quarter	4th Quarter	Final
Missouri	0	0	0	0	0
Nebraska	7	21	22	7	57

FIRST QUARTER
NU-Frazier 29 run (Brown kick), 7:08.

SECOND QUARTER
NU-Frazier 1 run (Brown kick), 5:24.
NU-Frazier 1 run (Brown kick), 3:00.
NU-Holbein 29 pass from Frazier (Brown kick), :00.

THIRD QUARTER
NU-Farley blocked punt for safety, 9:42.
NU-Green 9 run (kick failed), 8:22.
NU-Jackson 9 pass from Frazier (Brown kick), 4:40
NU-Turman 1 run (Retzlaff kick), 1:01.

FOURTH QUARTER
NU-Benning 16 run (Retzlaff kick), 11:26.

TEAM STATISTICS

	MU	NU
First downs	9	21
Rushing att.-yards	39-39	51-342
Passes	24-9-2	15-7-0
Passing yards	83	133
Total att.-yards	63-122	66-475
Returns-yards	0	11-123
Sacks by	0	4-30
Punts-average	11-34.5	5-33.4
Fumbles-lost	5-2	6-0
Penalties-yards	5-36	5-24
Time of poss.	35:16	24:44

INDIVIDUAL LEADERS

RUSHING:
MU: Blackwell 6-20-0; Janes 4-16-0; Olivo 11-10-0; Skornia 5-11-0.
NU: Green 15-90-1; Frazier 8-71-3; Benning 8-37-1.

PASSING:
MU: Corso 12-6-0, 59; Skornia 10-3-1, 24.
NU: Frazier 14-7-0, 133.

RECEIVING:
MU: Lingerfelt 3-29-0; Jones 3-25-0.
NU: Gilman 2-57-0; Vedral 1-36-0; Holbein 1-29-1.

INTERCEPTIONS:
MU: None.
NU: Veland 1-43-0.

TACKLES (UT-AT-TT):
MU: Cross 6-5-11; Chatman 5-4-9; Martin 2-5-7.
NU: Colman 4-4-8; C. Peter 0-7-7; Terwilliger 3-4-7.

SACKS:
MU: None.
NU: Kelsay 2-12; Williams 1-10; Hardin 1-8.

Nebraska 49
Kansas State 25

October 21, 1995 - Memorial Stadium

The first of several Big Eight challenges had arrived for No. 2 Nebraska. Kansas State, a program resurrected by coach Bill Snyder, was sailing along at 6-0 and was ranked eighth in the nation. The Wildcats were playing the best defense in the nation. K-State was allowing fewer than 85 passing yards per game to rank second in passing efficiency defense, less than 95 yards rushing to rank eighth and gave up just under 200 total yards each time out. Nebraska's defense was giving up 291 yards per game to sit 13th nationally by comparison.

Even the loss of graduated all-star quarterback Chad May wasn't proving to be that big a deal for K-State with the emergence of senior Matt Miller. Miller, the conference leader in total offense, was the No. 2-ranked passer in the Big Eight and had thrown for 1,191 yards and 13 touchdowns while completing nearly 67 percent of his passes in six games.

Miller also had a trio of gifted receivers in Kevin Lockett, Mitch Running and Tyson Schwieger. Lockett and Running already had 27 catches during the season, while Schwieger had 26.

K-State, 6-0 for the first time in 85 years, had gained enough national attention that ABC picked up their match at Nebraska (the homecoming game) for regional coverage. And the Huskers hadn't lost a homecoming game since K-State upset them by a score of 12-0 in 1968.

The 17-9 squeaker between the two teams at Manhattan, Kan., in 1994 was an incentive for the Huskers to pay attention. But, at that time, Nebraska was playing largely without its top two quarterbacks since Tommie Frazier was out with blood clots and Brook Berringer

(Above) Husker defenders let K-State quarterback Matt Miller know it was not going to be an easy day.
(Right) Frazier (left) scrambles into the Wildcat secondary, making another big play out of an apparent bust.

N
15
92

Fullback Brian Schuster (28) pulls through a tackle as the ground game punches ahead.

It would be the first of nine sacks the Huskers would record that day. The pressure on Miller and his backup Brian Kavanagh was relentless.

"It was a kind of personal thing," said Wistrom, noting that it was the K-State defense getting all the praise before the game. "Statistically, they were ranked as the No. 1 defense in the country, but we wanted to show them that we're as good. We just wanted to go out and play well."

Play well would be an understatement. K-State would manage minus-19 yards rushing and throw two interceptions despite 275 yards on 24-of-47 passing. Much of the passing yardage came on late scoring drives against the reserves.

Nebraska's scoring punch also started in overdrive when Mike Fullman returned the game's first punt 79 yards for a touchdown less than five minutes into the contest. It was the first punt return for a score by Nebraska in seven seasons. Fullman, a tiny (5-foot-7, 160 pounds) but speedy transfer from Rutgers, would provide more exciting moments as the fall progressed.

The Wildcats came right back with an 18-yard TD pass from Miller to Lockett but the extra point kick failed and Nebraska led 7-6.

The Huskers could do little wrong in this one, including fumble. Clinton Childs coughed the ball up on a Nebraska drive late in the first quarter but Jon Vedral fell on the loose ball rolling in the end zone for a score. That would open the flood gates for the Nebraska offense.

was on the sidelines in the first half after suffering a collapsed lung weeks earlier. It was almost run the ball or nothing against the Wildcats then. This was different. For one thing, Frazier was healthy.

Nebraska proved to be very focused for the game against the Wildcats and it didn't take long to show it. On Kansas State's second play, outside linebacker Grant Wistrom smashed Miller for a sack.

"He wasn't moving so good after Wistrom got him on that first sack," said Jared Tomich, who was bearing down from the other side of the Husker defense. "He was hurting. He was getting up slow."

Clinton Childs (26) tries to break loose from the stingy K-State defense.

Frazier threw 11 yards to tight end Sheldon Jackson for a touchdown five minutes into the second quarter. Freshman Ahman Green, getting his second start at I-back, took a shovel pass from Frazier 10 yards into the end zone on the Huskers' next possession.

The defense also got into the scoring act when freshman outside linebacker Chad Kelsay batted a shovel pass attempted by Miller and outside linebacker Luther Hardin was there to catch it and tumble 3 yards into the end zone for a 35-6 Nebraska lead. It was Nebraska's third interception return for a touchdown this season and it only added to Kansas State's helplessness.

"We weren't good in any aspect," Coach Snyder said. "The kicking game got us in a hole to begin with and then it happened to our offense and our defense. We just couldn't handle the emotion of the ballgame and that's my role.

"This football team came with the idea that if they played well and played hard, they'd win the football game. We played hard, but that's only half the point."

Snyder said that maybe he and his assistant coaches pumped up the team too much. "I think I've put them in a position where maybe they're destined to fail. I probably took it to a little higher level than I should have. You can't make some of the mistakes we made against a team like Nebraska and expect anything to happen other than what happened."

Nebraska added to its lead on a 32-yard pass from Frazier to Vedral in the third quarter, then Osborne let the reserves get some playing time.

Kansas State, however, was not ready to concede its 27th straight loss to the Huskers. Kavanagh threw a 7-yard TD pass to Running early in the fourth quarter. He hit Lockett with a 10-yard scoring toss less than six minutes later. And, after Clyde Johnson scored for KSU on a blocked punt with 5:59 left in the game to pull within 17 points, Osborne put the starters back in to make sure this K-State rally was going to fall short.

"We did an awful lot of good things and then we probably backed off too early," Osborne said. "We shouldn't have substi-

Freshman sensation Ahman Green (30) ran for over 100 yards against one of the nation's top defenses.

tuted so early on defense. I guess it's really nice to play a good football team and be able to pull your first team out."

While Osborne freely played many of his reserves, the physical punishment Nebraska was giving to Kansas State made Snyder substitute out of necessity.

K-State cornerback Joe Gordon had his helmet ripped off in a vicious block by linebacker Mike Rucker on Nebraska's touchdown punt return. Linebacker DeShawn Fogle was taken off the field on a stretcher with a neck injury. And Miller and Kavanagh were getting up slower and slower after their beatings, which included nine sacks for 82 yards in losses and the hits they regularly received immediately after throwing most of their passes.

"That has to be a little unnerving when you get hit almost every play, whether you release the ball or not," Osborne said. "Their quarterbacks got hit a lot and did a pretty good job of standing in there with the amount of pressure they had."

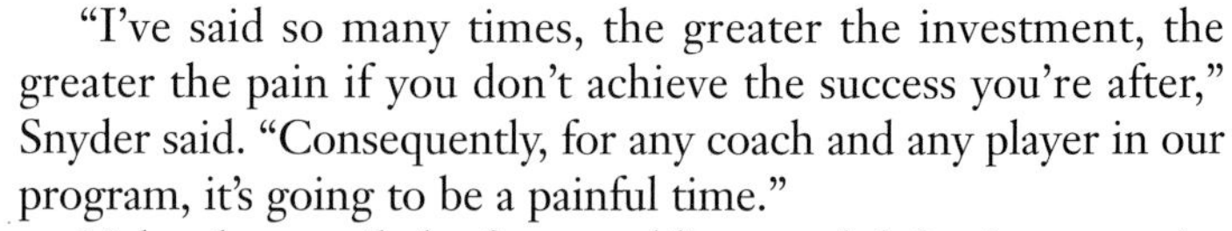

The pressure was on K-State's quarterbacks all game as they were sacked nine times and hurried a season high 19 times. (Right) Linebacker Terrell Farley (43) gets one of his two sacks and ten tackles. (Below) Jared Tomich's (93) clothesline sack dazes Matt Miller.

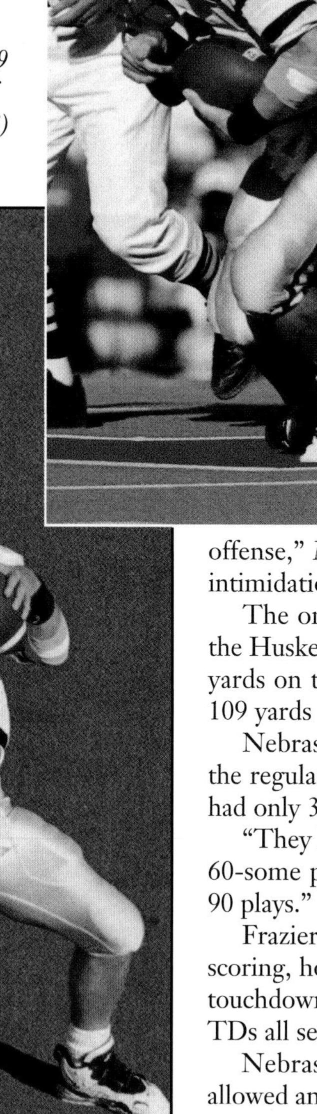

"I've said so many times, the greater the investment, the greater the pain if you don't achieve the success you're after," Snyder said. "Consequently, for any coach and any player in our program, it's going to be a painful time."

Nebraska unveiled a few new blitzes and defensive strategies for the Wildcats. Another change was a first start for linebacker Terrell Farley, the speedy junior college transfer who was proving to be a great addition. He ended this game with a team-high 10 tackles and two sacks.

"We've been saving some blitzes, but they kept jumping offside and we had to change the defensive plays," Farley said.

Doug Colman, who was making his second start at middle linebacker in place of the injured Phil Ellis, said the first half was more muscle than any new defenses.

"We didn't start blitzing a lot until the second half," he said. "I don't think it was a close game. The Blackshirts held them to six points, but the third and fourth teamer guys got in there and they started scoring a little bit more. I felt that after the first half, they freaked out a little bit."

Kansas State's players also were in shock over the outcome.

"I felt we were past the point where anyone could do this to us," Lockett said, referring to the lopsided score. "Nebraska took over every aspect of the game."

"They definitely put their licks on me and put their licks on our offense," Miller said. "They sure hit me hard. That's as much intimidation as I need."

The only negative for Nebraska was the rushing output by the Husker offense, according to Osborne. The season-low 190 yards on the ground came on 46 carries and included Green's 109 yards on 22 tries.

Nebraska did not run for a touchdown for the first time in the regular season since a 19-10 loss at Iowa State in 1992, and had only 338 yards of total offense on 63 plays.

"They held us to our lowest total, but what did we have, only 60-some plays?" Frazier asked. "Other games we've had 80 or 90 plays."

Frazier's passing game was good enough to keep the offense scoring, however. He hit 10-of-16 passes for 148 yards and four touchdowns against a team that had allowed only three passing TDs all season.

Nebraska also scored 49 points against a defense that had allowed an average of 7.5 points per game in the first six outings.

It wasn't really a bad afternoon at all, according to Osborne. "Any time you win by three touchdowns over Kansas State you have to feel good about the effort."

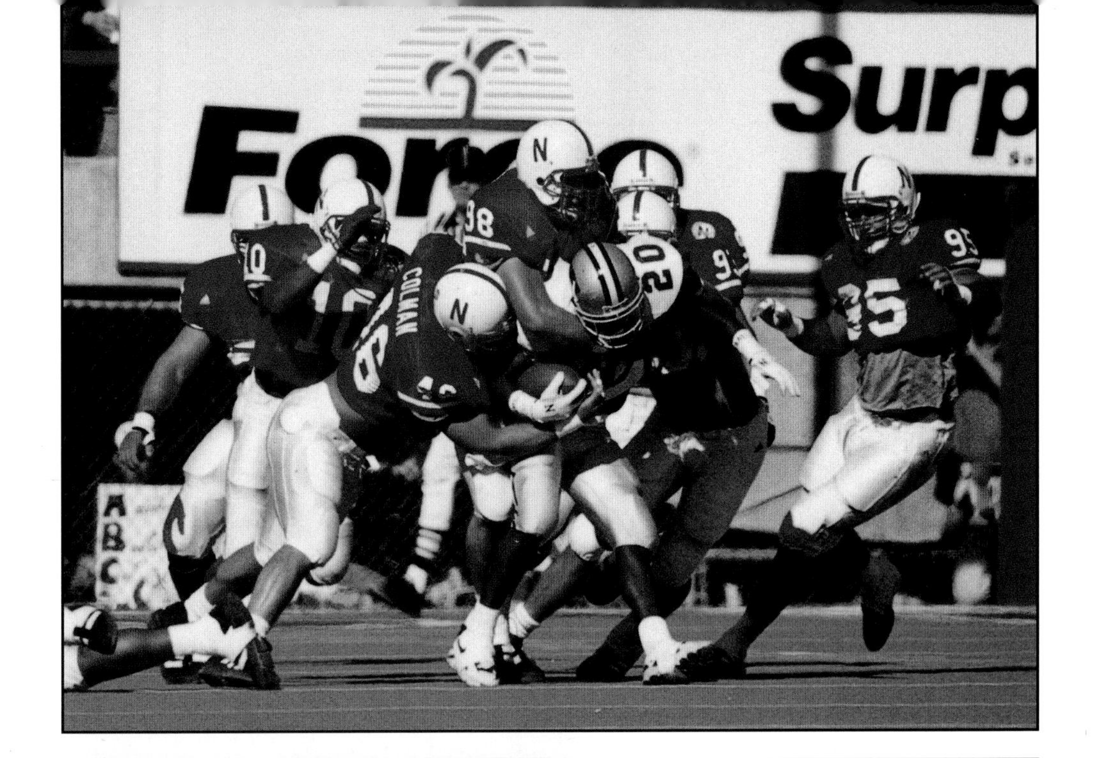

In one of the season's best efforts, Husker defenders trample all over K-State. The Wildcats were held to minus 19 yards total rushing.

Game 7 Statistics

	1st Quarter	2nd Quarter	3rd Quarter	4th Quarter	Final
Kan. State	6	0	0	19	25
Nebraska	14	21	7	7	49

FIRST QUARTER
NU-Fullman 79-yard punt return (Brown kick), 10:29.
KSU-Lockett 18-yard pass from Miller (kick failed), 7:23.
NU-Vedral fumble recovery (Brown kick), 02.

SECOND QUARTER
NU-Jackson 11-yard pass from Frazier (Brown kick), 9:46.
NU-Green 10-yard pass from Frazier (Brown kick), 5:21.
NU-Hardin 3-yard interception return (Brown kick), 4:31.

THIRD QUARTER
NU-Vedral 32-yard pass from Frazier (Brown kick), 5:09.

FOURTH QUARTER
KSU-Running 7-yard pass from Kavanagh (pass failed), 13:07.
KSU-Lockett 10-yard pass from Kavanagh (Gramatica kick), 7:33.
KSU-Johnson 6-yard blocked punt return (pass failed), 5:59.
NU-Green 12-yard pass from Frazier (Brown kick), 3:43.

TEAM STATISTICS

	KSU	NU
First downs	17	19
Rushing att.-yards	26-(-19)	46-190
Passes	47-24-2	17-10-0
Passing yards	275	148
Total att.-yards	73-256	63-338
Returns-yards	1-25	5-115
Sacks by	0	9-82
Punts-average	6-44.3	4-22.8
Fumbles-lost	0-0	1-0
Penalties-yards	14-113	7-64
Time of poss.	30:53	29:07

INDIVIDUAL LEADERS

RUSHING:
KSU: Hickson 6-26-0; Lawrence 6-15-0.
NU: Green 22-109-0; Frazier 6-36-0; Makovicka 6-21-0.

PASSING:
KSU: Miller 24-10-2, 109; Kavanagh 21-12-0, 136.
NU: Frazier 16-10-0, 148.

RECEIVING:
KSU: Running 10-110-1; Schwieger 4-58-0; Lockett 4-54-2.
NU: Green 3-41-2; Jackson 2-18-1; Vedral 1-32-1.

INTERCEPTIONS:
KSU: None
NU: Booker 1-22-0; Hardin 1-3-1.

TACKLES (UT-AT-TT):
KSU: Marlowe 4-6-10; Smith 1-9-10; Ochs 5-4-9.
NU: Farley 6-4-10; Wistrom 5-1-6; Booker 4-0-4; Colman 2-2-4; C. Peter 1-3-4.

SACKS:
KSU: None.
NU: Farley 2-22; Tomich 2-21; Cloman 2-13; Wistrom 2-10; Rucker 1-16.

Nebraska 44
Colorado 21

October 28, 1995 - At Boulder Colorado

For the eighth-straight season, Colorado and Nebraska were playing a game that likely would decide who would win the Big Eight championship. The Buffaloes had replaced Oklahoma as the perennial challenger for the steady Huskers in the title chase. Nebraska came to Boulder, Colo., with a 7-0 overall record and 3-0 league mark. The Huskers were ranked second nationally in both polls and had a chance to move up with top-ranked Florida State idle.

Colorado was 6-1 overall and 2-1 in the Big Eight after a shocking 40-24 loss to No. 6 Kansas at home two weeks before. But the Buffaloes, now ranked seventh, rebounded to thrash Iowa State 50-28 to get back in the proper frame of mind for Nebraska.

Colorado was taking a different approach to the Huskers this season. They were playing on their home turf this year under young head coach Rick Neuheisel, who took over for the retired Bill McCartney.

McCartney had made this game his designated rivalry and had the Buffaloes pumped to a feverish pitch when the Nebraska game came up. Neuheisel, displaying a great deal of diplomacy, tact and common sense for his 34 years, preferred to look at this as a big game and leave it at that. After all, Nebraska coach Tom Osborne refused to label Colorado a rival and that apparently was OK with Neuheisel.

"This game has special significance regardless of rivalry and it seems folly to me to have one team call it a rivalry and the other team not," Neuheisel said. "By mere definition, that means it's not."

Nebraska owned the last three wins in the series, but a victory over the Huskers could keep Colorado in the national championship picture.

(Above) The meeting of Colorado and Nebraska grows intense for both fans and players.
(Right) Even trying to block an extra-point kick is a supreme effort for the Husker Blackshirts as Jason Peter (95), Doug Colman (46) and Eric Warfield (3) can attest.

A fired up Husker team about to show the Buffaloes a 21-point first quarter.

"This is the second year in a row, playing this game, that we've got a chance to win the national championship if we win the game," Neuheisel said. "I would say there's no fear factor. Certainly, it's intimidating when you're losing on a consistent basis (to Nebraska). I think we all know that one of the reasons we've been unsuccessful is that we've put them on too high a plane. They're a great football team, I've said it time and time again, but so are we on a given, particular day."

The former UCLA quarterback had elected to emphasize Colorado's passing game and had had success behind the talents of Koy Detmer. He was leading the nation in passing efficiency when he was sidelined for the year with a knee injury.

Sophomore John Hessler stepped in and had thrown nine touchdown passes and 1,049 yards as a very adequate replacement. He entered this game with the 14th-best pass efficiency rating in the country.

Colorado averaged 503.8 yards per game (fifth-best nationally), 311.7 yards passing (sixth-best nationally) and 41.7 points per game (also sixth-best nationally).

"This year, their passing game has been emphasized," Osborne said. "They throw the ball very well, have great receivers, great speed at the receivers spots. Offensively, they are very dangerous and defensively, they have excellent athletes."

Hessler's targets included Phil Savoy (32 catches, 421 yards) and one of the fastest players in college football, Rae Carruth (30 catches, 668 yards). Both were sure-handed receivers and big-play players, especially Carruth, who could break a long one any time he ran a pass pattern.

Nebraska's offense entered the game No. 1 in rushing with an average of 426.9 yards per game. Nebraska was second in scoring with 54.4 points per outing and third in total offense averaging 584.9 yards per game.

Clester Johnson , after wrestling a pass away from the Colorado defenders, outraces them to the end zone for a 52-yard TD play.

The rushing defense for the Huskers also ranked second in the nation, allowing only 73.1 yards per game. Nebraska was 11th nationally in scoring defense with a yield of 16 points. The Husker Blackshirts were gaining momentum and were playing at a level comparable to that which had helped the team to the national title the year before. Their speed impressed just about everybody.

Nebraska had looked impressive throughout the previous weeks, including the 49-25 dismantling of Top 10-ranked Kansas State the week before. When the offense was hitting on all cylinders, the Huskers were scary.

On game day, the Huskers, after stopping the Buffaloes on the first offensive series, took the ball at their own 43.

Freshman Ahman Green, getting his third start at I-back, took a Tommie Frazier pitch and swept left end. Fullback Jeff Makovicka threw a block at the corner to take out a pair of Buffalo defenders, then split end Brendan Holbein threw another block down the sideline to spring Green, a state prep sprint champion at Omaha Central High School, who raced 57 yards to score. It took Nebraska all of 10 seconds to take the lead.

"Brendan did a great job as usual, and so did Jeff," Green said. "They made it easy for me to get to the outside."

"That was a new set," Osborne said. "We put an extra blocker out there, and that might have confused them."

Frazier wasn't confused and he knew Osborne wasn't, either.

"All week coach Osborne said we could score on the first play, and that's what we did," the senior quarterback said.

Colorado came right back. Hessler, using a quick, three-step drop to offset the Nebraska pass rush that had logged nine sacks against K-State the week before, took a couple of series to settle down. Once he did, he marched the Buffaloes on an 85-yard, seven-play drive capped by a perfect 18-yard touch pass to Savoy

30

15
54
NIKE

in the corner of the end zone.

Colorado, playing inspired defense now, stopped the Huskers on a fourth-and-one attempt, but linebacker Terrell Farley picked off a Hessler pass at the NU 45 on the next series and returned it 42 yards to the 13 yard line. The Huskers' lone junior college recruit continued to pay big dividends. He already had two interception touchdowns to his credit earlier in the season.

Four plays later, Green scored from the 1-yard-line, bulling two Buffalo defenders into the end zone. The crowd at Boulder and big-game atmosphere of this nationally televised test was not unsettling to the youngster from Omaha.

"It makes me better playing in a place like this," Green said. "I know now that I can go anywhere and play. It was a good feeling to come up here for the first time and do that."

But this was a team effort. Nebraska entered the game with a 22-4-1 road record over the past six years and had clinched a 34th-consecutive winning season, an ongoing NCAA record, the week before. It was tradition for Nebraska to play well and to win, home or away.

The Husker Blackshirts nearly picked off Hessler again on the next series and forced a punt after three plays. Frazier was in charge from there on out. Nebraska started their next possession on the NU 48. Frazier faked a handoff and found Clester Johnson breaking down the sideline. The NU split end wrestled the ball from a Buffalo defender and shook loose on his way to a 52-yard TD.

It was the sixth time Nebraska had scored on a one-play drive in the first eight games and the second time in this contest. The big-play team was ahead 21-7 in the first quarter.

Colorado was daring the nation's best running team to throw

Nebraska's power game sends the big boys directly at the Buffs, while Frazier (15) spins to hand off to fullback Jeff Makovicka (22).

with a defense that stacked seven or eight players on the line of scrimmage. Frazier had seen those types of efforts before. He knew what to do.

"We didn't expect him to be able to pass as well as he did," Colorado linebacker Matt Russell said. "We said all week long if we forced him into passing, we'd have the upper hand."

Maybe the Buffaloes should have checked the pregame statistics. Frazier threw for four touchdowns the week before when K-State loaded up to stop the run. That was his 16th career game throwing for 100 yards or more. He had 37 career passing touchdowns and this season had hit 46-of-85 passes with two interceptions and 11 touchdowns.

By game's end, Frazier would have completed 14-of-23 for a career-high 241 yards and two touchdowns. So much for thinking the guy can't pass!

"Frazier is a great player," Osborne said. "He kind of holds everything together. He threw the ball awfully well, and he showed a lot of poise."

Colorado came back again, this time mixing the run and pass to get into scoring position. Lendon Henry took a handoff and sliced off tackle but Nebraska linebacker Ryan Terwilliger met him in the hole and stripped the ball loose.

The football darted into the open end zone and Colorado lineman Heath Irwin was the first to get there, corralling the ball before it could skip out of bounds. The 15-play drive had burned more than seven minutes off the clock. Nebraska's defense wasn't making things easy for the Buffs, who nevertheless were keeping the ball away from Frazier and company.

The extra point made it a 21-14 game.

Nebraska answered after the kickoff. Frazier hit tight end Mark Gilman over the middle. It was a play similar to what Brook Berringer and the Huskers used to defeat an unbeaten Colorado team 24-7 the year before. They had made a day of hitting tight ends and the play was still there.

Frazier came up with a miracle play minutes later when he dropped back to pass, was hit from the blind side as he pump-faked, pulled the ball back up and hit Green in the flat. The freshman back carried the ball to the Colorado 8. Frazier was 5-of-6 passing at that point.

"Good teams bring out the best in me," he said.

But the Husker drive stalled and freshman kicker Kris Brown came in to boot a 25-yard field goal.

The Blackshirts turned up the pressure at that point. Outside linebackers Grant Wistrom and Jared Tomich led the pass rush with their backups Luther Hardin and Chad Kelsay. The Peter brothers, Christian and Jason, had all but owned the middle for the defense.

The Huskers forced another punt after three downs but this time NU was a long way away. Starting the drive at the 17 with 3:14 left in the half, Frazier mixed up runs, options and a handful of passes to march Nebraska down the field. Colorado, the most-penalized team in the Big Eight, helped the cause with a trio of penalties.

Frazier ran a quarterback draw from the shotgun to the 13. Damon Benning carried on an option to the 7. Then Frazier found wingback Jon Vedral over the middle for a touchdown with 10 seconds remaining in the first half.

"Frazier is quite a player," Neuheisel said. "We've seen a lot of great players. The running back (Iowa State's Troy Davis) we faced last week is a great player, and I'm not saying that to take anything away from Frazier. He's a good player."

"We've always respected him," added Russell. "But along with everybody else, I never really thought he was a great passer. He did a good job of finding open guys and teams down the road are going to have to respect that."

Nebraska had scored on four straight possessions to take a 31-14 lead. The Huskers had 295 yards of total offense by intermission and, surprisingly, 184 of that was through the air.

"We had a lot of guys in the box," Russell said of Colorado's overloading the line of scrimmage to stop the run. "I don't care who you are, if we stack that many guys up there on the line,

Freshman Kris Brown (35) gets off one of his three field goals on the day, proving to be a great find for the Huskers this fall.

75
25

A hit by Colorado linebacker Mike Phillips on a throwing Tommie Frazier (inset) knocked the quarterback to the ground but was not in time to break up the pass which was caught by Ahman Green (30) for a 35-yard gain. The reception led to a Husker field goal before halftime.

you're not going to be real effective on the ground."

Colorado still wanted to make a game of this one, however. On a fourth-and-one at the CU 49 midway through the third quarter, Hessler lofted a bomb down the sidelines to James Kidd for a score. That made it a 10-point game.

"When they scored and got it down to 10 we did what we had to do -- stop them in three plays," Nebraska rover Mike Minter said. "That was our big series of the game."

The Huskers answered with a 36-yard field goal by the freshman Brown near the end of the third quarter and a 37-yarder just over five minutes into the fourth period after Wistrom smacked Hessler from behind and Doug Colman picked off the wobbly pass at the CU 21.

Brown was booming his field goal kicks and could have been more than 10 yards farther back in his efforts. "It was one of those days where you feel like you can kick the ball a mile," he said, adding that he knew the third-quarter kick could have been a big one. "If I miss and Colorado scores a touchdown, it's a three-point game and anything could have happened."

But not to worry, Brown noted. "I'm kicking the best I ever have."

Frazier put the game away with a 2-yard TD run in the final minutes when the Huskers covered 74 yards on a drive that included a 20-yard pass to Gilman and a penalty for roughing the punter that allowed Nebraska to keep the ball.

"We wanted to come in here and show people that we could go on the road and win," Frazier said. "Everyone thought because we had five home games in a row that we were going to slack off on the road. But we're a better road team than we are at home because we like the hostile environment."

The win was near-perfection for the Huskers, who played without a turnover or a penalty. Colorado, on the other hand, had 12 penalties for 92 yards and had two interceptions.

"No penalties and no turnovers, I've never heard of that," said Colorado guard Irwin.

"We had to play with emotion and we did. We had to play hard and we did. But we also had to play mistake-free and we didn't," Neuheisel said.

The win was Nebraska's 126th straight scoring 35 or more points. Green moved to No. 2 on the Nebraska rushing charts for freshmen, behind two-time All-Big Eight Calvin Jones. The win also gave NU the upper hand in the run for a fifth-straight Big Eight championship and opened up two more topics for discussion.

Should Tommie Frazier win the Heisman? And, is Nebraska the No. 1 team in the nation, again?

"If they look at the best football player in the United States, Tommie Frazier is very deserving," Osborne said. But the coach noted quarterback passing statistics often are the measuring stick for great players at that position. He would say many more times before the season was over that Frazier had a lot more going for him than that. The kid just wins.

"Tommie Frazier is a phenomenal player," said NU center Aaron Graham. "He's got to be No. 1 in the minds of a lot of Heisman voters. The thing I like so much about him is the fact he's got this competitive fire that pumps you up every time you look at him."

"He's truly a great competitor and a gifted athlete," Neuheisel added. "He made all kinds of big plays, time and again. There's no question in my mind he's the front-runner for the Heisman."

Frazier had Buffalo cornerback T.J. Cunningham's vote.

"In all my years of playing and watching college football, Tommie is the best quarterback I've seen," Cunningham said. "It was a pleasure playing against him. He's a strong competitor."

So what about Nebraska as a team against the likes of top-ranked Florida State, Florida or Ohio State?

"I don't want to get into that No. 1 vs. No. 2 controversy," Osborne said. He remembered the flap over unbeaten Penn State's claim to the national title the year before. But Nebraska held the top spot in both polls with its win over Miami in the Orange Bowl.

"We'll just let the voters take a look," Osborne said.

Apparently they did. Nebraska jumped around idle Florida State to take the No. 1 spot, just as it had done by beating Colorado the year before.

Game 8 Statistics

	1st Quarter	2nd Quarter	3rd Quarter	4th Quarter	Final
Nebraska	21	10	3	10	44
Colorado	7	7	7	0	21

FIRST QUARTER
NU-Green 57 run (Brown kick), 13:13.
CU-Savoy 18 pass from Hessler (Voskeritchian kick), 8:19.
NU-Green 1 run (Brown kick), 2:52
NU-Johnson 52 pass from Frazier (Brown kick), 1:47.

SECOND QUARTER
CU-Irwin recovered fumble in end zone (Voskeritchian kick), 9:34.
NU-Brown 25 field goal, 5:15.
NU-Vedral 7 pass from Frazier (Brown kick), :10.

THIRD QUARTER
CU-Kidd 49 pass from Hessler (Voskeritchian kick), 8:18.
NU-Brown 36 field goal, 2:01.

FOURTH QUARTER
NU-Brown 37 field goal, 11:49.
NU-Frazier 2 run (Brown kick), 2:46.

TEAM STATISTICS

	NU	CU
First downs	26	20
Rushing att.-yards	54-226	24-106
Passes	23-14-0	43-21-2
Passing yards	241	276
Total att.-yards	77-467	67-382
Returns-yards	4-45	1-(-8)
Sacks by	2-6	0
Punts-average	2-42.0	6-41.7
Fumbles-lost	1-0	2-0
Penalties-yards	0-0	12-92
Time of poss.	35:48	24:12

INDIVIDUAL LEADERS

RUSHING:
NU: Green 18-97-2; Childs 10-44-0; Frazier 13-40-1; Je. Makovicka 8-24-0.
CU: Troutman 11-72-0; Henry 10-27-0.

PASSING:
NU: Frazier 23-14-0, 241.
CU: Hessler 43-21-2, 276.

RECEIVING:
NU: Johnson 3-72-1; Gilman 3-53-0; Green 2-44-0; Vedral 2-34-1.
CU: Savoy 8-74-1; Carruth 7-92-0; Kidd 1-49-1.

INTERCEPTIONS:
NU: Farley 1-42-0; Colman 1-0-0.
CU: None.

TACKLES (UT-AT-TT):
NU: Williams 3-7-10; Farley 3-4-7; Williams 3-2-5; Veland 2-3-5; Minter 3-2-5.
CU: Russell 7-7-14; Leomiti 9-4-13; Black 6-5-11.

SACKS:
NU: Wistrom 1-5; Hesse 1-1.
CU: None.

Nebraska 73
Iowa State 14

November 4, 1995 - Memorial Stadium

Ever since 1992, Nebraska had figured it had something to prove every time Iowa State came up on the schedule. This was the game that reminded the Husker players that any opponent is capable of winning on any given day. The 1992 Cyclones surprised a once-beaten, heavily favored Nebraska team 19-10 in Ames, Iowa. It was the only time a Tom Osborne-coached Husker team had lost to a team that would finish the season with a losing record.

Four years later, the fire still burned for the Huskers. "1992" was still in the backs of the minds of players who had been around long enough to remember that dark day.

There also were a few more incentives for the 8-0 Huskers against a 3-5 team that had not won a game the season before. New coach Dan McCarney had instilled a new attitude into the Cyclones and had learned that giving the ball to sophomore tailback Troy Davis was magic.

Davis was the nation's rushing leader and was the first player in NCAA history to rush for 1,000 yards in the first five games of the season. He averaged 190.8 yards per game and showed speed and durability in carrying the offensive load while option quarterback Todd Doxzon was shelved with a badly sprained ankle.

Nebraska also was carrying a new title: top-ranked team. The Huskers had moved around idle Florida State in both The Associated Press and USA Today/CNN polls with the 44-21 victory over No. 7 Colorado.

Even Florida State coach Bobby Bowden had been impressed by the defending national champions.

(Above) Tommie Frazier offers Coach Osborne some thoughts as defensive coordinator Charlie McBride watches his unit on the field.
(Right) Ahman Green goes toe-to-toe with a Cyclone defender. His three-touchdown, 176-yard day showed that the offense was as strong as ever.

N
ISU

Freshman wingback Lance Brown fights off the defense as Nebraska substituted liberally in the lopsided game.

"They've been the best team all year from what I've seen," he said. Bowden, who votes in the USA Today/CNN coaches' poll, admitted he had been voting Nebraska No. 1.

"They've got a great quarterback and tailbacks. But what really impresses me is their offensive line," he explained. "It doesn't make any difference who they put in there at tailback, that line just makes them all good."

Osborne, ever the one to temper something that looks too good to be true, would rather have waited a few more weeks to jump to the top spot.

"You attract a lot more attention when you're No. 1, and that sometimes takes more time and energy and everyone gives you their best shot," Osborne said. "The plus side, of course, is it puts you in the position you are striving for — to play for the national championship."

The Huskers were already getting plenty of media attention due to the return of I-back Lawrence Phillips. This would be Phillips' first game back, although he would not start ahead of developing freshman sensation Ahman Green.

Tommie Frazier, who limped through the team's light workout on Friday, showed no signs of having a recurring leg problem early in the game on Saturday. He ran 4 yards for Nebraska's first touchdown on its first possession.

On the ensuing kickoff, Husker freshman Kris Brown got too far under the ball and popped it up. NU safety Eric Stokes recovered the short kick on the Cyclone 41 yard line and, soon after, Green scored on a 6-yard pass from Frazier. Nebraska was up 14-0 and Iowa State had not yet touched the ball!

Green added a 17-yard touchdown run on the Huskers' third possession to end the first quarter with NU up 20-0. It was evident how one-sided this one was going to be.

"We made some real critical errors," McCarney said, noting that failing to field the short kickoff was the first. "On the first one, I don't know if they intentionally did that. There was a wind blowing in. We just misjudged it. Our front five guys just took off running to get in position to block someone and we didn't see it."

Iowa State finally got on the scoreboard when freshman quarterback Todd Bandhauer threw a 15-yard pass to Ed Williams early in the second quarter. But then the Huskers would score 46 unanswered points.

Green ran in from 26 yards out, Frazier hit Reggie Baul on a 36-yard TD pass and Brown kicked a 38-yard field goal for a 38-7 halftime lead.

McCarney's pregame plan had vanished in less than 30 minutes of football.

"We've got to try to establish a running game," he had said. "We've got to do all we can to sustain some drives, convert some

Fullback Jeff Makovicka (22) takes a shot from the Cyclone defense, but ISU slowed few Huskers down on a day of offensive record breaking.

third downs and try to keep the ball away from their offense. That means being able to run the football."

Davis was Iowa State's only hope of doing that. He would end the game with 28 carries and 121 yards rushing, well below his season average. Still, the ISU sophomore impressed Nebraska's main defensive man.

"Davis is one of those guys who has a special something," said NU defensive coordinator Charlie McBride. "He has that great vision, and can see things develop. I don't think he's a kid who can flat-out fly, but as far as quickness, vision and his ability to gain yards, I don't know how anybody can just flat shut him down. You give him the ball enough times, and he's going to break something."

Davis never broke into the end zone against Nebraska, however. He did have a 23-yard gain late in the first half but largely was held in check thereafter.

"It was real tough," Davis said. "Nebraska came out there swarming to the ball. Every time it was like six, seven people around me. I know our offensive line was trying its best to block, but Nebraska's got a good defense."

The Blackshirts held Iowa State to 264 yards of total offense despite liberal substituting throughout the game.

The Huskers showed good offense, too. Frazier hit 10-of-15 passes for 118 yards and two TDs. He rushed for 62 yards and didn't act like a man bothered by a sore leg.

I-Back Ahman Green (30) gets some additional yardage .

"I knew I would play," he said. "It was just a question of how effective I would be. My leg was real sore yesterday after practice. I got treatment and it was still sore after that."

"He moved awfully well today," Osborne said, "but I was afraid he might be one series and out of the game."

Green also came up big for the Huskers. The youngster had 176 yards rushing on 12 carries, a 14.7-yard-per-carry average. He scored on runs of 17, 26 and 64 yards, and the 6-yard TD pass from Frazier.

"We haven't been hitting well the last three weeks," Green said. "We needed to come out and show that our offense is still potent."

Phillips also showed that he remembered what to do with the football. He gained 68 yards on 12 carries and scored on a 13-yard run in the 28-point third quarter, although his quickness and cutting ability showed signs of being a little rusty.

"I did a few things that were all right, but the quickness and speed are things that, if I get a lot of repetitions, will come back," he said. "But right now, it's not there."

You couldn't have convinced McCarney and the Cyclones that anything was missing from Nebraska that afternoon.

"They're just a magnificent football team," McCarney said. "That's as fine a looking physical team as I've ever seen just standing on the sidelines and looking at them."

Nebraska not only broke McCarney's team in this one, it broke Cyclone records as well. Nebraska's 73 points were the most points Iowa State has ever given up to an opponent — one better than Nebraska's total points in the 1983 Nebraska versus Iowa State game. The 624 rushing yards Nebraska totaled against the Cyclones in 1995 bested the record 604 rushing yards Nebraska totaled in 1987. The 776 yards of total offense smashed the former record of 679 yards by Oklahoma against ISU in 1971.

"I know that no matter who we put on the field, we couldn't stop Nebraska and no matter who they put on the field, we couldn't stop them," McCarney said. "They substituted offensive linemen, receivers, quarterbacks — we didn't stop any of them."

All the talk in weeks previous about teams running up the scores to impress poll voters wasn't the case here, according to McCarney.

"Not at all. Tom's a class act. I've always said that and I believe that," he said. "He substituted freely and often. Not at any time of the game did I think they were trying to run it up. I think they were just in another league. We were not even close to the football team Nebraska has."

And the horror of it all, said McCarney, is that he didn't see anything he hadn't expected.

"They were about like what we thought. You don't see a weakness — the special teams, offense, defense, size, speed, strength are all outstanding. They physically dominated us. That is as fine a group of running backs as I've ever seen and they just keep coming at you. Plus, they have an operator at quarterback."

Nebraska used 15 ball carriers in the game and Frazier was sent to the bench midway through the third quarter. It didn't seem to matter who the Huskers sent in and they sent in everybody.

"I had a good idea that we would score every time we touched the ball," Frazier said. "When we execute like we can, we can score at any time."

The win also secured Osborne's 23rd season with nine wins or more, and continued Nebraska's NCAA record of 27 consecutive such seasons.

Game 9 Statistics

	1st Quarter	2nd Quarter	3rd Quarter	4th Quarter	Final
Iowa State	0	7	0	7	14
Nebraska	20	18	28	7	73

FIRST QUARTER
NU-Frazier 4-yard run (Brown kick), 11:48.
NU-Green 6-yard pass from Frazier (Brown kick), 6:10.
NU-Green 17-yard run (kick failed), :28.

SECOND QUARTER
ISU-Williams 15-yard pass from Bandhauer (Kohl kick), 11:35.
NU-Green 26-yard run (Frazier run), 7:46.
NU-Baul 36-yard pass from Frazier (Brown kick), 3:04.
NU-Brown 38-yard field goal, :27.

THIRD QUARTER
NU-Frazier 1-yard run (Brown kick), 12:39.
NU-Green 64-yard run (Brown kick), 10:00.
NU-Phillips 13-yard run (Retzlaff kick), 5:37.
NU-Childs 13-yard run (Retzlaff kick), 3:41.

FOURTH QUARTER
ISU-Norris 6-yard run (Kohl kick), 14:47.
NU-Makovicka 18-yard run (Retzlaff kick), 7:23.

TEAM STATISTICS

	ISU	NU
First downs	15	37
Rushing att.-yards	32-121	68-624
Passes	24-11-2	21-13-0
Passing yards	143	152
Total att.-yards	56-264	89-776
Returns-yards	0-0	6-73
Sacks by	0	1-4
Punts-average	6-35.8	0
Fumbles-lost	0-0	1-0
Penalties-yards	4-36	8-89
Time of poss.	24:01	35:59

INDIVIDUAL LEADERS

RUSHING:
ISU: Davis 28-121.
NU: Green 12-176-3; Childs 6-70-1; Phillips 12-68-1; Frazier 8-62-2.

PASSING:
ISU: Bandhauer 24-11-2, 143.
NU: Frazier 15-10-0, 118; Berringer 6-3-0, 34.

RECEIVING:
ISU: Horacek 5-66-0; WIlliams 4-45-1; Davis 1-13-0.
NU: Baul 4-48-1; Vedral 2-35-0; Green 2-22-1.

INTERCEPTIONS:
ISU: None.
NU: Fullman 1-11-0; Minter 1-0-0.

TACKLES (UT-AT-TT):
ISU: Brown 3-9-12; Cooper 2-9-11; Lincavage 6-4-10.
NU: Williams 2-5-7; Minter 2-4-6; Farley 0-5-5; Stokes 0-5-5.

SACKS:
ISU: None.
NU: Tomich 1-4.

Nebraska 41
Kansas 3

November 11, 1995 - At Lawrence Kansas

The trip to Lawrence, Kan., had a lot riding on it for both teams. The 10th- and 12th-ranked Kansas Jayhawks under coach Glen Mason still had a shot at a share of the Big Eight Conference title if they could knock off the nation's No. 1 team. Kansas, at 8-1 overall and 4-1 in the conference, had its best record and best national ranking ever facing a Nebraska team. But it also had been 26 years since the Jayhawks last beat the Huskers. No KU player was born in 1968 when that happened. And there still was a bowl game in KU's future. Which bowl depended, to a great extent, on this game.

Nebraska was 9-0 overall, 5-0 in the Big Eight and had its eyes firmly on a second-straight national championship and fifth-consecutive Big Eight title. Only Kansas and longtime rival Oklahoma remained between the Huskers and a trip to Tempe, Ariz., to play for the national title in the Fiesta Bowl on Jan. 2.

Coach Tom Osborne and his crew were locked in the ratings game battle with Ohio State and Florida. The unbeaten Buckeyes and Gators possessed powerful, high-scoring offenses that were tearing opponents apart. Nebraska needed to continue winning, and win convincingly.

That had not been a problem to date. But this was a nationally ranked opponent on the road, on television and against a KU coaching staff that had come within a missed two-point conversion of spilling Nebraska 21-20 two years ago.

Kansas also had manhandled Colorado 40-24 in Boulder, Colo., in early October, romped over Iowa State and Missouri, and belted Oklahoma 38-17. The Jayhawks' only loss was a stunner to Kansas State, 41-7, just two weeks earlier.

(Above) Everybody wanted a piece of Kansas and Doug Colman (46) helps Jason Peter (95) and Tony Veland (9) hog-tie this Jayhawk.
(Right) Frazier throws a dart outside of a Kansas defender's reach. He hit 10-of-15 for 86 yards.

15
57

56
KU
KU

(Left) Freshman linebacker Jay Foreman (56) fights through a block in another dominating defensive show by the Blackshirts.

Osborne saw the potential for a major battle against some talented, well-coached Jayhawks.

"When Glen first came there, they simply didn't have the athletes to give us a game, and we knew that," Osborne said. "The first few times we played them, we knew that barring something unusual, we were going to win the game. The last two-to-three years we haven't known that at all."

Mason knew something, too. He was well aware that Nebraska had size, speed, talent and all the other ingredients to wreak havoc on any opponent. The NU option offense was enough to make most defensive coaches cry.

"If Nebraska just ran the option with the players they have, it would be a full day's work," Mason said. "But when you add all the other things they can come at you with ... and what a great talent Frazier is. He's a 190-pound tailback playing quarterback."

Yes, Tommie Frazier was playing well enough to be considered one of the leading contenders for the Heisman Trophy. He was the trigger man for an offense that led the nation in rushing with a 426.4-yard average, in scoring at 55.3 points per game and was second in total offense with 593 yards per game.

Just the thought of playing Nebraska was enough to prompt a new mind-game for the Jayhawks. Don't mention the "N" word all week.

"By not mentioning Nebraska, it takes the godlike status away from them," said Kansas linebacker Keith Rodgers. "If you take them man-to-man, you find out they're human beings just like we are. That takes the mystique out of the whole thing, and you're not defeated before you play them. We look at it like Nebraska puts its pants on one leg at a time just like we do."

True enough, but those are bigger pants for the boys in red.

Nebraska turned opportunistic in the first half of this rugged game that showed, once again, how talented the Husker team really was. It had the potential to win ugly, even in a lopsided manner.

Nebraska's first points came on a turnover. Wingback Jon Vedral fell on a punt muffed by Jayhawk Isaac Byrd. The loose ball just happened to be in the end zone, giving the Huskers a 7-0 lead nearly six minutes into the game.

Nebraska would punt again soon afterwards and this time Jared Tomich's hit on June Henley knocked the ball loose for Tony Veland, whose recovery gave the Huskers possession at the KU 30.

Frazier ran 25 yards to set up his own 1-yard TD run for a 14-0 lead at the 1:17 mark of the first quarter.

But Kansas did a good job of playing keep away, too. Quarterback Mark Williams used short passes to move the ball effectively against the Husker defense. KU would have 199 yards of total offense by halftime, but managed just three points on a 19-yard Jeff McCord field goal about four minutes into the second quarter.

The ball-control offense and a stingy KU defense limited Nebraska to 79 yards rushing and 31 passing by intermission. Kansas was giving NU all the game it wanted.

"We felt like we were in the toughest dogfight of the year in the first half," said Nebraska defensive tackle Christian Peter. "But we gave up three points. We didn't give them any more."

Nebraska's defense did indeed rise to the occasion during the second half. Williams would complete only five more passes after halftime. He ended the game with 27 completions in 45 attempts for 242 yards.

But Nebraska's offense also answered the call. The Huskers scored on their first three possessions after intermission. Frazier marched his club 58 yards on eight plays, hitting tight end Vershan Jackson from 1 yard out for the first TD.

Frazier and I-back Lawrence Phillips teamed up on the next drive that began after a Phil Ellis interception. Ellis, a Butkus candidate linebacker, was playing himself back into shape after returning from suffering a broken foot in late September.

Frazier scrambled to the 20 yard line and picked up a face mask penalty to the 15. Phillips darted into the middle to drive to the

Grant Wistrom (98), Mike Minter (10) and Doug Colman (top right) show the Jayhawks' L.T. Levine (22) how to plug a hole. KU managed just 72 yards rushing.

6-yard line. On the next play, the big I-back used a Jeff Makovicka block to score with 4:04 to go in the third quarter. It was the 21st point Nebraska had scored as a result of KU turnovers in the game.

"Our mistakes really, really hurt us," Mason said. "I'm not saying that without the mistakes we would have won, but I don't think that final score is indicative of how that game went."

The Nebraska defense forced a punt after a pair of incompletions and a sack by Tomich. The Huskers took over at their own 40 and drove for pay dirt again.

Frazier scrambled for enough yards to break Jerry Tagge's all-time Nebraska record for total offense. The Husker senior ended up completing 10 of 15 passes for 86 yards and a touchdown, and rushed 10 times for 99 yards and two more scores. His career total offensive output reached 5,313 yards.

The TD pass to Jackson also broke David Humm's career record for touchdown passes with 42.

"He's a great leader," Kansas defensive tackle Kevin Kopp said of Frazier. "He really makes the difference for them."

The Husker quarterback capped the 60-yard scoring drive with a 5-yard run, resulting from a Makovicka block on a sweep right.

"We did what we had to do," Frazier said. "I thought this was pretty good. We can do better. We could have done worse."

Mason wasn't sure his team could have done much worse. KU had five turnovers, two interceptions and three lost fumbles. All of them led to Nebraska scores.

Nebraska's last score came on Mike Fullman's 86-yard interception return of a pass by former Nebraska backup quarterback Ben Rutz with just 6:56 to play.

"I don't know how many people would have thought coming into the game that Kansas would have 82 snaps and 345 yards and Nebraska would have 66 snaps and 375 yards," Mason said. "But that doesn't mean anything. The score is still 41-3. Turnovers were the big difference."

(Left and Above) KU quarterback Mark Williams has a menacing shadow in No. 93, Jared Tomich, and when he could get a pass away, Huskers like Terrell Farley (43) and Jason Peter (95) made him pay.

(Below) There is still weeks to go but a young Husker fan already knows the outcome of this TV game and the season.

Nebraska had a few turnovers, too. Frazier's string of 100 consecutive passes without an interception ended in the third quarter when Maurice Gaddie picked one off.

Nebraska's string of 17 quarters without a turnover ended with a lost fumble in the second period.

Frazier also put a scare into Husker fans during and after the game. Bothered by a tender heel and arch, he limped to the locker room early in the first half. He returned and played as though there were no problems but was on crutches after the game.

"The more I played, the more it hurt," said Frazier, who missed eight games of 1994 with blood clots in his leg. NU medical officials assured fans and the media that this was not blood-clot related.

Everyone breathed easier, except maybe the Huskers while reviewing how they played against Kansas.

"I don't know that we came out and played flat," said Tomich. "They were just really pumped up. It took the offense a little time to get moving, but once we got started, we played real well."

"Kansas played well," Osborne said. "I think they were more intense and excited than we were. We got better throughout the game. Kansas is very sound. They hung together and I didn't think they got tired."

"We didn't have a terrible game, but we did not have the yards production and the points," added offensive line coach Milt Tenopir. "Part of that was that we didn't execute. I also think Kansas did a good job of keeping the ball, but our defense kept them out of the end zone.

N
HUSKERS
18
16
adidas

(Left) Berringer (18) pivots away from Kansas defender Keith Rodgers (16), who had eight tackles for KU.

(Right) Nebraska fullback Jeff Makovicka (22) stiff-arms a Jayhawk as the Huskers grind out tough rushing yards.

Game 10 Statistics

	1st Quarter	2nd Quarter	3rd Quarter	4th Quarter	Final
Nebraska	**14**	**0**	**14**	**13**	**41**
Kansas	**0**	**3**	**0**	**0**	**3**

FIRST QUARTER
NU-Vedral recovered fumbled punt in end zone (Brown kick), 9:17.
NU-Frazier 1-yard run (Brown kick), 1:17.

SECOND QUARTER
KU-McCord 19-yard field goal, 11:23.

THIRD QUARTER
NU-Jackson 1-yard pass from Frazier (Brown kick), 11:57.
NU-Phillips 6-yard run (Brown kick), 4:04.

FOURTH QUARTER
NU-Frazier 5-yard run (Brown kick), 13:46.
NU-Fullman 86-yard interception return, (kick failed), 6:56

TEAM STATISTICS

	NU	KU
First downs	20	25
Rushing att.-yards	51-289	32-72
Passes	15-10-1	50-30-3
Passing yards	86	273
Total att.-yards	66-375	82-345
Returns-yards	4-108	1-19
Sacks by	2-9	0
Punts-average	3-41.7	4-33.3
Fumbles-lost	2-0	2-0
Penalties-yards	2-20	5-42
Time of poss.	28:36	31:24

INDIVIDUAL LEADERS

RUSHING:
NU: Frazier 10-99-2; Phillips 10-47-1; Green 10-45-0;
KU: Levine 13-47-0; Vann 8-40-0; Henley 7-14-0.

PASSING:
NU: Frazier 15-10-1, 86.
KU: Williams 45-27-2, 242.

RECEIVING:
NU: Johnson 4-50-0; Jackson 2-13-1; Holbein 1-14-0.
KU: Byrd 6-71-0; Levine 9-51-0; Smith 6-48-0.

INTERCEPTIONS:
NU: Fullman 1-86-1; Ellis 1-11-0; Williams 1-11-0;
KU: Gaddie 1-19-0.

TACKLES (UT-AT-TT):
NU: Williams 6-4-10; Booker 4-5-9; Farley 3-6-9; Colman 3-4-7; Minter 2-5-7.
KU: Thoren 3-9-12; Houston 3-6-9; Rodgers 2-6-8.

SACKS:
NU: Tomich 1-3; C. Peter 1-6.
KU: None

Nebraska 37
Oklahoma 0

November 24, 1995 - Memorial Stadium

What a fitting end to the Big Eight Conference. Oklahoma and Nebraska — the traditional rivals whose encounters so often decided the league championship. These were the teams that played some of the most memorable games in college football history while trying to lay claim to being the biggest "Big Red" in the land.

These two opponents had won or shared the Big Eight title every year from 1962 to 1988. Nebraska won the last four championships coming into the 1995 season. And now, the 10-0 Huskers also had clinched a fifth-straight title and the last Big Eight trophy. The Big Eight would expand to the Big 12 in 1996 and divisional play already meant OU versus NU would no longer be the traditional season finale.

The current Sooners (5-4-1), admittedly, were struggling, but this was still Oklahoma and Nebraska; records meant nothing. It has been that way with the two teams since the late 1950s. In the last 31 meetings, the winning team had come from behind 24 times.

Unranked Oklahoma teams had beaten ranked Nebraska teams three times in the Devaney-Osborne era, including 1990.

Most college football historians would call the 1971 game, won by No. 1 Nebraska over No. 2 Oklahoma 35-31, the best ever played.

Seldom did it matter who had the top billing in these head-knocking contests. Second-ranked Oklahoma upset No. 1 Nebraska 17-7 in 1987 and it was Nebraska that ended Sooner coach Bud Wilkinson's amazing string of 36 straight wins in 1959.

It was coach Tom Osborne who had the string going this time. The unbeaten defending national champions had not lost since the January 1994 Orange Bowl against top-ranked Florida State.

(Above) The Huskers come out fired up for the Oklahoma game, the last meeting of the rivals as Big Eight members: This was history.
(Right) Sooner quarterbacks never had a chance against the swarming Husker defense led by Jared Tomich (93) and Jason Peter (95).

95
TOMICH

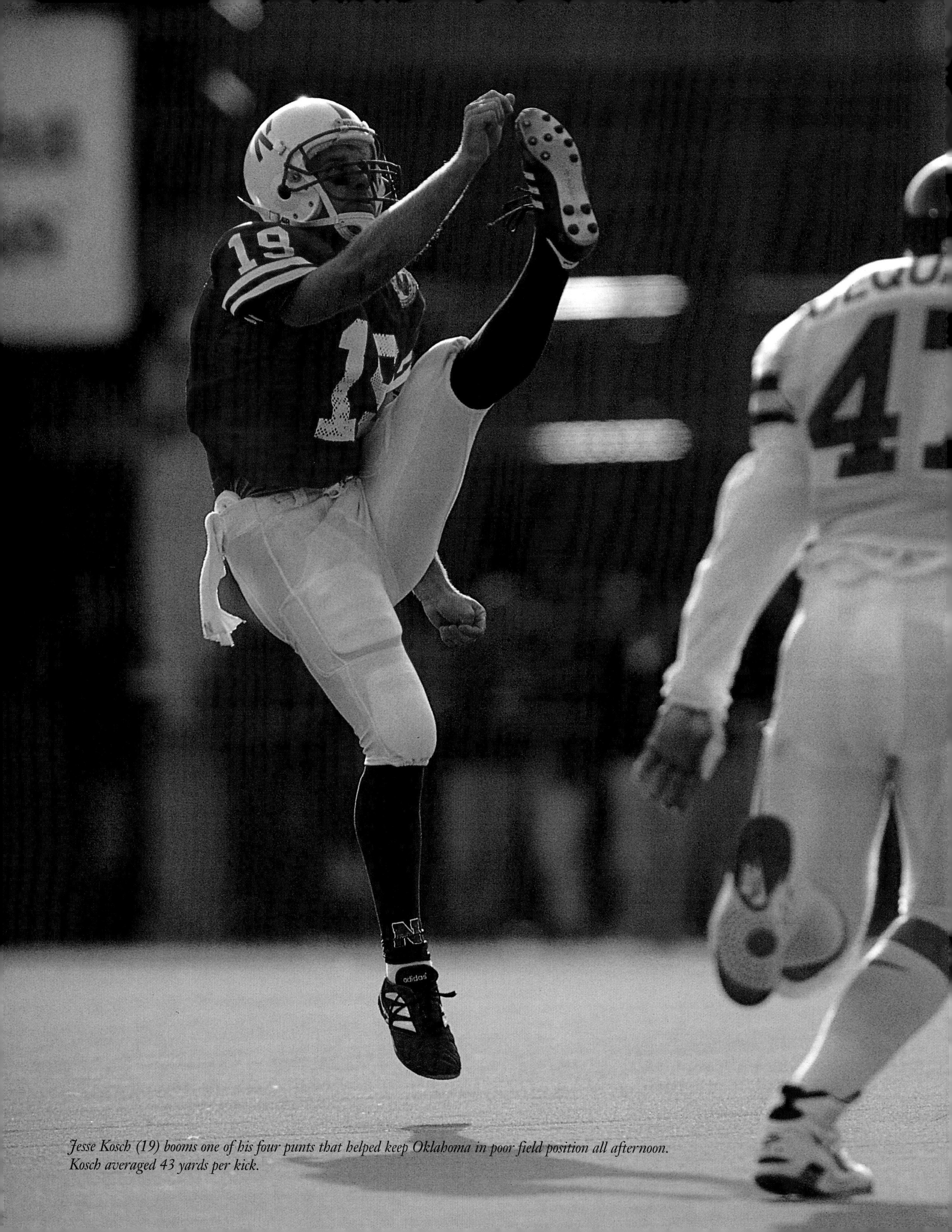

Jesse Kosch (19) booms one of his four punts that helped keep Oklahoma in poor field position all afternoon. Kosch averaged 43 yards per kick.

The Huskers were 33-point favorites for this game, a spread that made even Osborne gasp.

"Oklahoma is Oklahoma," NU linebacker Phil Ellis said. "It's something special to both teams, and point spreads don't matter."

The point spread, no doubt, took into consideration the struggles of OU under first-year coach Howard Schnellenberger. The Sooners had lost three of their previous four games before coming to Lincoln, had scored just 10 points in the last two games and were shut out in a 12-0 loss to Oklahoma State.

No doubt the odds makers also took into consideration what this game meant to Nebraska. It was the last in a series of hurdles to clear to gain a spot in the Fiesta Bowl on Jan. 2 and play in a third-straight national championship game. It was the final Big Eight game and the final home game for 22 seniors.

It also was what could be called payback time for Schnellenberger. It was, after all, Schnellenberger who stole Osborne's first and best chance for a national championship in the 1984 Orange Bowl.

In that game, Schnellenberger's Miami Hurricanes upset the powerhouse Huskers — with Turner Gill, Heisman Trophy winner Mike Rozier and All-Americans Irving Fryar and Dean Steinkuhler — by the score of 31-30 when Gill's two-point conversion pass attempt was tipped away from I-back Jeff Smith with 48 seconds to play.

Jared Tomich closes in on Sooner quarterback Garrick McGee. The All-America Husker managed two sacks on the day.

Schnellenberger had a gifted quarterback named Bernie Kosar then. He would start freshman Eric Moore now. And Nebraska owned a defense that was much better than the 1983 Blackshirts. Kosar would have had trouble throwing against these guys.

Oklahoma had a great defense, too. Osborne said it was the best front seven players his team would play all season. That meant the Nebraska running game, averaging a nation-leading 412.7 yards per game, would have its hands full with a Sooner defense against the rush that was ranked fifth nationally with a 92.9-yard allowance.

The going was tough on the early Nebraska possessions. The offense could manage only a 31-yard field goal by freshman Kris Brown in the first quarter. But linebacker Jamel Williams added a defensive touchdown for Nebraska when he picked off a Moore pass in the flat and raced 36 yards to score.

Brown would get another field goal just before halftime when he booted one 27 yards with one second left on the clock.

Nebraska's offense had not scored a touchdown in the first half for a second-straight year against the Sooners. Nevertheless, the Blackshirts were overpowering. By halftime, Oklahoma had minus 7 yards rushing, 125 yards passing, two turnovers and just three snaps in Nebraska territory.

Nebraska's offense managed only 134 yards rushing and 77 passing without a turnover.

"We knew the strongest part of Oklahoma's team was their defense," Osborne said. "So offensively we knew there would be a lot of second-and-eights and third-and-sixes early in the game."

All-America center Aaron Graham said the Sooner's speed was too much to handle. The OU linebackers were flying.

"Ordinarily, myself or one of our tackles is able to cut off a linebacker flowing to the option," Graham said. "But there was no way in heck we were able to catch them. Tommie Frazier and Lawrence Phillips wouldn't have been able to catch them, either."

"I thought we played our hearts out," said Sooner defensive tackle Martin Chase. "We showed the country that we have a real good defense. We showed we could play with Nebraska. They got a lot of breaks and took advantage of them."

Oklahoma, which had five punts and two interceptions to end seven first-half possessions, didn't do much more offensively the second half. It was three plays, a penalty and punt on the first possession after intermission.

But Nebraska gave the ball right back when Frazier threw an interception for the second time in two games.

The Sooners moved to the Nebraska 46 in three plays before NU outside linebacker Jared Tomich stripped the ball from James Allen and Husker safety Tony Veland scooped up the fumble and raced 57 yards for a touchdown.

The Peter brothers - Christian (55) and Jason (95) - stopped everything the Sooners tried up the middle. OU managed just 51 yards rushing.

It was the eighth defensive touchdown for Nebraska this season and second of the game. Only one other time had a Blackshirt defense scored twice during one game in Osborne's 23-year era.

"I wanted to go out with a bang," said Veland, a senior from Omaha, "and I guess I did. They had a little momentum going there, but that put them in a big hole."

The score was 20-0 and the Sooners still had not seriously threatened to score. Even a 13-play drive on the next possession could get OU only to the 45 yard line before it had to punt.

"I really never felt we were going to get beat," Osborne said. "But it took a lot of pressure off to go ahead 20-0. The way they were moving the ball, it didn't look like 20 points was something they were going to be able to overcome."

Brown added another field goal, this time from 35 yards out, to make it a 23-0 game heading to the fourth quarter.

Nebraska opened the fourth quarter with a drive that featured Jeff Makovicka and Clinton Childs hammering the middle. Then Frazier found wingback Jon Vedral between two defensive backs for a 38-yard TD pass play.

The Sooners' best chance to score came a few minutes later when an exchange of punts allowed Oklahoma to start a drive from its own 40 yard line, its best field position of the game. Garrick McGee and Jerald Moore scrambled and ran to the Nebraska 20 but the Huskers' Grant Wistrom stuffed Allen on a fourth-and-one play and NU took over on downs.

Brook Berringer came in at quarterback for the Huskers and marched the team back down the field. He scrambled on a fourth-and-long to pick up a first down at the 17. From there, Joel Makovicka, the freshman backup to junior brother Jeff at fullback, broke three tackles and found the end zone.

The touchdown broke Nebraska's own Big Eight record with a scoring average of 52.479 points per game. The 1983 Huskers averaged 52.089 in 12 games.

But the offense had struggled against Oklahoma. Nebraska finished with 271 rushing yards on 56 attempts, and added 136 yards through the air. The Husker offense also didn't score until the fourth quarter.

It didn't matter though; the Nebraska defense scored twice and held OU to 241 total yards, including only 51 on the ground.

"Sometimes the offense carries us, but I thought we did a pretty good job," defensive tackle Christian Peter said. "I think we've showed throughout the year that we have a great offense, but we also have a great defense."

It was the first Nebraska shutout of Oklahoma since 1942. The Sooners helped with three turnovers and 97 yards in penalties.

"We're our own worst enemy," Schnellenberger said. "If it isn't throwing interceptions and fumbling, it's penalties."

If Nebraskans felt disappointed in the outcome of the game, it was probably for Frazier. He was in the Heisman Trophy running against Ohio State running back Eddie George and Florida quarterback Danny Wuerffel but didn't have a great game in his regular-season finale on national television.

Frazier finished the game with 35 yards rushing on 10 carries and 12-of-25 passing for 128 yards and a touchdown. He also threw one interception.

"I don't know if it hurt me, but right now I really don't care about that," said Frazier, who improved to 32-3 as a starter at Nebraska.

"I didn't think he was pressing," Osborne said. "He had people in his face a couple of times. On the interception, he couldn't see where he was throwing. I will say that if you look at four years in productivity and results, the guy has produced. He's a great player."

"I don't think I played a bad game," Frazier said. "I did everything I normally do. It's just that things didn't fall into the right places for me today. They were doing some things that caught us off guard. They were shifting around up front a lot."

The record books still will show Frazier with school career records for 5,476 yards of total offense, 43 passing touchdowns and 32 victories as the starting quarterback. He also had 36 career rushing touchdowns.

He ended the regular season completing 56.4 percent of his passes for 1,362 yards and 17 touchdowns. He also ran for a team-leading 14 TDs.

Freshman I-back Ahman Green also added 44 yards to his school freshman rushing record to end the season with 1,086, which was 41 yards short of the Big Eight freshman record set by Kansas' June Henley in 1993.

Freshman kicker Brown scored 13 points against OU to finish with a school freshman scoring record 97 points, one better than Green. The 97 points by Brown also was a season record for kick-scoring at the school.

Tommie Frazier (15) gets some downfield blocking help, as the Sooners' Broderick Simpson (51) tries to stop the quarterback's progress. OU played well defensively, limiting Frazier to just 35 rushing yards.

(Top) Jason Peter (95) rushes OU quarterback Garrick McGee (8). This kind of pressure helped Nebraska limit OU to 51 yards rushing and 16-of-31 passing with two interceptions.

(Right) Phil Ellis (41) wraps around Sooner rushing star Jerald Moore for a tackle. Moore managed just 39 yards on 14 carries against the inspired Blackshirts.

Mike Fullman (12) darts back with a punt against the Sooners. The Huskers had 225 yards on 10 returns in the contest, showing new scoring potential for Nebraska's kick return game.

Game 11 Statistics

	1st Quarter	2nd Quarter	3rd Quarter	4th Quarter	Final
Oklahoma	0	0	0	0	0
Nebraska	10	3	10	14	37

FIRST QUARTER
NU-Brown 31-yard field goal, 10:44.
NU-J. Williams 36-yard interception return (Brown kick), 8:36.

SECOND QUARTER
NU-Brown 27-yard field goal, :01.

THIRD QUARTER
NU-Veland 57-yard fumble return, (Brown kick), 7:41.
NU-Brown 35-yard field goal, :28.

FOURTH QUARTER
NU-Vedral 38-yard pass from Frazier, (Brown kick), 14:12.
NU-Jo. Makovicka 17-yard run (Brown kick), :44.

TEAM STATISTICS

	OU	NU
First downs	12	26
Rushing att.-yards	30-51	56-271
Passes	34-16-2	27-13-1
Passing yards	190	136
Total att.-yards	64-241	83-407
Returns-yards	2-16	10-225
Sacks by	0	2-15
Punts-average	10-41.7	4-43.0
Fumbles-lost	3-1	4-1
Penalties-yards	9-97	3-24
Time of poss.	27:14	32:46

INDIVIDUAL LEADERS

RUSHING:
OU: Moore 14-39-0; Allen 7-19-0; McGee 5-18-0.
NU: Phillips 15-73-0; Jo. Makovicka 4-45-1; Green 13-44-0; Frazier 10-35-0.

PASSING:
OU: McGee 30-15-1, 159.
NU: Frazier 25-12-1, 128.

RECEIVING:
OU: Alexander 6-71-0; Mills 4-76-0; Penny 3-27-0.
NU: Baul 4-38-0; Holbein 2-20-0; Johnson 2-19-0.

INTERCEPTIONS:
OU: Bush 1-16-0.
NU: J. Williams 1-36-1; Booker 1-22-0.

TACKLES (UT-AT-TT):
OU: Wesley 6-8-14; Peters 9-4-13; Fogle 2-7-9.
NU: Veland 5-2-7; Wistrom 4-2-6; Minter 3-3-6; Tomich 2-4-6; Farley 2-4-6.

SACKS:
OU: None.
NU: Tomich 2-15.

Nebraska 62
Florida 24

January 2, 1996 — At Tempe Arizona

Tommie Frazier met the press three days before the Tostitos Fiesta Bowl game, his last as a Nebraska football player. His arrival in the ballroom at the Tempe Mission Palms Hotel drew a majority of the print and electronic reporters assembled in the room. It was as if he were someone with game tickets on the 50-yard line to sell at face value or less and they were fans who had come to the Valley of the Sun without a means of admission to the "Duel in the Desert" for the national championship.

Within seconds of entering the room, Frazier was surrounded. Frank Solich, the Huskers assistant head coach and running backs coach, spoke from the podium at the front of the room to a handful of newspaper reporters spread among several dozen chairs. Frazier's teammates Aaron Taylor, Clester Johnson and Ahman Green were left only with small groups in other parts of the room.

By then, Frazier had answered every conceivable question, several times. But that didn't stop reporters driven by a need to file stories about the dream matchup of No. 1 Nebraska and No. 2 Florida. Frazier was cooperative enough. He answered every question with a patience born of four seasons in the media spotlight.

Earlier, Florida quarterback Danny Wuerffel, the nation's most efficient passer, told reporters that he would surprise a lot of people if he were playing in an option offense and that Frazier would surprise a lot of people if he were asked to be a dropback passer. Wuerffel's point was that, both he and Frazier had the skills to be successful quarterbacks regardless of the system in which they performed.

"Do you think that's right?" a reporter asked Frazier.

The question was much longer than Frazier's answer.

(Above) During this pre-Fiesta Bowl meeting of the coaches, Florida's Steve Spurrier does most of the talking, no doubt about Osborne's running game. (Right) Husker defender Michael Booker concentrates on coverage in one of his best career games. He had a TD interception and three breakups that day.

Stopping the run was Nebraska's first priority. Jared Tomich (93) closes on this tackle, helping the Gators net a minus 28 yards for the day.

"Yes," he said.

There was silence as Frazier looked at the reporter and shrugged. Next question.

"Is the I-back situation the same as the quarterback situation last year?" another reporter asked.

"No," Frazier said. He paused, then added: "What was the quarterback situation last year?"

Frazier's interest was clearly elsewhere.

His focus was the game three nights later. Check that: THE GAME. Nebraska, the defending national champion, was 11-0 and riding a 24-game winning streak dating back to the 1994 Orange Bowl game. Except for an 18-16 loss to Florida State, the Huskers would have been playing for a third-consecutive national title. Florida was 12-0 after winning a third-consecutive Southeastern Conference championship. The teams had been brought together by the Bowl Alliance, without which Nebraska would have been in Miami to play in the Orange Bowl for the fifth year in a row and Florida would have been in New Orleans representing the SEC in the Sugar Bowl.

Another reporter, grasping for an angle, pointed out to Frazier that the Huskers' national championship the previous season, capped by a dramatic 24-17 victory against Miami, was fashioned with emotion that carried over from the near-miss in 1993. Nebraska had a mission, some unfinished business, in 1994. The Huskers didn't have any business to finish on the night of Jan. 2, 1996.

"The makeup (of this team) is different," Frazier said. "But we're still on a mission."

A little more than 72 hours later, no one would have disputed that. By then, Tom Osborne was calling the 1995 Huskers the best in his 23 years as head coach. "This is the most complete team I've coached," he said during a news conference on the morning after the game.

Confident and ready, the Huskers gather to thunder into Sun Devil Stadium for an impressive show.

HUSKERS

CELEBRATING NEBRASKA'S 27TH CONSECUTIVE BOWL GAME

Tostitos BRAND

FIESTA BOWL

NEBRASKA vs. FLORIDA
JAN. 2, 1996
TEMPE, ARIZONA

CELEBRATING A TRADITION
BIG EIGHT
CONFERENCE
1907-1996

Perfect 11-0 1995 Season • NCAA Record 35-1 Last Three Years • Fifth Consecutive Big Eight Championship

TOMMIE FRAZIER

Johnny Unitas Golden Arm Award Winner • Heisman Trophy Runner-Up • Davey O'Brien Finalist • Maxwell Award Finalist • Walter Camp Offensive Player-of-the-Year Finalist • UPI Player-of-the Year • ESPY Awards College Football Player-of-the-Year • TD Club of Columbus Quarterback-of-the-Year • Football News Offensive Player-of-the-Year Finalist •

Johnny Unitas
Golden Arm Award
Tommie Frazier

Oh yes, the game: Nebraska won it 62-24. In the context of its month-long buildup, THE GAME was much ado about nothing. It turned out to be, simply, the game.

What the Huskers did to Florida was not to be believed. They so overwhelmed what almost certainly was a worthy opponent with a 29-0 second quarter that Gator fans began leaving Sun Devil Stadium soon after the halftime show. By game's end, the stadium was awash in red.

Actually, red was the color of choice from the opening kick-off. Nebraska fans comprised well over half a Fiesta Bowl-record crowd of 79,864. It wasn't the same as playing at Memorial Stadium in Lincoln, where the Huskers' NCAA-record string of sellouts is 208. But it must have seemed close for a program that had been matched against Florida State or Miami in four straight Orange Bowl games.

Florida was as good or better than any of the Florida State and Miami teams. "This is as good a team as we've played in a bowl game since I've been here," Nebraska defensive coordinator Charlie McBride said of the Gators, who overwhelmed opponents with the nation's second-ranked passing offense, nicknamed the "Fun 'n Gun." Coach Steve Spurrier's team averaged 44.5 points and 534.4 yards (including 360.8 through the air) per game. Wuerffel passed for 3,266 yards and 35 touchdowns with only 10 interceptions. Florida's offense was so efficient that Spurrier didn't even use Wuerffel in a 58-20 non-conference victory against Northern Illinois in the eighth game of the season.

Danny Wuerffel (7) couldn't escape the Husker pass rush as Terrell Farley (43) gets his sack.

Eric Kresser, Wuerffel's back-up and also a junior, passed for 458 yards and six touchdowns, causing some people to suggest that Wuerffel was merely a product of an offensive system.

McBride disagreed, comparing Wuerffel to the best quarter-

Even Nebraska's freshman backups were too much for the Gators. Mike Rucker (84) makes the stop before Chad Kelsay (57) can get there.

15

The Husker defensive line never gave Florida a chance to go forward.

backs Nebraska had faced in his 19 seasons as a Husker assistant. Such a group is select. Among those it has included are Troy Aikman, Chad May, Scott Mitchell and Heisman Trophy winners Gino Torretta and Charlie Ward.

Wuerffel finished third in voting for the Heisman Trophy in 1995. Frazier was second to Ohio State's Eddie George. The ballots were counted a month before the bowls. If Frazier's performance against Florida had been included, Nebraska probably would have had its third Heisman winner.

Frazier's play was the linchpin in the 38-point victory, which is why he was chosen as the game's outstanding offensive performer by CBS television. And his 75-yard touchdown run on the final play from scrimmage in the third quarter dramatically underscored his extraordinary skills.

Nebraska was second-and-five at its own 25-yard line. Fans in Florida blue and orange continued to filter through the stadium exits, the first step in what, for most, would be a long journey home. With about 18 seconds remaining on the game clock, Frazier took the snap from center Aaron Graham.

Frazier faked a handoff to fullback Brian Schuster, who blocked a defender assigned to keep Frazier from getting to the outside. Schuster pushed the Gator toward the sideline.

As he cut behind Schuster's block, it appeared as though Frazier might pitch the ball to I-back Clinton Childs, but only for a split second. Two defenders tried unsuccessfully to pull Frazier down by his jersey, but they were left clutching at the cool desert air. Frazier faked a defender near his own 35-yard line as five Gators converged each with a shot at bringing him down, including four at once.

Gator Terry Jackson (22) finds no hole as Huskers Terrell Farley (43) and Jason Peter (95) snuff the play.

Ben Hanks and Lawrence Wright appeared to have the best chance of stopping him but couldn't.

Husker guard Jon Zatechka smashed into the clutter from behind in an attempt to boost Frazier along. Childs also tried to help extricate Frazier. But mostly, he did it on his own through force of will.

Suddenly, Frazier was free again and heading south. Florida's Fred Weary was the last to get his hands on Frazier, near the Nebraska 45-yard line. But, like everyone else, his effort was in vain.

The Gators seemed to be in a state of denial following the game.

"We had guys trying to strip the ball and make things happen," said Hanks, a senior nickelback and defensive co-captain. "When we weren't able to do that, he broke some tackles."

The official play-by-play sheet credited Frazier with breaking seven tackles during the first 20 yards of his remarkable run. Husker defensive tackle and co-captain Christian Peter, who watched from the sideline, disputed that total. "There were 11 of them," he said. "I counted them all."

Senior Clinton Childs (26) pulls in the ball and heads up field, averaging 26 yards plus on three kickoff returns.

Frazier was typically low-key. "I don't know how many guys [there were] or whether they were trying to take the ball." They kept contacting me, but I kept my legs going, he said. I felt them trying to take the ball. Next thing you know, I just came out the other end."

Apparently, Florida's defenders were, at least in part, victims of misinformation. "We knew we were going to have a tough time stopping (Lawrence) Phillips," Hanks said, "but I think we were surprised by the toughness of Frazier. He showed me and our team that he's a guy with a lot of character."

The touchdown, Frazier's second of the game, and Kris Brown's extra-point kick increased the lead to 49-18. Even though Florida had just scored its second touchdown and added a two-point conversion, the game's outcome had long since been determined, and the suspense was gone. But it provided an appropriate exclamation point, not only to the game but also to Frazier's extraordinary career at Nebraska.

A couple of hours earlier, no one imagined the second half would be nothing more than window dressing for a lopsided Husker victory. In the days before the game, there was considerable discussion about a tie-breaker instituted for bowls — and used in the Las Vegas Bowl.

The Fiesta Bowl game very well might be decided by that.

The first quarter didn't change such an opinion. Florida took the opening kickoff and drove to a first-and-goal at the Husker 5-yard line before settling for a 23-yard field goal by Bart Edmiston. Seven of the 10 plays preceding Edmiston's kick were Wuerffel passes. Four were complete.

Florida's scoring drive was impressive. But there were indications of what was to come.

On the second play from scrimmage, Nebraska linebacker Terrell Farley deflected a Wuerffel pass and nearly caught the ball for an interception. Two plays later, Husker outside linebacker Jared Tomich tackled Wuerffel for a 4-yard loss, the first of seven sacks by Nebraska's Blackshirts. And the Gators gained nothing on three downs from the 5-yard line before settling for the field goal.

"We felt good about the first (defensive) series," said Nebraska middle linebacker and co-captain Phil Ellis, who was credited with six tackles, three of them unassisted.

Limiting Florida to three points "was a big boost for the defense," he said.

The Huskers needed only six plays to cover 52 yards and take the lead on a 16-yard pass play from Frazier to Phillips, who was starting at I-back for the first time after serving an Osborne-imposed, six-game suspension resulting from some much-publicized, off-the-field problems.

The extra-point kick was deflected and Nebraska led 6-3.

The Gators regained the lead with a 10-play, 54-yard touchdown drive that began after Frazier threw an interception on a third-and-12 at the Florida 34. The big plays in the drive were two passes from Wuerffel to wide receiver Reidel Anthony, good for a combined 40 yards. Wuerffel finished the drive by extending the ball over the goal line from one yard out despite being stopped short himself. Edmiston added the extra-point kick. With 1:17 remaining in the first quarter, Florida led 10-6. The question was: Could the Huskers keep up? The answer was: Yes.

Nebraska was well on its way to taking the lead for good when the first quarter ended. On the second play of the second quarter, Phillips broke off right guard and ran 42 yards for his second touchdown. Brown kicked the extra point to make the score 13-10, Huskers. Service Florida.

(Right) Tommie Frazier (15), made all the right moves again. Frazier (15) and Phillips (1), combining for 364 yards, ran almost at will against Florida behind the NU line.

After two penalties, the Gators faced first-and-28 at their own 4-yard line. Farley, who made a team-high eight tackles, including two sacks, burst through the line and pulled down Wuerffel for what appeared to be a safety. The officials, however, ruled that Wuerffel had gotten the ball out of the end zone, delaying the inevitable until second down, when an untouched Jamel Williams tackled Wuerffel to score the safety.

Nebraska led 15-10. The race, and rout, was on. The Huskers took Florida's free kick and drove 51 yards on seven plays for their third touchdown, scored by I-back Ahman Green on a 1-yard run. The key play in the drive was a 32-yard run by Frazier on third-and-7 at the Florida 48-yard line.

Time and again, Frazier frustrated Florida with such plays, beginning with the Huskers' first possession when he gained 4 yards on a third-and-2 at the Gators' 20-yard line.

"Tommie Frazier: he's a big, big factor," said Ellis.

On Nebraska's next possession, Frazier converted a fourth-and-1 from the Florida 32, set up by a 7-yard pass to wingback Clester Johnson. The drive culminated in the first of two Kris Brown field goals, this one from 26 yards. With 3:46 left in the first half, the Huskers were at 25 and counting.

"There was a point in time, maybe the second quarter or so, when they weren't flying around like they had been," said Nebraska center and co-captain Aaron Graham. "In order to defense our offense, you've got to be flying up the field. It's a no-win situation. Coach Osborne has such a great scheme."

The Husker defense continued to fly around, however, disguising blitzes and coverages and generally frustrating Wuerffel, who had seemed unflappable before the game. "I think we had him flustered," Ellis said. "I was up there eye-to-eye. He was wide-eyed. That was good. That was the plan. I think some of their offensive players were acting a little gun-shy after a while."

Any doubt that Nebraska had the game in-hand was eliminated barely a minute after Brown's field goal. On first-and-10 from his own 30-yard line, Wuerffel threw a pass that was intercepted by Husker cornerback Michael Booker and returned 42 yards for yet another touchdown.

"I must say, that was an ugly pass. No spiral on it," said Booker, who was selected as the game's outstanding defensive player by CBS television. "They came out there with a game plan to pick on me. Probably 70 percent of the passes came my way the first half."

In addition to his interception, one of three by the Huskers, Booker deflected three passes and made four tackles. Picking on Booker proved to be one of many miscalculations.

Before the game, the Gators "were doing their little choo-choo thing, like they were going to run over us," Booker said. "After the game started, they stopped the trash talking.

15
RODGERS
54

Lawrence Phillips (1) finds a way to advance from a big block by tackle Eric Anderson (70). He burned the Gators for 165 yards, two touchdowns on the ground and one from a pass reception. Nebraska's front line opened wide running lanes like this all game.

(Below) A touchdown celebration after Tommie Frazier's early game swing pass results in the first of Phillips' three end zone visits.

"They came and talked the game. We played it."

Florida, which had averaged 534.4 yards per game during the regular season to rank No. 4 in Division I-A of the NCAA, was limited to a season-low 269 total yards. The Gators finished with a net of minus-28 rushing yards, the second-lowest total in school history. In marked contrast, Nebraska gained 629 total yards, including 524 on the ground, the Huskers' fourth-highest total of the season.

Frazier rushed for 199 yards, the most by a quarterback in Nebraska history. Phillips finished with 165 yards and two touchdowns rushing on 25 carries. The Huskers' previous best rushing total in a bowl game was 147 by Heisman Trophy winner Mike Rozier in the 1984 Orange Bowl.

The last Nebraska ball carrier to rush for 100 or more yards in a bowl game was I-back Doug DuBose, who gained 102 yards on 20 carries in a 28-10 victory against LSU in the 1985 Sugar Bowl.

"I knew we were going to run the ball a lot and try to run them down. Basically, that's what happened," said Phillips, whose second rushing touchdown came on a 15-yard run in the fourth quarter.

"I think they just got tired of getting cut and blocked. We kind of wore them down."

Michael Booker's touchdown and Brown's extra-point kick didn't finish the first-half scoring. The Huskers got the ball one more time before the intermission and turned the possession into an eight-play, 59-yard drive that took just over a minute, culminating in a 24-yard Brown field goal with eight seconds left in the half.

The halftime score was 35-10. Even so, Nebraska's defense didn't relax. "We had watched a lot of the Tennessee-Florida game (on film)," Ellis said. "We knew what we were up against."

Florida rallied from a first-half deficit of 30-14 to defeat Tennessee 62-37. The Gators scored 48 unanswered points during that game. The Blackshirts were determined to prevent a repeat.

Any thought that Florida would rally in the second half was quickly dispelled. Nebraska took the kickoff and drove to the Gators' 15-yard line before an injudicious pass by Frazier was intercepted. Less than four minutes later, the Huskers' Eric Stokes returned the favor by intercepting a pass from Wuerffel.

Nebraska needed just six plays, two of them carries by Frazier, to make the Gators pay for the error in judgment. The first carry initiated the series and produced an 11-yard gain. The second concluded as Frazier ran right through the heart of the Florida defense on a quarterback draw for 35 yards and his first rushing touchdown.

The Gators responded with a touchdown of their own just 2 minutes and 20 seconds later, after Wuerffel had teamed with Ike Hilliard on a 35-yard touchdown pass.

The Huskers scored two touchdowns in the fourth quarter on runs by Phillips and Brook Berringer, Frazier's back-up. Florida managed one, on Anthony's 93-yard kickoff return.

Nebraska almost scored a ninth touchdown in the closing seconds when James Sims, the No. 5 I-back, broke a 32-yard run to the Florida 1-yard line. But third-string quarterback Matt Turman dropped to one knee after taking the center snap as time expired. The Huskers had made their point(s).

Unlike the previous season, when Penn State also finished undefeated and untied, and tried to lay claim to the national championship, Nebraska's repeat title was unquestioned. The vote in both the Associated Press and USA Today/CNN polls was unanimous. The Huskers again were the best in the nation in a conference that could claim a similar distinction. In the final season of its existence, the Big Eight placed four teams in the final Top 10. Colorado, Kansas State and Kansas were the others.

Osborne noted that the conference was as strong as it had been since 1971 when Nebraska, Oklahoma and Colorado finished first, second and third, respectively, in the final AP rankings.

In winning a second national championship, "there's not nearly as much emotion," said Osborne. "There's not the newness of it

Brenden Holbein (5), running away from the Gators on a 33-yard pass play, sets up a 24-yard field goal just before the half.

this year." Even so, a rally for the team at the Bob Devaney Sports Center on the day after the Fiesta Bowl victory drew an estimated 8,000 fans — not bad, considering it was a work day.

"We were supposed to do this," Osborne said. "People expected it. I'm sure in five years or 10 years, the players will look back and have a better sense of what they did."

What the Huskers did was win 12 games, none of which were particularly close. Florida had taken heart in the fact that Nebraska's smallest margin of victory, 14 points, had come at home in a non-conference game against Washington State. The Cougars were pass-oriented.

The Gators thought their passing attack might be too sophisticated for Nebraska and that their speed, particularly at wide receiver, would be too much to handle with man-to-man coverage.

"They all feel we can't run with them," said George Darlington, Nebraska's secondary coach. "But quite frankly, I thought Colorado had more speed than Florida. We knew we had seen it before."

On the other side of the field, Spurrier had never seen anything quite like the Huskers. "I'm really embarrassed that we couldn't match up with Nebraska," he said afterward. "They're too good for us.

"That's all you can say. They clobbered us up and down the field, about everywhere. They're by far the best team I think we've played in the six years I've been at Florida. I don't have any answers. As coaches, we did a lousy job (of preparing), somehow or another. But we were outmatched."

Immediately after the game, with Nebraska fans trying to surge onto the field, Sheldon Jackson, a reserve tight end, took a large red flag with a white "N" on it and ran a partial victory lap.

A large group, which included Osborne and his wife, Nancy, stood on a podium near mid-field for the trophy presentations. While Frazier received the trophy as the game's outstanding offensive player, his 75-yard touchdown run was replayed for all to see on a massive videoscreen.

The crowd chanted: "Frazier, Frazier, Frazier."

The Huskers were no more friendly to Florida's Eric Kresser (10) than to Danny Wuerffel (above). The Gators were sacked seven times and seldom threw without pressure.

Congratulations are in order. Frazier (15), rushing 199 yards for two TDs and passing for 105 yards for a third, earned his third-straight bowl Most Valuable Player award.

The Fiesta Bowl Statistics

	1st Quarter	2nd Quarter	3rd Quarter	4th Quarter	Final
Florida	10	0	8	6	24
Nebraska	6	29	14	13	62

FIRST QUARTER
UF-Edmiston 23-yard field goal, 11:06.
NU-Phillips 16-yard pass (kick blocked), 8:10.
UF-Wuerffel 1-yard run (Edmiston kick), 1:17.

SECOND QUARTER
NU-Phillips 42-yard run (Brown kick), 14:28.
NU-Williams sacks Wuerffel for safety, 12:42.
NU-Green 1-yard run (Brown kick), 9:13.
NU-Brown 26-yard field goal, 3:46.
NU-Booker 42-yard interception return (Brown kick), 2:40.
NU-Brown 24-yard field goal, 0:08.

THIRD QUARTER
NU-Frazier 35-yard run (Brown kick), 2:21.
UF-Hillard 35-yard pass from Wuerffel (conversion pass good) 0:52.
NU-Frazier 75-yard run (Brown kick), 0:01.

FOURTH QUARTER
NU-Phillips 15-yard run (kick blocked), 8:25.
NU-Berringer 1-yard run (Retzlaff kick), 4:44.
UF-Anthony 93 yard kickoff return, (conversion failed) 4:31.

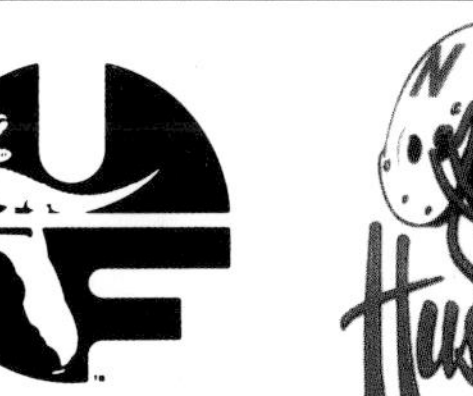

TEAM STATISTICS

	UF	NU
First downs	15	27
Rushing att.-yards	21-(-28)	68-524
Passes	38-20-3	15-6-2
Passing yards	297	105
Total att.-yards	59-269	83-629
Returns-yards	11-260	9-102
Sacks by	7-40	0-0
Punts-average	4-41.3	1-36
Fumbles-lost	1-1	1-0
Penalties-yards	9-78	4-30
Time of poss.	24:43	35:17

INDIVIDUAL LEADERS

RUSHING:
UF: Williams 6-6-0; Jackson 4-4-0; Anthony 2-(-1)-0; Wuerffel 9-(-37)-0.
NU: Frazier 16-199-2; Phillips 25-165-2; Green 9-68-1; Sims 2-35-0; Je. Makovicka 6-32-0; Childs 3-14-0; Schuster 1-4-0; Jo. Makovicka 2-4-0; Benning 1-3-0; Berringer 1-1-0; Legate 1-1-0; Turman 1-(-2)-0.

PASSING:
UF: Wuerffel 31-17-255-1; Kresser 7-3-42-0.
NU: Frazier 14-6-105; Phillips 1-0-0-0.

RECEIVING:
UF: Doering 8-123-0; Hillard 6-100-1; Anthony 2-40-0; McGriff 2-19-0; Jackson 1-10-0; Evans 1-5-0.
NU: Johnson 2-43-0; Holbein 1-33-0; Phillips 1-16-1; Je. Makovicka 1-8-0; Vedral 1-5-0.

INTERCEPTIONS:
UF: Brown 1-5-0; Lott 1-0-0.
NU: Booker 1-42-1; Stokes 1-11-0; Veland 1-(-3)-0.

TACKLES (UT-AT-TT):
UF: Bates 8-4; Daniels 8-4; Hanks 5-4; Chester 3-3; Brown 6-3; .
NU: Farley 4-4-8; Minter 4-2-6; Ellis 3-3-6; J. Williams 4-1-5; Wistrom 3-2-5; Booker 3-1-4; Foreman 1-2-3; Tomich 1-2-3; J. Peter 1-2-3; C. Peter 1-1-2.

SACKS:
UF: None.
NU: Farley 2-9; Warfield 1-10; Wistrom 1-9; Rucker 1-7; Tomich 1-4; J. Williams 1-1;

The Celebration

(Above) Husker fans and players had plenty of reason to celebrate, and celebrate they did with their version of the Gator chomp.

(Right) CBS Television sideline reporter Michele Tafoya gets Tom Osborne's thoughts shortly after capturing his second-consecutive national championship. Fiesta Bowl MVP Tommie Frazier waves to the crowd while awaiting his turn at the microphone.

(Above) The celebration begins on the sideline for defensive tackle Christian Peter (55) and continues as he and the Huskers return home. Peter proudly hoists the national championship trophy awarded by the Associated Press.

(Right) Senior Center Aaron Graham, who anchored an offensive line that was "reloaded" prior to the start of the season, tells the victory celebration crowd where the Huskers rank in his poll.

Season Statistics

11-0-0 Overall / 7-0-0 in Big Eight, Conference Champions, National Champions

TEAM STATISTICS		Nebraska	Opponents
Total First Downs		298	170
	By Rush	212	51
	By Pass	70	111
	By Penalty	16	8
Total Offensive Yards		6,119	3,235
	Avg. Per Game	556.3	294.1
	Total Plays	855	726
	Avg. Gain Per Play	7.2	4.5
Net Rushing Yards		4,398	862
	Avg. Per Game	399.8	78.3
	Rushing Attempts	627	341
	Avg. Per Attempt	7.0	2.5
	Yards Gained Rushing	4,571	1,263
	Yards Lost Rushing	173	401
Net Passing Yards		1,721	2,373
	Avg. Per Game	156.4	215.7
	Avg. Per Attempt	7.5	6.2
	Avg. Per Completion	14.0	12.4
	Attempts	228	385
	Completions	123	191
	Completion Percentage	53.9	49.6
	Had Intercepted	6	20
	NCAA Rating	138.14	103.00
Interceptions By		20	6
	Yards Returned	369	48
	Avg. Per Return	18.5	8.0
	Touchdowns	5	0
Punting Avg.		38.6	40.8
	Number of Punts	29	84
	Yards	1,118	3,426
	Had Blocked	1	2
	Net Punting Avg.	38.1	34.2
Punt Returns		50	5
	Yards Returned	552	12
	Avg. Per Return	11.0	2.4
	Touchdowns	1	1
Kickoff Returns		21	65
	Yards Returned	441	1,059
	Avg. Per Return	21.0	16.3
	Touchdowns	0	0
Fumble Returns		1	0
	Yards Returned	57	0
	Touchdowns	1	0
Penalties/Yards		47/434	80/656
	Avg. Yards Per Game	39.4	59.6
Fumbles Lost		28/9	23/8
Total Turnovers		15	28
3rd Down Conversions		66/143	49/165
	Conversion Percentage	46.1	30.0
4th Down Conversions		15/27	6/16
	Conversion Percentage	56	38
Sacks By/Yards Lost		32/231	0
Time of Possession		31:56	28:03
Touchdowns		77	21
	By Rush	51	6
	By Pass	18	14
	By Return	8	1
PAT Kicks Made/Att.		69/72	18/19
PAT Run-Pass Made/Att.		2/4	0/2
Field Goals Made/Att.		13/16	2/3
Safeties		1	0
Total Points		574	150
Avg. Per Game		52.3	13.6

RUSHING

	G/GS	Att.	Gain	Loss	Net	Avg./ Play	Avg./ Game	Long Play	TD
A. Green	11/6	141	1,108	22	1,086	7.7	98.7	*64 (ISU)	13
T. Frazier	11/11	97	655	51	604	6.2	54.3	*29 (Missouri)	14
L. Phillips	5/2	71	568	21	547	7.7	109.4	*80 (OSU)	9
C. Childs	8/1	55	447	16	431	7.8	53.9	*65 (ASU)	3
D. Benning	9/2	63	421	14	407	6.5	45.2	62 (Pacific)	4
Jeff Makovicka	11/11	63	384	13	371	5.9	33.7	54 (Wash. St.)	1
J. Sims	9/0	30	273	3	270	9.0	30.0	*80 (Mich. St.)	3
B. Schuster	11/0	28	246	0	246	8.8	22.3	55 (ISU)	0
Joel Makovicka	11/0	22	187	2	185	8.4	16.8	39 (OSU)	2
B. Berringer	9/0	21	105	24	81	3.9	9.0	17 (OSU)	0
R. Washington	8/0	3	49	5	44	14.7	6.1	40 (Missouri)	0
M. Turman	9/0	13	37	2	35	2.7	3.9	25 (Pacific)	1
C. Johnson	11/10	3	35	0	35	11.7	3.2	15 (ISU)	0
B. Legate	9/0	5	21	0	21	4.2	2.3	7 (ISU)	0
C. Eicher	3/0	6	16	0	16	2.7	5.3	6 (ISU)	0
J. Cobb	4/0	3	8	0	8	2.7	2.0	5 (ISU)	0
R. Baul	11/10	1	8	0	8	8.0	0.7	8 (Pacific)	0
C. Norris	1/0	2	3	0	3	1.5	3.0	2 (Pacific)	0
J. Vedral	11/1	0	0	0	0	0.0	0.0	0	1
Nebraska	**11**	**627**	**4,571**	**173**	**4,398**	**7.0**	**399.8**	***80**	**51**
Opponents	**11**	**341**	**1,263**	**401**	**862**	**2.5**	**78.3**	***87**	**6**

* Indicates touchdown scored.

RECEIVING

	G/GS	No.	Yards	Avg.	Long Play	TD
C. Johnson	11/10	22	367	16.7	61 (ASU)	2
R. Baul	11/10	17	304	17.9	*76 (OSU)	2
M. Gilman	11/5	16	256	16.0	*35 (WSU)	1
J. Vedral	11/1	14	272	19.4	*38 (OU)	5
B. Holbein	11/7	14	151	10.8	*29 (MU)	1
A. Green	11/6	12	102	8.5	35 (CU)	3
S. Jackson	10/0	6	52	8.7	15 (Pacific)	2
K. Cheatham	5/0	4	31	7.8	10 (ASU, Pac)	0
L. Phillips	5/2	4	14	3.5	7 (OSU)	0
R. Washington	8/0	3	24	8.0	11 (KSU)	0
L. Brown	11/0	2	44	22.0	*39 (ASU)	1
D. Benning	9/2	2	40	20.0	23 (KSU)	0
C. Childs	8/1	2	19	9.5	10 (MSU)	0
V. Jackson	11/0	2	13	6.5	12 (ASU)	1
T. Carpenter	9/1	1	15	15.0	15 (Pacific)	0
Jeff Makovicka	11/11	1	10	10.0	10 (CU)	0
J. Lake	9/0	1	7	7.0	7 (OSU)	0
Nebraska	**11**	**123**	**1,721**	**14.0**	***76**	**18**
Opponents	**11**	**191**	**2,373**	**12.4**	***80**	**14**

* Indicates touchdown scored.

PASSING

	Att.	Comp.	Pct.	Yds.	Avg./ Att.	Avg./ Game	Int.	TD	Pct.	NCAA Rating
T. Frazier	163	92	.564	1,362	8.4	123.8	4	17	.104	156.14
B. Berringer	51	26	.510	252	4.9	28.0	0	0	.000	92.49
M. Turman	12	4	.333	73	6.1	8.1	2	1	.083	78.60
C. Childs	1	1	1.000	34	34.0	4.3	0	0	.000	385.60
A. Green	1	0	.000	0	0.0	0.0	0	0	.000	.00
Nebraska	**228**	**123**	**.539**	**1,721**	**7.5**	**156.5**	**6**	**18**	**.079**	**138.14**
Opponents	**385**	**191**	**.496**	**2,373**	**6.2**	**215.7**	**20**	**14**	**.036**	**103.00**

Season Statistics

TOTAL OFFENSE

	G/GS	Plays	Rush	Pass	Total	Avg./ Play	Avg./ Game
T. Frazier	11/11	260	604	1,362	1,966	7.6	178.7
A. Green	11/6	142	1,086	0	1,086	7.6	98.7
L. Phillips	5/2	71	547	0	547	7.7	109.4
C. Childs	8/1	56	431	34	465	8.3	58.1
D. Benning	9/2	63	407	0	407	6.5	45.2
Jeff Makovicka	11/11	63	371	0	371	5.9	33.7
B. Berringer	9/0	72	81	252	333	4.6	37.0
Nebraska	**11**	**855**	**4,398**	**1,721**	**6,119**	**7.2**	**556.3**
Opponents	**11**	**726**	**862**	**2,373**	**3,235**	**4.5**	**294.1**

FIELD GOALS

	Season	1-19	20-29	30-39	40-49	50+
K. Brown	13-16	0-0	6-7	6-7	1-2	0-0
Nebraska	**13-16**	**0-0**	**6-7**	**6-7**	**1-2**	**0-0**
Opponents	**2-3**	**1-1**	**1-1**	**0-0**	**0-1**	**0-0**

PUNT RETURNS

	G/GS	Rets.	Yards	Avg.	Long Play	TD
M. Fullman	11/0	21	285	13.6	*79	1
R. Baul	11/10	10	96	9.6	28	0
K. Cheatham	5/0	8	102	12.8	33	0
D. Benning	9/2	5	34	6.8	14	0
T. Williams	11/11	2	15	7.5	12	0
O. McFarlin	11/0	2	11	5.5	9	0
T. Farley	11/5	1	5	5.0	0	0
M. Minter	11/11	1	4	4.0	4	0
Nebraska	**11**	**50**	**552**	**11.0**	***79**	**1**
Opponents	**11**	**5**	**12**	**2.4**	**??**	**0**

* Indicates touchdown scored.

SCORING

	G/GS	TD	PAT1	PAT2	FG	TP
K. Brown	11/11	0	58-61	0	13-16	97
A. Green	11/6	16	0	0	0	96
T. Frazier	11/11	14	0	1	0	86
L. Phillips	5/2	9	0	0	0	54
J. Vedral	11/1	7	0	0	0	42
D. Benning	9/2	4	0	0	0	24
J. Sims	9/0	3	0	0	0	18
C. Childs	8/1	3	0	0	0	18
S. Jackson	10/0	2	0	0	0	12
T. Farley	11/5	2	0	0	0	12
C. Johnson	11/10	2	0	0	0	12
M. Fullman	11/0	2	0	0	0	12
Joel Makovicka	11/0	2	0	0	0	12
T. Retzlaff	7/0	0	11-11	0	0	11
Jeff Makovicka	11/11	1	0	0	0	6
V. Jackson	11/0	1	0	0	0	6
L. Brown	11/0	1	0	0	0	6
J. Williams	11/0	1	0	0	0	6
M. Gilman	11/5	1	0	0	0	6
T. Veland	11/11	1	0	0	0	6
M. Turman	9/0	1	0	0	0	6
L. Hardin	11/1	1	0	0	0	6
B. Holbein	11/7	1	0	0	0	6
B. Schuster	11/0	0	0	1	0	2
Nebraska	**11**	**77**	**69-72**	**2**	**13-16**	**576**
Opponents	**11**	**21**	**18-19**	**0**	**2-3**	**150**

PUNTING

	G/GS	Punts	Yards	Avg.	Net. Avg.	Inside Opp. 20	Blk
J. Kosch	10/10	27	1,088	40.3	39.9	11	0
B. Lafleur	1/0	1	30	30.0	30.0	0	0
Team	1/0	1	0	0.0	0.0	0	1
Nebraska	**11**	**29**	**1,118**	**38.6**	**38.1**	**11**	**1**
Opponents	**11**	**84**	**3,426**	**40.8**	**34.2**	**9**	**2**

PUNTING / DISTANCE IN YARDS

1-19	20-29	30-39	40-49	50-59	60-69	70+	Long
1	3	10	9	3	0	1	74
0	0	1	0	0	0	0	30
0	0	0	0	0	0	0	0
1	3	10	9	3	0	1	74
1	8	26	35	8	2	2	83

ALL PURPOSE LEADERS

	G/GS	Rush	Rec.	PR	KOR	Total	Avg./ Game
A. Green	11/6	1,086	102	0	71	1,259	114.5
C. Childs	8/1	431	19	0	223	673	84.1
T. Frazier	11/11	604	0	0	0	604	54.9
L. Phillips	5/2	547	14	0	0	571	112.2
D. Benning	9/2	407	40	34	79	560	62.2
R. Baul	11/10	8	304	96	0	408	37.1
C. Johnson	11/10	35	367	0	0	402	36.5
Nebraska	**11**	**4,398**	**1,721**	**552**	**441**	**7,112**	**646.5**
Opponents	**11**	**862**	**2,373**	**12**	**1,059**	**4,306**	**391.5**

KICKOFF RETURNS

	G/GS	Rets.	Yards	Avg.	Long Play	TD
C. Childs	8/1	10	223	22.3	40	0
A. Green	11/6	4	71	17.8	34	0
D. Benning	9/2	3	79	26.3	42	0
K. Cheatham	5/0	2	56	28.0	33	0
J. Vedral	11/1	1	2	2.0	2	0
Nebraska	**11**	**21**	**441**	**21.0**	**42**	**0**
Opponents	**11**	**65**	**1,059**	**16.3**	**51**	**0**

INTERCEPTIONS

	G/GS	Int.	Yards	Avg.	Long Play	TD
T. Farley	11/5	3	92	30.7	42	2
M. Booker	11/9	3	50	16.7	22	0
M. Fullman	11/0	2	97	48.5	*86	1
M. Minter	11/11	2	0	0.0	0	0
T. Veland	11/11	1	43	43.0	43	0
J. Williams	11/0	1	36	36.0	*36	1
J. Ogard	11/0	1	19	19.0	19	0
T. Williams	11/11	1	11	11.0	11	0
P. Ellis	8/5	1	11	11.0	11	0
A. Skoda	4/0	1	7	7.0	7	0
L. Hardin	11/1	1	3	3.0	*3	1
L. Dennis	9/0	1	0	0.0	0	0
D. Colman	11/6	1	0	0.0	0	0
D. Schmadeke	??/0	1	0	0.0	0	0
Nebraska	**11**	**20**	**369**	**18.5**	***86**	**5**
Opponents	**11**	**6**	**48**	**8.0**	**19**	**0**

Season Statistics

DEFENSIVE STATISTICS

		(Tackles)					(Fumbles)					QB	Int
	G/GS	UT	AT	TT	Sacks*	Loss	Csd.	Rec.	BK	PBU	Int.	Hurry	Csd.
T. Farley	11/5	27	35	62	5-40	9-45	0	0	2	5	3-92	12	0
M. Minter	11/11	27	26	53	0	2-12	1	0	0	6	2-0	0	0
J. Williams	11/0	22	25	47	1-10	6-27	1	0	0	2	1-36	4	0
D. Colman	11/6	19	27	46	2-13	6-25	0	1	0	1	1-0	4	0
C. Peter	11/11	12	34	46	2-15	5-27	2	0	0	1	0	9	0
G. Wistrom	11/11	21	23	44	4-23	15-55	0	0	0	0	0	13	1
T. Veland	11/11	22	16	38	0	1-1	1	2	0	2	1-43	2	0
J. Hesse	11/0	20	17	37	1-1	6-7	1	0	0	0	0	0	0
R. Terwilliger	11/6	18	17	35	0	4-6	1	0	0	0	0	4	0
M. Booker	11/9	20	13	33	0	1-3	0	0	0	6	3-50	0	0
J. Foreman	11/11	10	22	32	0	2-5	0	0	0	0	0	2	0
J. Peter	11/11	9	21	30	0	5-13	1	0	0	1	0	7	1
T. Williams	11/11	19	9	28	0	1-9	0	1	0	3	1-11	1	0
P. Ellis	11/5	11	16	27	2-9	4-11	0	0	0	2	1-11	5	0
J. Tomich	11/10	18	9	27	10-75	12-79	3	2	0	3	0	24	1
O. McFarlin	11/0	13	8	21	0	0	0	1	0	0	0	0	0
C. Kelsay	11/0	13	7	20	2-12	3-13	0	0	0	3	0	5	0
E. Stokes	11/2	7	11	18	0	0	0	0	0	2	0	0	0
A. Penland	11/0	6	11	17	0	1-1	0	0	0	0	0	0	0
M. Fullman	11/0	11	5	16	0	0	0	0	0	0	2-97	0	0
E. Warfield	11/0	7	9	16	0	0	0	0	0	2	0	1	0
M. Rucker	9/0	3	10	13	1-6	1-16	0	0	0	0	0	2	0
S. Saltsman	10/0	5	8	13	1-9	2-10	0	0	0	0	0	2	0
L. Dennis	9/0	5	5	10	0	0	0	0	0	1	1-0	0	0
L. Hardin	11/1	5	4	9	1-8	1-8	0	0	0	0	1-3	3	0
J. Ogard	11/0	2	5	7	0	1-1	0	0	0	2	1-19	1	0
B. Legate	9/0	2	5	7	0	0	0	0	0	0	0	0	0
L. Arnold	5/0	1	5	6	0	0	0	0	0	1	0	0	0
J. Jenkins	9/0	2	4	6	0	1-1	0	0	0	2	0	0	0
Q. Hogrefe	4/0	2	4	6	0	0	0	0	0	1	0	0	0
B. Schuster	11/0	1	3	4	0	0	0	0	0	0	0	0	0
A. Skoda	4/0	1	3	4	0	0	0	0	0	0	1-7	0	0
T. Toline	4/0	1	2	3	0	1-2	0	0	0	0	0	0	0
Joel Makovicka	11/0	1	2	3	0	0	0	0	0	0	0	0	0
R. Worthy	3/0	2	1	3	0	0	0	0	0	0	0	0	0
K. Brown	11/11	2	0	2	0	0	0	0	0	0	0	0	0
D. Schamdeke	9/0	2	0	2	0	0	0	0	0	1	1-0	0	0
E. Nelson	2/0	0	2	2	0	0	0	0	0	0	0	1	0
C. Blahak	5/0	1	1	2	0	0	0	0	0	0	0	0	0
M. Hoffman	2/0	0	2	2	0	0	0	0	0	0	0	0	0
V. Jackson	11/0	1	0	1	0	0	0	0	0	0	0	0	0
B. Holbein	11/7	1	0	1	0	0	0	0	0	0	0	0	0
R. Held	4/0	0	1	1	0	0	0	0	0	0	0	0	0
K. Cheatham	5/0	0	1	1	0	0	0	0	0	0	0	0	0
D. Alderman	5/0	1	0	1	0	0	0	0	0	0	0	0	0
M. Roberts	5/0	0	1	1	0	0	0	0	0	0	0	1	0
E. Walther	4/0	1	0	1	0	0	0	0	0	0	0	0	0
L. Townsend	5/0	1	0	1	0	0	0	0	0	0	0	0	0
D. Benning	9/2	1	0	1	0	0	0	0	0	0	0	0	0
A. Green	11/6	1	0	1	0	0	0	0	0	0	0	0	0
S. Jackson	10/0	1	0	1	0	0	0	0	0	0	0	0	0
A. Treu	11/0	0	1	1	0	0	0	0	0	0	0	0	0
J. Vedral	11/1	1	0	1	0	0	0	0	0	0	0	0	0
J. Benes	4/0	0	0	0	0	0	0	0	0	1	0	0	0
D. Brummond	1/0	0	0	0	0	0	0	0	0	0	0	1	0

*Sacks included in Tackles for Loss

Season Statistics

1995 HIGHS AND LOWS

Nebraska	High	Low
Points Scored	77 vs. Arizona State	35 vs. Washington State
First Downs	37 vs. Iowa State	19 vs. Kansas State
Rushing Attempts	70 vs. Pacific (569 yards)	46 vs. Kansas State (190 yards)
Rushing Yards	624 vs. Iowa State (68 attempts)	190 vs. Kansas State (46 att.)
Passes Attempted	36 vs. Pacific (16 comp.)	14 vs. Michigan State
Passes Completed	16 vs. Pacific (162 yards)	7 vs. Michigan State (14 att.)
Had Intercepted	2 vs. Pacific	0, five times
Passing Yards	292 vs. Arizona State	86 vs. Kansas
Total Plays	106 vs. Pacific (731 yards)	63 vs. Kansas State (338 yards)
Total Yards	776 vs. Iowa State (89 attempts)	338 vs. Kansas State (63 plays)
Possession Time	39:44 vs. Pacific	24:44 vs. Missouri
Fumbles	6 vs. Missouri	0 vs. Oklahoma State, Kansas State
Fumbles Lost	3 vs. Washington State	0 six games
Turnovers	3 vs. Washington State, Kansas	0 vs. Missouri, Kansas State, Colorado, Iowa State
Turnover Margin	+4 vs. Missouri	-3 vs. Washington State
Penalties	8 vs. Iowa State (89 yards)	0 vs. Colorado
Yards Penalized	89 vs. Iowa State (8 penalties)	0 vs. Colorado
Sacks By	9 vs. Kansas State	1 vs. Arizona State, Pacific, Iowa State, Kansas

Opponents	High	Low
Points Scored	28 by Arizona State	0 by Missouri, Oklahoma
First Downs	25 by Kansas	7 by Pacific
Rushing Attempts	45 by Arizona State (171 yards)	17 by Pacific (60 yards)
Rushing Yards	171 by Arizona State (45 att.)	-19 by Kansas State (26 att.)
Passes Attempted	50 by Kansas (30 comp.)	24 by Missouri (83 yards), Iowa State (143 yards)
Passes Completed	30 by Kansas (50 att.)	9 by Missouri (24 att.)
Had Intercepted	3 by Oklahoma State, Kansas	1 by Michigan State, Pacific
Passing Yards	290 by Michigan State (35 att.), Arizona St. (33 att.)	83 by Missouri (24 att.),
Total Plays	82 by Kansas (345 yards)	48 by Pacific (197 yards)
Total Yards	461 by Arizona State (78 att.)	122 by Missouri (63 att.)
Possession Time	35:16 by Missouri	20:16 by Pacific
Fumbles	6 by Michigan State	0 by Arizona State, Pacific, Kansas State
Fumbles Lost	2 by Michigan State, Kansas	0 six games
Turnovers	5 by Kansas	0 by Washington State
Turnover Margin	+3 by Washington State	-4 by Missouri
Penalties	14 by Kansas State (113 yards)	2 by Pacific (20 yards)
Yards Penalized	113 by Kansas State (14 penalties)	20 by Pacific (2 pen.)
Sacks By	None	0 11 games

INDIVIDUAL HIGHS

Most Rushing Attempts: 22; Lawrence Phillips, vs. Michigan State (206 yards); Ahman Green, vs. Kansas State (109 yards)
Most Net Rushing Yards: 206; Phillips, vs. Michigan State (22 att.)
Most Rushing TDs: 4; Phillips, vs. Michigan State
Longest TD Run: 80; Phillips, vs. Oklahoma State; James Sims, vs. Michigan State
Longest Run, No TD: 62; Damon Benning, vs. Pacific
Most Pass Attempts: 25; Tommie Frazier, vs. Oklahoma (12 completions)
Most Completed Passes: 14; Frazier, vs. Colorado (23 attempts)
Most Passing Yards: 241; Frazier, vs. Colorado (23 attempts)
Longest TD Pass: 76; Frazier to Reggie Baul, vs. Oklahoma State
Longest Pass, No TD: 61; Frazier to Clester Johnson, vs. Arizona State
Most Pass Receptions: 4; Clester Johnson, vs. Arizona State, Washington State; Reggie Baul, vs. Iowa State (48 yards); Johnson, vs. Kansas (50 yards); Baul 4 vs. Oklahoma (38 yards).
Most Receiving Yards: 129; Johnson, vs. Arizona State (4 rec.)
Most TD Receptions: 2; Ahman Green, vs. Kansas State
Most Total-Offense Attempts: 36; Frazier, vs. Colorado
Most Total-Offense Yards: 281; Frazier, vs. Colorado
Most All-Purpose Attempts: 25; Ahman Green, vs. Kansas State
Most All-Purpose Yards: 242; Ahman Green, vs. Washington State (16 att.)
Most Touchdowns Scored: 4; Phillips, vs. Michigan State; Green, vs. Iowa State
Most Field Goals Attempted: 4; Kris Brown, vs. Oklahoma
Most Field Goals Made: 3; Kris Brown, vs. Michigan State, Colorado, Oklahoma
Longest Field Goal: 47; Kris Brown, vs. Michigan State
Most Interceptions: 1; 20 times
Longest Interception TD Return: 86 yards; Mike Fullman, vs. Kansas
Longest Interception Return, No TD: 43; Veland, vs. Missouri
Longest Punt Return: 79; Mike Fullman, vs. Kansas State
Longest Kickoff Return: 42; Damon Benning, vs. Kansas
Most Punts: 4; Jesse Kosch, vs. Washington State (37.0 avg.), Missouri (34.3 avg.), Oklahoma (43.0 avg.)
Highest Punting Average: 61.0; Kosch, vs. Arizona State (2 punts)
Longest Punt: 74; Kosch, vs. Arizona State
Most Total Tackles: 10; Terrell Farley, vs. Kansas State; Jamel Williams, vs. Colorado; Williams, vs. Kansas
Most Solo Tackles: 6; Phil Ellis, vs. Michigan State; Jamel Williams, vs. Kansas
Most Tackles for Loss: 4; Grant Wistrom, vs. Washington State (16 yards); Wistrom, vs. Kansas State (13 yards)
Most Yards Lost: 22; Jared Tomich, vs. Oklahoma State (2 tackles); 22; Farley vs. Kansas State (2 tackles)
Most Quarterback Sacks: 2, seven times
Most Yards Lost: 22; Tomich, vs. Oklahoma State; 22; Farley, vs. Kansas State

SCORE BY QUARTER

	1st quarter	2nd quarter	3rd quarter	4th quarter	Final
Nebraska	**158**	**175**	**136**	**107**	**576**
Opponents	34	38	31	47	150

AVERAGE SCORE BY QUARTER

	1st quarter	2nd quarter	3rd quarter	4th quarter	Final
Nebraska	**14.4**	**15.3**	**12.4**	**9.7**	**52.3**
Opponents	3.1	3.4	2.8	4.3	13.6

OPPONENTS LONG PLAYS

Rush: 87; Frank Madu, Washington State
Pass: 80; Jake Plummer to Keith Poole, Arizona State
Field Goal: 24; C, Gardener, Michigan State
Punt return: 25; Clyde Johnson, Kansas State
Kickoff return: 51; Mike Lawrence, Kansas State
Interception return: 19; Maurice Gaddie, Kansas
Punt: 83; Chris Salani, Michigan State

1995 Nebraska Roster

NO.	LTRS.	NAME	POS.	HT.	WT.	BIRTHDATE	YR.	HOMETOWN
47		Aden, Matt	WLB	6-2	215	11/23/74	So.	Omaha, Neb. (Northwest)
48		Alderman, Dave	Rover	5-10	185	9/10/74	Jr.	Omaha, Neb. (North)
61		Allen, Derek	DT	6-3	275	4/25/77	Fr.	Russellville, Ark.
27		Allen, Jacques	WB	6-2	210	11/29/73	Sr.	Kansas City, Mo. (Raytown)
70	*	Anderson, Eric	OT	6-4	300	7/16/75	So.	Lincoln, Neb. (Southeast)
52		Baldwin, Matt	C	6-1	260	11/27/76	Fr.	Arvada, Colo. (Bear Creek)
87		Bassett, Chris	OLB	6-0	230	8/24/74	So.	Tracy, Minn.
7	**	Baul, Reggie	SE	5-8	170	4/19/73	Sr.	Bellevue, Neb. (Papillion-LaVista)
11		Benes, Jason	FS	5-11	180	2/21/75	So.	Valparaiso, Neb. (Raymond-Central)
21	**	Benning, Damon	IB	5-11	205	3/2/74	Jr.	Omaha, Neb. (Northwest)
18	***	Berringer, Brook	QB	6-4	225	7/9/73	Sr.	Goodland, Kan.
50		Bilanzich, Andy	P	6-0	235	10/2/76	Fr.	Salt Lake City, Utah (Judge Memorial Cath.)
17		Blahak, Chad	RCB	5-9	190	8/20/73	Jr.	Lincoln, Neb. (Lincoln High)
20	*	Booker, Michael	LCB	6-2	195	4/27/75	Jr.	Oceanside, Calif. (El Camino)
35		Brown, Kris	PK	5-11	190	12/23/76	Fr.	Southlake, Texas (Carroll)
14		Brown, Lance	WB	5-11	190	3/24/75	Fr.	Papillion, Neb. (Papillion-LaVista)
80		Brummond, Darren	OLB	6-2	215	12/19/74	Fr.	Englewood, Colo. (Cherry Creek)
90	*	Carpenter, Tim	TE	6-4	240	11/27/74	So.	Columbus, Neb.
6		Cheatham, Kenny	SE	6-4	200	8/11/76	Fr.	Phoenix, Ariz. (South Mountain)
26	**	Childs, Clinton	IB/FB	6-0	215	5/27/74	Sr.	Omaha, Neb. (North)
9		Christo, Monte	QB	6-0	195	7/10/76	So.	Kearney, Neb.
56		Clausen, Jeff	OL	6-6	275	1/9/77	Fr.	Dixon, Ill.
42		Cobb, Josh	FB	5-11	240	2/26/76	Fr.	Wallace, Neb.
46	***	Colman, Doug	MLB	6-3	245	6/4/73	Sr.	Ventnor, N.J. (Ocean City)
45		Cook, Steve	MLB	6-2	240	9/20/75	Fr.	Blair, Neb.
84		DeBates, T.J.	TE	6-3	235	5/3/77	Fr.	Stewartville, Minn.
2	*	Dennis, Leslie	RCB	5-8	165	3/21/75	So.	Bradenton, Fla. (Southeast)
75	**	Dishman, Chris	OT	6-3	310	2/27/74	Jr.	Cozad, Neb.
73		Drum, Brandon	DT	6-3	240	9/18/76	Fr.	Columbus, Neb. (Scotus)
23		Eicher, Chad	IB	6-3	210	11/23/74	So.	Seward, Neb.
41	***	Ellis, Phil	MLB	6-2	225	1/26/73	Sr.	Grand Island, Neb.
43		Farley, Terrell	WLB	6-0	200	8/16/75	Jr.	Columbus, Ga. (Independence, Kan., College, Kendrick HS)
56		Foreman, Jay	SLB	6-1	220	2/18/76	Fr.	Eden Prairie, Minn.
15	***	Frazier, Tommie	QB	6-2	210	7/16/74	Sr.	Palmetto, Fla. (Manatee)
35		Froehlich, Russell	SLB	6-0	200	6/23/76	Fr.	Omaha, Neb. (Bellevue East)
7		Froeschl, Nate	RCB	5-11	185	9/10/76	Fr.	Falls City, Neb. (Sacred Heart)
16		Frost, Scott	QB	6-3	215	1/4/75	So.	Wood River, Neb.
12		Fullman, Mike	RCB	5-7	160	8/9/74	Jr.	Roselle, N.J. (Rutgers)
80		Gard, Sean	OLB	5-11	210	7/9/75	So.	Omaha, Neb. (Central)
72		Gessford, Ben	OT	6-2	260	8/12/76	Fr.	Lincoln, Neb. (East)
87	***	Gilman, Mark	TE	6-4	240	7/5/72	Sr.	Kalispell, Mont. (Flathead)
54	***	Graham, Aaron	C	6-4	275	5/22/73	Sr.	Denton, Texas
30		Green, Ahman	IB	6-0	210	2/16/77	Fr.	Omaha, Neb. (Central)
81		Gumm, Trent	OLB	6-2	215	6/21/75	Fr.	Columbus, Neb.
80		Haafke, Billy	IB	5-11	180	3/19/75	Fr.	South Sioux City, Neb.
58	***	Hardin, Luther	OLB	6-2	245	11/16/73	Sr.	O'Fallon, Ill. (Althoff Catholic)
82		Held, Ryan	SE	6-3	190	11/23/74	So.	Overland Park, Kan. (Blue Valley North)
6		Herron, Chris	Rover	5-10	180	12/16/75	Fr.	Scottsbluff, Neb.
59		Heskew, Josh	C	6-3	270	9/2/75	So.	Yukon, Okla. (Mustang)
44	*	Hesse, Jon	OLB	6-4	245	6/6/73	Jr.	Lincoln, Neb. (Southeast)
50		Hoffman, Michael	DT	5-9	225	2/28/75	So.	Spencer, Neb. (Spencer-Naper)
49		Hogrefe, Quint	MLB	5-11	200	8/26/75	Fr.	Auburn, Neb.
5	**	Holbein, Brendan	SE	5-9	190	11/28/73	Jr.	Cozad, Neb.
66		Horst, Joe	OG	6-1	250	3/18/74	So.	Wood River, Neb.
62		Hoskinson, Matt	OG	6-1	285	1/22/75	So.	Battle Creek, Neb.
53		Hunting, Matt	LB	6-3	220	12/28/74	So.	Cozad, Neb.
32		Jackson, Julius	SLB	6-0	210	11/7/76	Fr.	Gainesville, Texas
88		Jackson, Sheldon	TE	6-4	240	7/24/76	Fr.	Diamond Bar, Calif. (Damien)
34		Jackson, Vershan	TE	6-0	240	2/27/75	So.	Omaha, Neb. (South)
96	*	Jenkins, Jason	DT	6-5	280	7/26/73	Sr.	Hammonton, N.J. (Oakcrest/Dodge City CC)
33	**	Johnson, Clester	WB	5-11	210	2/18/73	Sr.	Bellevue, Neb. (West)
58		Johnson, Marcus	OG	6-4	265	1/13/77	Fr.	Oceanside, Calif. (Vista)
76		Julch, Adam	OT	6-5	310	1/31/77	Fr.	Omaha, Neb. (Burke)
57		Kelsay, Chad	OLB	6-3	230	4/9/77	Fr.	Auburn, Neb.
19		Kosch, Jesse	P	6-0	180	9/20/74	So.	Columbus, Neb. (Scotus)

23		Lafleur, Bill	P	5-11	195	2/25/76	Fr.	Norfolk, Neb. (Catholic)
89	*	Lake, Jeff	SE	6-4	205	9/6/74	So.	Columbus, Neb. (Lakeview)
53		Langan, Troy	C	6-1	250	7/6/74	Jr.	Columbus, Neb. (Scotus)
31		Leece, Charlie	MLB	5-9	230	4/22/76	Fr.	Grand Island, Neb.
40		Legate, Billy	FB	5-11	215	12/6/75	Fr.	Elgin, Neb. (Clearwater)
12		London, Frankie	QB	6-0	175	11/24/76	Fr.	Lake Charles, La. (LaGrange)
58		Macken, Casey	LB	6-0	220	12/30/75	Fr.	Cozad, Neb.
22	***	Makovicka, Jeff	FB	5-11	225	9/24/72	Sr.	Brainard, Neb. (East Butler)
45		Makovicka, Joel	FB	5-11	225	10/6/75	Fr.	Brainard, Neb. (East Butler)
5		Matthews, Karnell	Rover	5-10	160	8/19/77	Fr.	St. Peters, Mo. (Francis Howell North)
21		McClymont, Alex	LCB	5-9	160	12/7/76	Fr.	Holdrege, Neb.
4	*	McFarlin, Octavious	Rover	5-11	190	8/10/75	So.	Bastrop, Texas
43		McIntyre, Corey	FB	6-1	190	11/22/76	Fr.	Grand Island, Neb. (Northwest)
78	*	Mikos, Kory	OT	6-5	285	10/15/73	Jr.	Seward, Neb.
83		Miller, Andy	SE	5-10	180	5/17/75	Fr.	Papillion, Neb. (Papillion-LaVista)
83		Miller, Bryce	OLB	6-4	220	11/16/73	Jr.	Elmwood, Neb. (Elmwood-Murdock)
10	**	Minter, Mike	Rover	5-10	190	1/15/74	Jr.	Lawton, Okla.
10		Morro, Brian	P	5-9	165	12/11/75	Fr.	Middletown, N.J. (South)
65		Nelson, Erik	DT	6-3	270	9/29/76	Fr.	Iowa City, Iowa (City High)
63	*	Nunns, Brian	OT	6-2	295	4/13/73	Sr.	Lincoln, Neb. (Lincoln High)
97	*	Ogard, Jeff	DT	6-6	310	9/1/73	Jr.	St. Paul, Neb.
33		Ortiz, Tony	SLB	6-0	205	7/3/77	Fr.	Waterbury, Conn. (Crosby)
69	***	Ott, Steve	OG	6-4	290	8/6/72	Sr.	Henderson, Neb.
52	***	Penland, Aaron	WLB	6-1	220	5/22/73	Sr.	Jacksonville, Fla. (University Christian)
9		Perino, Jeff	QB	6-2	195	12/18/76	Fr.	Durango, Colo.
55	**	Peter, Christian	DT	6-3	300	10/5/72	Sr.	Locust, N.J. (Middletown South)
95	*	Peter, Jason	DT	6-4	285	9/13/74	So.	Locust, N.J. (Milford Academy)
25		Peterson, Jerome	LCB	5-8	180	4/28/76	Fr.	Port Allen, La.
1	**	Phillips, Lawrence	IB	6-0	220	5/12/75	Jr.	West Covina, Calif. (Baldwin Park)
73	*	Pollack, Fred	OT	6-4	295	12/27/74	So.	Omaha, Neb. (Creighton Prep)
32		Reddick, David	WB	5-9	190	9/21/76	Fr.	Camden, N.J. (Woodrow Wilson)
13		Retzlaff, Ted	PK	6-0	180	4/15/75	So.	Waverly, Neb.
39		Roberts, Mike	Rover	6-1	185	9/19/72	Jr.	Omaha, Neb. (Central)
86		Roy, Dorrick	TE	6-3	220	4/2/75	Fr.	Inglewood, Calif. (Montclair Prep)
27		Royce, Tom	RCB	5-10	165	11/9/73	Jr.	Council Bluffs, Iowa (Abraham Lincoln)
84		Rucker, Mike	OLB	6-5	240	2/28/75	Fr.	St. Joseph, Mo. (Benton)
74	*	Saltsman, Scott	DT	6-2	275	10/22/73	Jr.	Wichita Falls, Texas (Rider)
37	**	Schmadeke, Darren	LCB	5-8	175	2/5/73	Sr.	Albion, Neb.
66		Schmode, Anthony	OG	6-1	280	3/14/76	Fr.	Battle Creek, Neb.
28	*	Schuster, Brian	FB	5-11	225	9/19/73	Jr.	Fullerton, Neb.
57		Seaman, Doug	C	6-1	270	5/8/75	So.	Bellevue, Neb. (Bellevue East)
40		Sears, Kareem	MLB	6-2	230	12/17/76	Fr.	Enid, Okla.
65		Sherman, James	OG	6-2	300	10/23/77	Fr.	LaVerne, Calif. (Whittier)
31		Sims, James	IB	6-1	215	11/3/69	So.	Omaha, Neb.(Omaha Cent./W.Memphis, Ark.)
36		Skoda, Adam	MLB	6-1	220	11/24/74	Fr.	Lincoln, Neb. (Lincoln High)
16	**	Stokes, Eric	LCB/FS	5-11	185	12/18/73	Jr.	Lincoln, Neb. (East)
67	*	Taylor, Aaron	OG	6-1	305	1/21/75	So.	Wichita Falls, Texas (Rider)
91	**	Terwilliger, Ryan	WLB	6-5	225	5/31/73	Jr.	Grant, Neb.
77		Tessendorf, Ross	DT	6-1	255	12/22/75	Fr.	Columbus, Neb. (Lakeview)
92		Toline, Travis	OLB	6-3	230	11/12/75	Fr.	Wahoo, Neb.
93	*	Tomich, Jared	OLB	6-2	250	4/24/74	Jr.	St. John, Ind. (Lake Central)
94	*	Townsend, Larry	DT	6-4	300	9/16/74	Jr.	San Jose, Calif. (Yerba Buena)
76		Tully, Kyle	OL	6-0	290	2/29/76	Fr.	Jefferson, Wis.
77	*	Treu, Adam	OT	6-6	295	6/24/74	Jr.	Lincoln, Neb. (Pius X)
11	*	Turman, Matt	QB	5-11	185	12/13/73	Jr.	Wahoo, Neb. (Neumann)
24		Uhlir, Todd	IB	5-10	220	1/8/75	So.	Battle Creek, Neb.
71		Van Cleave, Mike	OG	6-2	275	4/20/74	So.	Huffman, Texas (Hargrave)
25	*	Vedral, Jon	WB	5-11	200	4/9/74	Jr.	Gregory, S.D.
9	***	Veland, Tony	FS	6-2	210	3/11/73	Sr.	Omaha, Neb. (Benson)
68	*	Volin, Steve	OG	6-2	290	1/13/73	Sr.	Wahoo, Neb.
51	*	Vrzal, Matt	C	6-1	300	7/12/74	Jr.	Grand Island, Neb.
61		Wade, Brandt	OG	6-2	295	9/30/75	Fr.	Springfield, Neb. (Platteview)
29		Walther, Eric	FS	6-0	170	11/6/75	Fr.	Juniata, Neb. (Hastings Adams Central)
3		Warfield, Eric	FS	6-1	195	3/3/76	So.	Texarkana, Ark. (Arkansas HS)
3	**	Washington, Riley	WB	5-9	165	7/31/73	Jr.	Chula Vista, Calif. (San Diego SW)
85		Wieting, Sean	WB	5-9	185	6/19/75	So.	Tulatin, Ore. (Tigard)
29		Wiggins, Shevin	SE/WB	5-11	180	9/27/74	So.	Palmetto, Fla. (Manatee)
28	*	Williams, Jamel	WLB	6-2	200	11/23/76	Jr.	Merrillville, Ind.
8	**	Williams, Tyrone	RCB	6-0	195	5/31/73	Sr.	Palmetto, Fla. (Manatee)
81		Wills, Aaron	TE	6-2	235	10/24/76	Fr.	Omaha, Neb. (Burke)
99		Wiltz, Jason	DT	6-3	285	11/23/76	Fr.	New Orleans, La. (St. Augustine)
98	*	Wistrom, Grant	OLB	6-5	240	7/3/76	So.	Webb City, Mo.
86		Zahl, Brendan	OLB	6-3	230	6/17/75	So.	Stratton, Neb.
64	*	Zatechka, Jon	OG	6-2	280	6/10/75	So.	Lincoln, Neb. (East)

Roster includes all players who played in games in 1995 as well as scholarship freshmen who redshirted.

Final Football Polls

Final 1995 Associated Press Poll

	Team (First-Place Votes), Record	Points
1.	**Nebraska, (62), 12-0-0**	**1,550**
2.	Florida, 12-1-0	1,474
3.	Tennessee, 11-1-0	1,428
4.	Florida State, 10-2-0	1,311
5.	Colorado, 10-2-0	1,309
6.	Ohio State, 11-2-0	1,162
7.	Kansas State, 10-2-0	1,147
8.	Northwestern, 10-2-0	1,124
9.	Kansas, 10-2-0	1,029
10.	Virginia Tech, 10-2-0	1,015
11.	Notre Dame, 9-3-0	931
12.	Southern Cal., 9-2-1	886
13.	Penn State, 9-3-0	867
14.	Texas, 10-2-1	724
15.	Texas A&M, 9-3-0	661
16.	Virginia, 9-4-0	603
17.	Michigan, 9-4-0	474.5
18.	Oregon, 9-3-0	416
19.	Syracuse, 9-3-0	382
20.	Miami, Fla., 8-3-0	352
21.	Alabama, 8-3-0	313
22.	Auburn, 8-4-0	276
23.	Texas Tech, 9-3-0	197
24.	Toledo, 11-0-1	170
25.	Iowa, 8-4-0	133.5

Final 1995 USA Today/CNN Poll

	Team (First-Place Votes), Record	Points
1.	**Nebraska, (62), 12-0-0**	**1,550**
2.	Tennessee, 11-1-0	1,438
3.	Florida, 12-1-0	1,434
4.	Colorado, 10-2-0	1,308
5.	Florida State, 10-2-0	1,280
6.	Kansas State, 10-2-0	1,129
7.	Northwestern, 10-2-0	1,121
8.	Ohio State, 11-2-0	1,105
9.	Virginia Tech 10-2-0	1,101
10.	Kansas, 10-2-0	994
11.	Southern Cal, 9-2-1	898
12.	Penn State, 9-3-0	857
13.	Notre Dame, 9-3-0	813
14.	Texas, 10-2-1	768
15.	Texas A&M, 9-3-0	703
16.	Syracuse, 9-3-0	593
17.	Virginia, 9-4-0	585
18.	Oregon, 9-3-0	441
19.	Michigan, 9-4-0	426
20.	Texas Tech, 9-3-0	329
21.	Auburn, 8-4-0	292
22.	Iowa, 8-4-0	205
23.	East Carolina, 9-3-0	163
24.	Toledo, 11-0-1	150
25.	Louisiana State, 7-4-1	110

Managers and Trainers

1995 Husker Student Trainers, Back Row (from left): Head Student Trainer Josh Heller, Jim Ohrt, Zane Harvey, Brent Todd, Stacia Weaver, Matt Olberding, Jason Masek. Middle row: Dannika Nelson, Jen Ogle, Josh Nichter, John Meyer, David Maloley. Front row: Sonya Simonson, Ciji Miller, Megan Armbruster, Sandra Kulken and Peggy Pope.

1995 Husker Undergraduate Assistant Coaches, Back Row (left to right): Ed Morrow, Merritt Nelson, Chad Young, Front Row: Abdul Muhammad, Damon Schmadeke, Chad Stanley.

1995 Husker Student Managers, Back Row (from left): Jon Meier, Adam Kucera, Ryan Ricenbau, Mike Schukei, John McNeely, Jason Joseph, Jason McNeely. Front row: Reed Devall, Lowell Miller, Jeff Knox, Kyle McMurray, Ryan Hutsel and Kevin Ridley.

1995 Husker Equipment Managers (from left): Troy Williams, Mark Lewin, Assistant Equipment Manager Mike Mason, Head Equipment Manager Glen Abbott, Matt Geiser and Shawn Davis.

University of Nebraska

Athletic Department

Bill Byrne
Athletic Director

Glen Abbott
Equipment Manager

Dr. Lonnie Albers
Director of Athletic Medicine

Chris Anderson
Sports Information Director

Mike Arthur
Assistant Director of Performance-Programs

Chris Bahl
Licensing Coordinator

Bryan Bailey
Coordinator of Reconditioning

Gary Bargen
Assistant Compliance Director

Cindy Barker
Assistant Athletic Trainer

Cindy Bell
Ticket Manager

Kevin Best
Assistant Sports Information Director

Orval Borgialli
Devaney Center Coordinator

Jon Bostick
Development Officer

Don Bryant
Associate A.D., Public Relations

Craig Busboom
Accounting Manager

Clayton Carlin
Graduate Assistant Football Coach

Bryan Carpenter
Computer Video Technician

Dr. Pat Clare
Chief of Staff, Orthopedic Surgeon

Kevin Coleman
West Stadium Strength Coach

Heidi Cuca
Marketing Director

Bob Devaney
Athletic Director Emeritus

Joni Duff
Football Secretary

Dr. Robert Dugas
Team Orthopedist

Dave Ellis
Coodinator of Performance Nutrition

Boyd Epley
Assistant A.D., Director of Athletic Performance

Dave Finn
Director of Video Operations

Gary Fouraker
Associate A.D., Business & Finance

Dr. Samuel Fuenning
Director Emeritus, Athletic Medicine

Randy Gobel
Assistant Director of Performance-Operations

Mike Gooding
Assistant Athletic Trainer

Mike Grant
Graduate Assistant Football Coach

Dr. Tom Heiser
Team Physician, Orthopedist

Dr. Barbara Hibner
Associate A.D., Senior Women's Administrator

Butch Hug
Events Manager

John Ingram
Facilities Operations Manager

Nick Joos
Director of Basketball Operations

Shot Kleen
Electronic Technician

Norma Knobel
Administrative Services Manager

Paul Koch
Devaney Center Strength Coach

Trina Kudlacek
Academic Counselor

Roland "Duke" LaRue
Assistant Athletic Trainer

Dennis Leblanc
Assistant A.D., Academic Programs/Services

Doug Lillie
Devaney Center Superintendent

Pat Logsdon
Assistant to the Director of Football Operations

Keith Mann
Assistant Sports Information Director

Mike Mason
Assistant Equipment Manager

Paul Meyers
Development Officer

Brian Mohnsen
Computer Video Technician

Marc Munford
Development Officer

Jack Nickolite
Associate Director of Athletic Medicine

Dr. James O'Hanlon
Institutional Representative

Doak Ostergard
Associate Head Athletic Trainer

Tom Osborne
Assistant A.D., Head Football Coach

Al Papik
Senior Associate A.D., Compliance Coordinator

Steve Pederson
Associate A.D., Dir. of FB Operations

Jack Pierce
Director of Athletic Development

Dr. Matt Reckmeyer
Team Physician, Orthopedist

Jeff Schmahl
Video Production Specialist

Rick Schwieger
Production Specialist P.A. Announcer

Joe Selig
Associate A.D., External Operations

Bill Shepard
Grounds Manager

Dr. Jack Stark
Performance Psychologist

George Sullivan
Head Trainer Emeritus, Medical Consultant, PT, ATC

Curt Thompson
Coordinator of Performance Ed. Services

Sonya Varnell
Coordinator of Multicultural Programs

Jerry Weber
Head Athletic Trainer

Sara Weinberg
Assistant Athletic Trainer

Mary Lyn Wininger
Coach Osborne's Secretary

Kathi Woody
Football Secretary

Mel Worster
Asst. Equipment Manager, Devaney Sports Center

Keith Zimmer
Asst. Director of Academic & Student Services

1995 NATIONAL CHAMPIONSHIP ISSUE

Huskers Illustrated

• $4.95 •
Volume 16, No. 2

Nebraska's Dynasty Solidified With Second-Straight National Title

TWO FOR TOM

WEDNESDAY, JANUARY 3, 1996

Who loves L.A.?

Los Angeles doesn't have an NFL team, but four stadium sites are being considered. One of as many as 18 teams could move in. In Focus, **Thursday**

USA TODAY

Open arms: Los Angeles wants to lure an NFL team with a new stadium. The leading site is at Hollywood Park racetrack.

SPORTSLINE

A QUICK READ ON THE TOP SPORTS NEWS OF THE DAY

BASKETBALL/NBA Coverage, 8C

Portland 101, New York 92
Houston 105, Minnesota 100
New Jersey 81, Milwaukee 72
Utah 102, Dallas 92
Cleveland 108, Washington 100
Indiana 102, Denver 87
Seattle 111, Atlanta 88
Philadelphia 90, L.A. Lakers 89

MEN'S COLLEGE TOP 25 Coverage, 6, 9C

3-Kansas 100, Cornell 46
11-Wake Forest 81, Furman 49
8-Villanova 76, Notre Dame 57
16-Utah 83, Brigham Young 77

WOMEN'S COLLEGE TOP 25 Coverage, 6, 9C

Syracuse 62, **2**-Connecticut 59
15-N.C. State 98, Maryland 57
4-Tennessee 87, **18**-Florida 67
South. Utah 78, **16**-Okla. St. 60
Clemson 63, **5**-Virginia 59
17-Old Domin. 79, Richmond 36
7-Arkansas 70, Dayton 53
19-Purdue 84, Butler 53
10-Colorado 81, Baylor 59

FOOTBALL/FIESTA BOWL Coverage, 3, 6C

Nebraska 62, Florida 24

HOCKEY/NHL Coverage, 7C

Chicago 5, Boston 2
Calgary 10, Tampa Bay 0

LARKIN REMAINS: The Cincinnati Reds locked up shortstop Barry Larkin, the National League's Most Valuable Player last season, through 1999 with a $16.5 million contract extension. *(Baseball, 7C)*

GOLDEN OLDIE: Buffalo Bills end Bruce Smith, in his 11th NFL season, took his run-stopping skills to a new level and was an easy pick for columnist Gordon Forbes' all-pro team. *(Story, 4C)*

USA TODAY

Smith: Makes Forbes' team.

WALKER CHARGED: Former Kentucky and NBA star Kenny Walker was arrested in Lexington, Ky., and charged with fourth-degree assault on his wife. Police said Rosalind Walker was choked. Walker is scheduled to be arraigned today.

BARNETT UPDATE: Northwestern football coach Gary Barnett met with UCLA officials Saturday about their vacancy and spoke with athletic director Pete Dalis Tuesday, The Associated Press reported. His lawyer also met with UCLA. Dalis wants a new coach by week's end.

GEARING UP: Three-time world champion Jackie Stewart apparently will return to Formula One next year as head of Ford's factory-backed team, with a news conference scheduled Thursday at the North American International Auto Show in Detroit.

ASHE MEMORIAL: After all the haggling, Richmond, Va., might reconsider its plan to put a statue of the late Arthur Ashe on historic, Confederate-lined Monument Avenue because of a commentary in the *Richmond Times-Dispatch* by Ashe's wife, Jeanne Moutoussamy-Ashe. The statue, she wrote, "honors Richmond more than it does its son, his legacy and his works." But she favors the city's plan to build an African-American Sports Hall of Fame.

SKATING BY: Boston University moved past Colorado College into first place in the USA TODAY/*American Hockey* college hockey poll. *(Poll, 9C)*

JOCKEY INVESTIGATED: The California Horse Racing Board is investigating the alleged whipping of a 2-year-old colt by jockey Corey Nakatani past the finish line in the sixth race at Santa Anita last Friday. Tillie's Joy broke down following the race with a complete fracture of the cannon bone in his left foreleg. He was destroyed.

JORDAN TRIAL: The audio on a videotaped rap song, which includes a description of shooting someone, will not be allowed in the murder trial of a man charged with killing Michael Jordan's father, the judge ruled. *(Story, 3A)*

STILL NO. 1: Teams from Tennessee, California, Wisconsin and Ohio are new in this week's USA TODAY high school girls basketball Super 25. Oregon City, Ore. (10-0) stays No. 1. *(Super 25, high school notes, 5C)*

By Rachel Shuster

SPORTS HOT LINE: $0.95/min.
Sheridan's latest line: 1-900-884-4400
Sagarin's ratings: 1-900-370-3703 (touchtone only)

USA SNAPSHOTS®

A look at statistics that shape the sports world

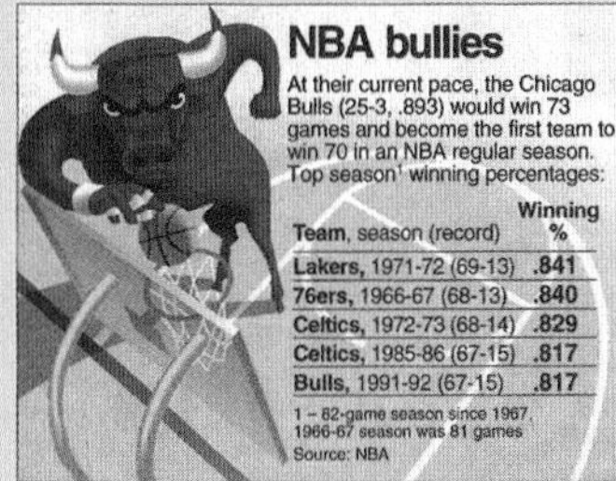

By Scott Boeck and Sam Ward, USA TODAY

'Huskers repeat No. 1 feat

By Robert Hanashiro, USA TODAY

Giving Gators the slip: Nebraska's Lawrence Phillips escapes Florida's Ben Hanks, center, and Mike Harris, right, Tuesday on his way to a second-quarter touchdown in the Tostitos Fiesta Bowl. Phillips carried for more than 100 yards in the opening half.

By Steve Wieberg
USA TODAY

TEMPE, Ariz. — Nebraska stepped into history Tuesday night.

Check that. The Huskers stomped into history. They stampeded. They embarrassed Florida 62-24 in the Tostitos Fiesta Bowl, becoming the first college football team in 16 years to win a second national championship in succession — and the first in almost four decades to put undisputed titles back to back.

"Just unbelievable," linebacker Mike Ellis said afterward. "Everything clicked."

Not unexpectedly, Nebraska's option running game overpowered Florida's defense, piling up 524 yards and six touchdowns.

Quarterback Tommie Frazier ran for 199 yards and two touchdowns, a school record in a bowl, and threw for another TD. I-back Lawrence Phillips, starting for the first time since his September arrest for assault and a six-game suspension, ran for 165 yards and two TDs and caught the scoring pass.

Less expected was the way the Huskers' defense pounded the Gators' complex, ultra-productive passing offense. Quarterback Danny Wuerffel was sacked seven times, once for a safety, and harassed into three interceptions. One was returned 42 yards for a TD.

The Huskers (12-0) devastated Florida (12-1) with 29 unanswered points in a 14:20 span in the second quarter, turning an early 10-6 deficit into a 35-10 lead by the half.

"We don't have any answers," Florida coach Steve Spurrier said afterward. "They're just too good for us. ... I'm embarrassed."

Nebraska extended a two-season winning streak to 25 games and its record spanning three seasons of college football dominance to 36-1.

FIESTA REPORT

Tennessee sets mark in 87-67 win

By Harry Blauvelt
USA TODAY

Abby Conklin scored 13 of her game-high 23 points down the stretch as No. 4 Tennessee topped No. 18 Florida 87-67 Tuesday in Knoxville in college women's basketball and set an NCAA Division I record for consecutive home wins.

It was the Volunteers' 69th consecutive victory at Thompson-Boling Arena, breaking Auburn's record of 68 from 1986-91. Tennessee is 11-1 and 1-0 in the Southeastern Conference.

Conklin hit five of seven three-point attempts. "We ran some special options which opened it up for Abby," Tennessee coach Pat Summitt said.

Conklin scored 13 points during a 21-4 run to end the game after the Gators pulled within 66-63 with 6:33 left. Tennessee's Chamique Holdsclaw had 16 points and 10 rebounds.

Tennessee hosts No. 2 Connecticut Saturday (3 p.m. ET, CBS) in a rematch of last season's NCAA Division I title game won by UConn 70-64.

▶ UConn, Virginia lose, 6C
▶ Scores, 9C

USA TODAY/CNN Top 25 Coaches Poll

Unofficial

The USA TODAY/CNN Top 25 Coaches football poll, with first-place votes in parentheses, record, total points based on 25 points for first through one point for 25th, and previous ranking:

Rank/School	(First)	Record	Points	Previous
1. Nebraska	(56)	12-0	1,400	1
2. Tennessee		11-1	1,297	4
3. Florida		12-1	1,296	2
4. Colorado		10-2	1,184	7
5. Florida State		10-2	1,154	8

▶ Top 25 poll, **9C**; Official poll will appear in Thursday's paper

Richter sidelined for 4 weeks

By Mike Brehm
USA TODAY

New York Rangers backup goaltender Glenn Healy, who began the team's 17-game home unbeaten streak, will have to carry it on for now.

Mike Richter had an MRI examination late Tuesday afternoon and learned he'll be out four weeks with a strained groin muscle.

Richter, 11-1-2 in his last 14 games, left Saturday's victory at Edmonton after feeling a sharp pain while stretching for a shot.

"It's getting better," Richter said Tuesday after treatment. "I'm starting to be able to do a little bit of stretching, a lot of icing and therapy."

The Rangers try to extend their streak tonight against the Montreal Canadiens. Healy, a former No. 1 goaltender with the New York Islanders, won Oct. 24 to start the streak and tied the Canadiens 2-2 at Montreal last month.

Contributing: Rick Carpiniello
▶ **NHL report, statistics, 7C**

COVER STORY

Nebraska ends trying season on top — again

Says Osborne, 'It's been more of a mixed year than any I can remember'

By Steve Wieberg
USA TODAY

TEMPE, Ariz. — Tom Osborne is convinced. The first national championship of his coaching tenure at Nebraska last year carried a price: too many prying eyes, all too intent on finding a flaw.

Maybe, the Cornhuskers' coach suggested near the end of a long and trying 1995 season, after his football program and judgment were questioned anew on CBS' *48 Hours*, it would be best to hand the trophy back.

They didn't, of course. They claimed another.

Nebraska extended its winning streak to two full years and 25 games Tuesday night, defeating Florida 62-24 in the Tostitos Fiesta Bowl.

Running back Lawrence Phillips, one of the primary subjects of controversy this season, scored three touchdowns, including Nebraska's first two, and rushed for 165 yards — more than 100 in the first half alone. Quarterback Tommie Frazier ran for two more touchdowns and 199 yards, and the defense sapped the Fun and the Gun from the Gators' high-yield offense.

Osborne has built a certified powerhouse on the plains,

Please see COVER STORY next page ▶

Seles heads for Australian Open

By Doug Smith
USA TODAY

Monica Seles resumes her comeback in Australia next week, healthy and full of confidence.

"I've always done well in Australia, haven't lost a match (21-0) there yet," said Seles, 22, Australian Open champion in 1991, '92 and '93.

For the first year since '92, Seles plans a full schedule, including the four majors, events in Tokyo, Indian Wells, Calif., Key Biscayne, Fla., Hilton Head, S.C. and the Olympics in Atlanta.

Seles returned to the WTA TOUR last summer after a 2½-year absence. She won the Canadian Open and lost the U.S. Open final to Steffi Graf.

She says the left-knee injury that forced her to skip several events, including the season finale in New York, has healed. She has recovered from a recent virus that threatened her return.

"Two weeks ago, I wasn't sure I was going to be able to make the (trip)," said Seles, who opens a tournament Monday in Sydney.

By Robert Hanashiro, USA TODAY

Wet and wild: Jubilant Nebraska players give coach Tom Osborne a victory shower after the Cornhuskers' 62-24 drubbing of Florida in the Tostitos Fiesta Bowl Tuesday night.

NEBRASKA

vs.

FLORIDA

THE NATIONAL CHAMPIONSHIP

25th ANNIVERSARY

JANUARY 2, 1996

TEMPE, ARIZONA